AF732446

Esther's Journey

Other Books by Chiche Scaglia Davis

The Art of Meditation

Esther's Journey

a novel by

Chiche Scaglia Davis

RoseHeart Publishing

RoseHeart
IMPRINT

This book is a work of fiction. Names, characters, places and incidents are either a product of the author's imagination or are used fictitiously. Any resemblance to actual events, locales, persona, living or dead, is entirely coincidental.

ESTHER'S JOURNEY

All Rights Reserved © 2009 by Chiche Scaglia Davis

Cover Design by CH Creations
Interior Layout and Design by CH Creations

No part of this book may be reproduced or transmitted in any form or by any means, electronic or mechanical, including photocopying, recording, or by information storage and retrieval system except by a reviewer who may quote brief passages in a review to be printed in a magazine or newspaper without written permission from the author.

Published October 2009
RoseHeart Publishing
www.roseheartbooks.com

ISBN 10: 0-9841870-2-2
ISBN 13: 978-0-9841870-2-7

Printed in the United States of America

To my son Eduardo

CHAPTER I
AFRAID OF TOMORROW

Odessa, 1905, November

"No matter how much wood you put in the fireplace, the house doesn't get warm. We are not prepared for this kind of weather here in Odessa. It has been so cold and crazy, and it is not December yet. I want to live in one of those modern houses with steam radiators in each room," Rebecca said as she carried an armful of dry wood.

She stopped at the back door of the kitchen to clean her feet on the mat and shook loose some of the snow from the hem of her skirt. Carefully she placed the logs next to the fire. She wiped her hands on the white apron and turned to face Esther.

"The snow is so heavy! We haven't had anything like this in ages. If it doesn't melt by tomorrow, I will ask Yuri to shovel a path on the back and the front entrances. It is almost impossible to get through," Rebecca continued.

Perhaps Esther didn't hear, since she didn't answer but instead continued to sit motionless next to the window. Her lips too tight to open in answer, she stared at the old birch tree near the kitchen. The black of her dress accentuated her pale face. Her blue eyes were red from tears and so many nights with little or no sleep. Mechanically, she tried to pull up some locks of dark hair that had escaped the prison of her earlier perfect chignon and were now resting on her shoulders.

Unlike Esther, the sad circumstances had not changed Rebecca. She remained calm and in control of the moment. Since childhood, she had thought of each difficult moment she had to overcome as a soul lesson and an opportunity for spiritual growth. She looked at life with optimism. She believed in the spiritual world. She saw death as a start, not an end of the soul.

"I'm waiting for the water to boil to make tea." Rebecca reached for the woolen crocheted shawl she had lost in so much confusion. "There you are." With a graceful movement she swung the shawl over her shoulders and rubbed her cold hands together. "Snow falling in Odessa, unbelievable." she declared. "The ceremony was really beautiful, wasn't it? Pity it snowed so much. Such weather. It kept everybody from going to the cemetery. Do you know what the problem was? I think people were afraid of catching influenza and dying too." She picked up the kettle top and added, "Good, almost boiling. I need a big glass of hot tea. I'm still cold."

Rebecca didn't expect an answer for her monologue. She involved herself in the small ceremony of tea making. Steam rushed out of the kettle in a stream. She picked it up and poured the boiling water into the teapot. Immediately after, she covered the teapot with a tea cozy, and placed two glasses in the holders on the kitchen table. Without disturbing the quietness in the room, she took some preserves, a loaf of bread, a piece of cheese, and the sugar dish from a cabinet, and placed them in the center of the table. She pulled two napkins from a drawer in the hutch. As she walked back to the table to put them next to the glasses, she said, "Yingele, please come to the table. In less than five minutes, you'll get a perfect glass of tea."

Esther didn't move, but her eyes closed, and the insinuation of a smile showed on her lips. She was far back in time outside the window. She could see herself at play with her father. She could hear her mother laugh while she watched them cavort from that same kitchen window. That was in that distant past when they were alive. Now, the garden was empty of happy play and laughter. The silence was so profound, she could hear the snow fall.

Rebecca got an apple from the fruit bowl on the counter, cut a slice, and walked to the big cage that held a noisy multicolored bird, a Brazilian yellow and red plumaged Papa Gallo. She placed the apple on a metal pan. "Here, Rita, have some apple. I'm sure you are hungry. We have not paid much attention to you lately, have we?" Turning away from Rita, she asked her cousin, "Esther, please, do I have to beg you? At least you must have a piece of bread. You only had a boiled egg hours ago. Come to the table and keep me company. I need to eat something."

The sound of Rebecca's voice calling her name brought Esther back from the memories of those long ago happy times, drawing her back into the late afternoon in the warm kitchen.

Cousin Rebecca was all the family Esther had left in Odessa. She couldn't count on Uncle Ishmael, the "Black Sheep" as her parents used to call him. Nobody knew of his whereabouts, not even Rebecca, his daughter. Esther didn't know if she had relatives alive in some other part of Russia. She was six the summer they visited her father's family in St. Petersburg. It wasn't frequent the family went on vacation. That was the first time Esther had made such a long trip all by train. She loved it. She remembered her grandmother was an old lady then. Her father had two sisters. Aunt Esther had never married and seemed old, at least in the eyes of the young Esther. She wondered if that dried up old spinster could have ever married. She inherited her name from that aunt. Sarah, Esther's other aunt, was a small, plump woman. Esther thought her aunt was as pretty and young as her own mother. Aunt Sarah was special. She was her father's favorite sister and became Esther's favorite aunt. Until that visit, Esther hadn't known that side of the family. They never came to Odessa. The second and last time she saw her paternal relatives, she was almost eleven.

On that occasion, her father's ship had suffered some damage and had to be repaired. Esther and her mother went to St. Petersburg to be with him. It wasn't often they had the opportunity to enjoy the company of her father for a full month, and visit relatives at the same time. In that second trip, Esther became very close to her Aunt Sarah. Since then, they had corresponded regularly. Esther was twelve when she received a letter with the news her aunt was about to marry and she cried disconsolately. She felt abandoned. Her Aunt Sarah had met an American businessman in St. Petersburg by the name of Frank Bernstein. In her goodbye letter, Sarah explained to Esther she and Frank were in love. He made her immensely happy and they were moving to America soon after their marriage.

For a time, Sarah continued to write to her niece from New York, but Esther hadn't heard from her aunt since the winter of 1904. She would need to let her aunt know about her parents.

Esther's maternal grandparents had died before the turn of the century. Just that morning, they had buried her mother. Not to have any elders left on either side of the family brought her a sudden fear. She was only eighteen and not prepared to face that reality.

Jacob Vainer, her father, had died in the early spring of that same year. He disappeared with the rest of the crew when his ship was sunk in Japanese waters. In the straits of Tsushima, the Japanese Fleet under Admiral Togo, intercepted and practically destroyed the Russian Fleet, which was enroute to the Port of Vladivostok. Russia suffered tremendous casualties in lives and ships. Jacob was an officer under Commandant Serebriakoff, the captain of the Borodino. The ship was one of the most modern of the Russian fleet at that time. On May 27, 1905, the Borodino with all hands aboard sank in the attempt to cross the Straits of Tsushima.

His wife, Esther's mother, Miriam, tried to battle the grief of the death of her husband. For weeks she lacked the will to get out of bed. Slowly the pink on her cheeks vanished, dark circles appeared under her eyes, and she became fragile. Her health improved some after an intensive treatment in a rehabilitation clinic at the edge of the Black Sea, but not enough to restore her will to live.

Often, Esther tried to convince her mother to go back to her garden, to sit in the conservatory among the flowers, or to go to the beach for a walk and wet her feet in the waters at the edge of the Black Sea. Her pleas were all in vain. She wasn't able to get Miriam out of the house. Suddenly, her mother became a recluse, and late that same fall, she became ill. All the efforts from Esther, Rebecca and Olga, the old maid, were futile. They administered the medicines prescribed by the doctor, followed the instructions with intelligent precision, and added a big amount of love to their care.

Miriam did not recuperate. At the end of November 1905,

Miriam died. Her spirit was broken, and she battled illnesses for which there were no known medicines. She missed her husband terribly, and was tired of being alive.

"I can see you are following my suggestion." Rebecca smiled at Esther. "The tea is perfect. It is warming up my feet. They were frozen from the walk in the snow. It is so unusually cold out there." Gesturing toward the window with her chin to make her point, she wrapped the shawl more tightly around her body, shivering a little from the cold. She turned to reach the corner of the table and took a platter with a cake on it, cut a piece, placed it on a small plate and passed it to Esther.

"Have a piece of this cake. It looks divine. Mrs. Kaufman brought it early this morning and told me to be sure you eat some." As she cut a piece for herself, she added, "I think Mrs. Kaufman has obscure intentions, and she is trying very hard to please you. She has several sons, you know."

Esther nodded. The insinuation made her smile a little. Her voice betrayed her concern when she spoke. "Oh, Becca, what are we going to do? I'm so worried."

"We are also tired. This is not the time to find answers."

"While mother was alive, I had no time to think of tomorrow, but, since this morning, it is all I can think of."

"Esther, you are your own tormentor, please stop that."

"The reality is I'm an orphan. Right now the thought is a paralyzing truth." Her eyes were red and wet with tears when she spoke.

The desperate look on her face worried Rebecca. "Come, come now, Esther, don't you think I understand?"

"You are right, I'm sorry. I'm an egotist."

"Why don't you let time heal your heart? You are driving yourself mad trying to foresee into tomorrow. Be patient, wait with confidence for the future to arrive." Rebecca placed her hand on the hand of her cousin. "We've time, we're young and pretty. We may not be rich, but we're not poor either."

The words said by Rebecca, with a touch of humor, fulfilled the purpose. Esther stopped her sobs, sighed, and used the wrinkled handkerchief to dry her teary eyes. She regained some of her lost control and serenity.

Esther was two years younger than Rebecca. They looked

alike. People often asked if they were sisters. Rebecca's father and Esther's mother were brother and sister. Rebecca's mother died while giving birth to her second child. After Rebecca's father buried his wife and the baby, he sold their home. He gave no explanation for his decision, and his daughter was too young to ask. Distraught with grief, he felt dead inside. He could not console his daughter, and ignored her sadness. He prepared two suitcases, one for Rebecca and the other for himself. He told Rebecca they would go to Odessa to visit his sister and her family. Rebecca still remembered the last time she saw him. Just a few weeks after they arrived in Odessa, her father had a loud argument with his sister and brother-in-law. Without further words or letting them know his destination, her father kissed her on both checks, said goodbye, and left forever. Rebecca had neither seen her father nor heard from him since. From that day on, her Aunt Miriam and Uncle Jacob became her parents and Esther, her little sister.

"I don't know about you, but I'm so sleepy. The tea and the food warmed me up and now I can hardly keep my eyes open." Rebecca pressed her fingers against her mouth to avoid a big yawn and asked, "Don't you think it is time for bed? We spent so many vigilant nights and for so long. To go to bed early will be a welcome change, at least for me." She got up from the table, picked up the teapot in one hand and reached for Mrs. Kaufman's cake with the other.

Still without words, Esther moved the chair back, stood and helped her cousin clear the table. "I don't want to dwell on our adversity," Esther cried, "but you know as much as I, we can't use our small fortune in food or clothes."

"Stop worrying, Esther."

"Neither can we use our dowry money."

Rebecca laughed and talked at the same time. "My dear little cousin, if we spend our dowry, we'll never find a suitable husband, and you may end up marrying the ugly rich son of Mrs. Kaufman." With a smile and much tenderness she asked, "Sweetheart, where is your optimism?"

There was so much they could do. They could find jobs if they had to. "I believe we'll be all right."

She tried to convince Esther, but she was not completely

sure her words were true. Rebecca knew they had always lived very well, and until that moment the family never had money troubles. They also had the large inheritance of the grandparents Prusky, Miriam's parents. They were both well-educated, and if it came down to them needing to work, they could teach piano lessons or maybe tutor some school children, but she was so tired. She did not want to think any more that evening. They needed to wait until they could talk to Mr. Resnik, the executor, and ask him. In a week the lawyer would give them detailed information about their financial situation. Rebecca started her way out of the kitchen with the thought that first thing in the morning, she had to talk to Olga and explain the situation.

Poor Olga had gone to bed as soon they returned from the cemetery. The big woman was cold, wet and so sad that she had to go to her room to pray, and, as she told Rebecca, "To ask the Spirits for tomorrow to come as a better day."

The salary for a maid was the first money they could save if they had to, but Olga was not just a maid. She was part of the family. She had been with them forever and now she was a bit old. Where could she go? Maybe she could go live with her sister, but that was highly unlikely. Olga had never gotten along with her sister. Rebecca decided Olga should stay with them as long as she desired.

Esther locked the back door, turned off the gaslight next to the stove, and hurried to catch up with Rebecca. They walked together to the stairs. Rebecca left a candle and matches on the newel post. Both girls were startled by the black cloth draped over the mirror at the side of the stairs. Their faces were shadowed by the reminder of death, the funeral and procession to the cemetery. There was so much snow that even when they both opened their umbrellas, it was impossible to prevent the snow from falling on top of the coffin.

"Come with me to lock the front door and turn off the lights. I'm afraid to walk in the dark tonight," Rebecca remarked.

"Yes, I know you need company," Esther agreed.

"I see strange shadows." Involuntarily, Rebecca made Esther smile again. "Oh, please don't laugh about it. I do get scared…"

The phrase remained unfinished, interrupted by a gust of strong wind that pushed the front door wide open. The two girls screamed, huddled very close together, their arms touching, their eyes fixated into the dark, unable to talk.

"A ghost!" Rebecca shouted.

Regaining her calm and a bit amused by the incident, Esther said, "There are no ghosts out there. It is so cold tonight they would freeze their spiritual tuchies off."

Then she got behind the heavy door, wrestled the wind and the snow, closed and locked it. She lowered the gaslight to the minimum, and with one hand, tried to repair the damage the wind did to her hair as she took Rebecca by the shoulder.

"Zeesa meidel, let's go to sleep." Esther told her cousin.

CHAPTER II
MIRIAM

Odessa, the winter of 1902

The events that changed her promising future into a tragic life began to meld over twenty years earlier. Miriam, Esther's mother, was almost a child then.

As with most Jewish women of her time, Miriam was well-educated and well-mannered. Since early age, she took music lessons, learned how to cook, and most importantly, she learned how to raise a family. She walked with grace and spoke with a soft voice she could control, even in moments of anger. Like her father, she had large gray eyes and black hair she combed in an elaborate fashion. She was pretty, small, slender, and fragile. She was the second child in her family. Her brother, Ishmael, was three years her senior.

Her father, Boris Prusky, was a kind and respected man. He had a small but prosperous business for the import and export of fabrics. His office was close to the old Turkish Fort, and within walking distance from the port. His house at Balkovskaya Street, was just a few miles away, and in ten minutes he could be home from work.

Miriam's mother, Irina Prusky, was a nervous and irritable woman, quick to harsh criticism. She loved Miriam, but had a special weakness for her son, Ishmael. He could do no wrong. Irina used the fact that her husband spent more time at work than at home, as an excuse to indulge in pastries and Spanish sherry.

The life of Miriam was an intriguing and mysterious fantasy in the eyes of her daughter and niece. “Oh, Mama, please tell me again,” Esther would beg her mother. She lay on the brown leather sofa, her hands under her chin. “You know I never tire of listening to that story.” She paused for an instant and sat next to her mother. With closed eyes, she smiled, sighed and said, “It is so romantic.”

In the winter afternoons, when the cold weather kept them in, the three women gathered close to the fire to hear music on the phonograph. Jacob brought the instrument home from one of his trips to Germany and gave it to Miriam for her birthday.

“My beloved, Miriam, the music will keep you company when I’m not around.” He embraced and kissed her with much tenderness and restrained passion.

They had several records of Viennese waltzes composed by Johan Strauss, and those were Esther’s favorite. In St. Petersburg, Jacob bought two records of Russian folk music, but it was not played often. The girls disliked them, and after a few seconds, they mocked the balalaika players and the baritone singer. Everyone loved the Italian arias sung by Enrico Caruso, but they only had four records of the famous tenor. Miriam kept a record of Braham’s lieders hidden from her daughters. She reserved the romantic songs for those times, when alone, she could cry over the absence of her husband. Records were expensive, but not easy to find in Odessa. They depended on Jacob to bring the latest recorded music.

Esther and Rebecca tired easily. They hated to listen to the same music again and again. Quite often they provided the entertainment. Both girls could act, play the piano, and also the violin, which they inherited from Grandfather Boris, Miriam’s father.

When they played, music arrived in every corner of the house. Olga left her fortress and her kitchen chores to join them. She sat next to Miriam to listen. Once the girls finished and the room was in silence for an instant, Olga left her place as spectator. Before she abandoned the room, she repeated once more to Miriam, “Madam, those two girls are prodigies.” From the door she turned to remark, “Madam, they should be playing in a concert hall.” Her hands wrapped in her enormous white apron, she disappeared from their view, returning to her domain of the warm kitchen.

To be sure they would remember, Miriam showed her daughters the albums filled with sepia-colored photographs. She told the girls a small history about each one of the portraits found in the page. Most of them were dead people or relatives the girls did not know. She explained where, and the way they were related to the Prusky's or the Vainer's. The people in the pictures looked stiff and out of fashion. It was tedious to sit still and listen with attention for a long time. When they began to yawn with boredom, Miriam closed the album and placed it on the baroque wooden table.

Esther and Rebecca always received the stories Miriam told them with joy. She had a creative imagination. They listened, captivated by the romantic tales with intrepid cavaliers and romantic heroines as protagonists. Nonetheless, their favorite story was about Miriam, when she saw Jacob for the first time and the almost impossible way they met. The girls knew they only had to ask once. Miriam would agree to tell them, with endless patience, the detailed story from start to finish once more. The tale helped her to bring Jacob's presence home. In all those years she never became accustomed to the fact he was at sea so many months at a time. She missed him as much as the first time he went away.

Miriam drifted into her past, and submerged her spirit into a golden mist of memories. Every time before she started, she paused in silence, a sigh escaping her lips while praying, and she would say, "It happened in the late spring of 1886. I was so young then. I met your father the week of my seventeenth birthday."

Miriam waited with barely contained anxiety for her birthday the next week. Her mother, who missed her son, Ishmael and planned a visit to St. Petersburg to see him, had promised to take her too. Certainly she would visit her brother. He left Odessa in 1884 to study at the University of St. Petersburg.

She had never been far from home before, but, an avid reader, she had collected mountains of information about the city. She found all sorts of information in books. She knew the climate, population, even the distance from Odessa to the Russian capital. In magazines, she found all the places she wanted to visit, cut them out and glued them to a scrap album. There were so many possibilities, theaters, elegant restaurants and hundreds of shops. She would need the full month, from morning to night, to visit them all. She completed her research booklet months before the journey began. She made so many plans. "I did not know then, I was about to meet the love of my life and my future husband," Miriam told the girls.

Her mother had promised to take her shopping for new clothes, shoes and hats. Miriam's father told her what she already knew. The weather in St. Petersburg was never as good as in Odessa. She hoped for that spring to be different, and counted on good weather to walk in the lovely boulevards and parks she had read about. Possibly, the thing she wanted the most for that trip as part of her seventeenth birthday present was an evening at the Aleksandrovky Theater, or to listen to some of the music of the composer who had produced an uproar with his symphonies and concertos, Pyotr Il'yich Tchaikovsky. Borodin was her second choice and only if they could not find a balcony at the Concert Hall. She knew the director of the Symphony that year was Maestro-Rimsky Korsakov. Miriam had heard wonderful words of praise of the young director-composer.

"We were so lucky, the weather was perfect. From the moment we placed foot out of the train, the magic accompanied me." It was mid-afternoon when they followed a porter who carried their luggage out of the station. He trusted the suitcases to a quite circumspect driver, then opened the door of the carriage for the Prusky family to enter. "The most cosmopolitan street was in front of my eyes, Nevsky Prospect. Never before that day had I seen such a display of perfection. Hundreds of elegant shops and hotels adorned both sides of the wide avenue. The people on the sidewalks were as elegant as the shops, looking like mannequins-vivants," Miriam said.

Their hotel was just a few miles ahead on the same street. As soon as they entered, the impact of so much opulence made Miriam breathless. The view in front of her was magnificent. The hotel lobby was painted royal blue and had silver stars on the ceiling. There was a round, royal blue velvet upholstery seat in the center, striped divans under the windows, and so many beautiful people around.

Her father went to the front desk and the concierge handed him the keys and the guest book to sign. Without wasting time, Mr. Prusky spoke to the clerk, giving him a good tip to buy theater tickets for them.

Four nights later, Miriam had one of her wishes fulfilled. They went to the Mariinsky Theater. The magnificent building, built in a baroque style, was larger than she thought it would be. The seats, the balconies and the curtains were done in red velvet. Gold was everywhere. Even the curtain fringes were golden. In that visit to St. Petersburg, everything bedazzled the young woman from Odessa and her seventeen provincial years.

"That Friday evening in May of 1886, I saw the most incredible piece of art, Swan Lake. I was bewitched by the charm of the Mariinsky Theater, the most romantic music, the most beautiful dance and dancers, and in the interval, by the most handsome man in a naval uniform I had ever dreamed to meet."

Miriam felt tired and suddenly feverish. With her eyes closed, she had to recline her back on the sofa as she felt fatigue embrace her. The two girls understood and smiled. They knew their mother was remembering her Jacob, reliving the first encounter and the impact caused by him with his white uniform. They never interrupted that time of privacy in their mother's thought. To avoid disturbing her, they talked in a whisper to each other and waited until she was ready to continue. Esther left the sofa and sat next to Rebecca on the floor on the brown bear fur carpet, her feet close to the fire. They waited and moved with anticipation.

Miriam had to use her memories frequently as a reminder that she had a husband. No doubt they loved each other very much, but in recent years, the wars and political unrest had kept Jacob at sea more and his visits were short and far apart. She never protested the long separations, but memories of their happy times were not enough to fill the emptiness in her heart.

After a prolonged pause, she opened her eyes, but they could not see the present, they were far away in her past. She sighed, took the little handkerchief from the sleeve of her gray silk blouse and dried an indiscreet tear. "I was wearing the most beautiful brocade pale pink dress you can imagine. I bought the dress with Mother the day before, just two blocks from the hotel in a fashionable shop call Alexandrine. For the first time I was wearing shoes with high heels."

Miriam was stopped by the two girls who said at once as rehearsed, "You forgot to tell us the color of the shoes, Mother."

"You are right, my dears, I forgot. The shoes were as beautiful as my dress, made in pink sateen and embroidered with red and purple gems like stones. In the interval between the second and third act, Father's unexpected behavior astounded Mother and me. He brought a stranger to the balcony with him.

"He had gone out to smoke one of those horrendous cigars that you both knew. When he came back in, he was accompanied by your father, Esther, and he said, 'Allow me to present to you, Jacob Vainer.' Mother and I were astonished. We could not articulate a word. We smiled at the officer. Mother crossed a strange but meaningful gaze with Father. She expected a good explanation once the officer abandoned their balcony, and she did not have to wait.

"'He is a Lieutenant Commander in the Tsar's Navy,' my father said to explain the uniform Jacob was wearing. 'It was a great coincidence to find him in the theater,' he exclaimed with obvious happiness. Mr. Prusky told them the officer was the son of an old and dear friend. Maybe it was the magic of the moment, the candlelight, or destiny, but Miriam and Jacob fell in love instantly and forever.

Trying not to be noticed, an almost impossible task for the corpulent woman, Olga arrived in the parlor. She carried a silver tray with the tea service for Miriam, two very big steamy cups with chocolate and a platter with cake and cookies for the girls.

Olga was tall. She had a thick layer of fat from head to toe that made her look more like a wrestler than a cook. In the summer, when the sand was so hot it could burn the girls' feet, she was able to walk with both of them in her arms from the edge of the sea to the carriage, more than a hundred yards, without even panting.

She was probably in her forties, but she looked no more

than thirty-five. She had all her teeth. She never said her age and, until then, nobody asked how old she was. Olga had been hired by Irina Prusky to serve the Vainer family, and she had been in the house since the day before Miriam got married. She knew the family history from the beginning. Despite her Amazon look, she had a sweet disposition, was a great cook and a wonderful storyteller. In the afternoons when she baked cakes and cookies, Esther and Rebecca spent hours in the kitchen with her. They learned how to cook while they laughed at her tales about Cossack lovers. Only once, Olga, after a few glasses of vodka to commemorate the Tsar's birthday, mentioned a son she had when she was very young.

When Olga entered the room, Miriam stopped her tale. Esther and Rebecca were not happy at the interruption and protested. Both girls abandoned their place on the fur rug close to the fire. They crawled close to the table, sat on the floor and drank in silence. Without enthusiasm, but hurriedly, they finished their chocolate and placed the cups back on the tray. Esther got a cookie and passed the plate to Rebecca.

"Have one, Becca, they are delicious."

"Thank you, Esther, I had enough. Mother Miriam, please continue." Rebecca was on her knees, her voice was comical and her eyes squinted. Her forehead wrinkled and her hands were together as in prayer.

"Mama, please. The story is as romantic as a fairytale," Esther said, and joined Rebecca in the plea.

"We can't go to bed until we've heard every last word, Mother Miriam."

She could hear impatience in the voice of Rebecca, and laughed at her exaggeration. "It is not even dinner time, sweetie; I'll finish my tale before then."

Miriam loved Rebecca as much as her own daughter. From the moment her brother abandoned the girl ten years earlier, Miriam became her defender and protector. Nobody would take Rebecca away from her. She would prevent it at any cost.

Under their severe scrutiny, Miriam poured tea in her cup, rested her back on the sofa, drank some tea before continuing, "Next day, we received an invitation for dinner."

They were downstairs in the hotel's breakfast room when

Mr. Prusky told his wife and daughter that, earlier the bellboy had brought him a letter from Karl Vainer, Jacob's father. They had planned a party with some friends and Mr. Prusky and his family were expected.

Mr. and Mrs. Vainer had the rare opportunity to be with their son for almost three weeks. They wanted to make his stay pleasant and his agenda not too busy. They expected to entertain him, but keep him at home and enjoy his company. The ship on which Jacob served as an officer was anchored at the port of St. Petersburg, and it was not scheduled to sail for eighteen days.

"The evening of the party and for the rest of the eighteen days your father and I spent many hours together, possibly displeasing your paternal grandparents, Mr. and Mrs. Vainer. We began to learn about each other, but always under the acute eyes of my parents, who were glued to my heels. We walked in the parks, had tea together, and went to the theater. We crossed many bridges in our long rides in carriages visiting sights of St. Petersburg."

"Mama, please stop your tale for an instant and have some tea. You must drink it before it gets cold," Esther said.

Miriam looked at her daughter from that other time in May, smiled and drank the rest of her tea. She placed the cup and saucer on the tray and sat back. Before she restarted the story, she straightened the wrinkles in her dark gray skirt, and with her face down, she stayed with her thoughts a little longer. Then she sighed, and said, "One early morning in June, he left. I went with Father to the port to bid him goodbye. I got drenched. It rained as very often it does in St. Petersburg, but I did not move until the ship disappeared over the horizon.

"Oh, Mama, such a sentimental farewell," Esther lamented. Saddened by the image, she reached for her mother's hand, holding it.

"After Jacob left, I lost my earlier enthusiasm for knowing St. Petersburg. I had visited many places with him. Without him, the city became meaningless and empty. I was ready to go back to Odessa to wait at home for my prince."

In the fireplace, the embers began to smoke. The golden light of the wintry sun was almost gone. The two girls were silent and very close together. Their backs arched in expectation, their faces forward, their curiosity still hungry. They never talked about it, not even after her death, but Esther and Rebecca pitied Miriam. They were permanent witnesses to her life of loneliness.

"Father was a bit disappointed, but he was unable to convince me to stay, so he changed the train tickets to Odessa that same day."

A week later, in the late afternoon, they arrived home. The train station was a large building next to the railroad. In one corner of the room behind a long wooden stand with metal bars on it, sat a bored clerk. The room was completed with two rows of wooden benches that divided the space into small rectangles. The station was smelly. A peculiar mix of the odors of paper, ink, and horse urine was suspended in the air. When Miriam stepped down from the train, she felt the provincial change. That evening, and for the next six months, at the end of each day she marked a red circle on the calendar.

The room was almost in darkness. Miriam interrupted the narration. She got up with tremendous difficulty as if her legs could not support the weight of her small body. She took a match from a holder on the mantle. Then she picked up the glass globe of a kerosene lamp, placed it on the side table next to the sofa and lit it. Still with her mind in the past, she placed the globe back. Automatically, she shook the match and threw it into the smoky fireplace.

The second part of the nineteenth century in which Miriam lived most of her life, was a time of significant changes. The wheel of progress, that inevitably turns, brought to Russia immense innovations into the arts, literature and music. As the country approached the twentieth century, the discontent among the countrymen was more notorious. Political unrest continued to wash the streets of the cities with human blood.

"From the moment I met Jacob, my life changed. I was grateful for his love and happy for being in love." She was disturbed by a new feeling that was born simultaneously with love—dread. Miriam feared for his life.

"Those were turbulent years. The Russian people grew discontented with the government, and more violent times were yet to come." Miriam finished the words, got up from the sofa and walked to the fireplace. She felt as if she walked on cotton. An instant of dizziness made her vacillate. She took a deep breath. Then she kneeled, got a log and placed it over the smoky embers. She blew with a bellows until the signs of flames appeared. Slowly, she walked back, while she organized her thoughts, followed by the glance of the two attentive girls.

"It was getting chilly in here. Don't you think, girls?"

"Yes it was, Mama. My hands and feet are frozen." Esther's exaggeration made them laugh.

There was a short pause before Miriam continued her tale.

"I have already told you this, but you may not remember. In 1887, a group of students among whom was a young man called Lenin, attempted and failed to assassinate our Tsar Alexander III. Since that moment and until now, a younger brother of that Lenin called Vladimir has caused innumerable problems for Tsar Nicholas and his government."

The country's political situation had become an obsession for Miriam. She had to wait until her father finished with the newspaper. No one could touch the paper before he did. "The paper becomes untidy when you read, darling," he used to complain. As soon as her father left for work, she ran to get the paper from his study and impatiently looked for the political news. She was so well informed of the country's state of turmoil, she became afraid with the possibility of a war. Violence could take Jacob's life. The Russian instability brought sadness into her soul. Jacob's letters arrived, but not frequently enough to soothe her torment. The mail was very slow. Often a letter had to go across half the European continent to reach her.

"Mother was worried about me. She did not like the idea of me marrying a seaman. On more than one occasion Mother tried to show me how wrong Jacob was for me. She mentioned many times the loneliness I would face having a husband whose first love was the sea. One afternoon, when we were walking in the park near the house, Mother confessed to me that her biggest fear was to lose me. She was upset supposing that once married to Jacob, I could move to St. Petersburg to live in his family's household. She was afraid I would not be able to visit with her or walk in the park as we were used to doing every afternoon. She could not bear to have me far from home and from her life. Mother asked Nanette to cook all my favorite dishes, to pamper me. She found pretexts to meet for tea with her friends that had suitable bachelor sons."

Esther laughed out loud. She couldn't imagine her mother married to someone else. Her father was the most handsome and loving man in the world when he was around to show his feeling. Surprised by her daughter's outburst, Miriam smiled.

"We were back in Odessa at the beginning of the summer of 1887. Mother was disappointed because Ishmael did not come back with us. He stayed at the university in St. Petersburg."

That summer, Odessa was a bit more humid than normal, and it reminded her of St. Petersburg's weather. She used to go with her mother for long walks in the country until then. However, since she came back, she wanted to walk or ride the carriage on the shores, close to the port filled with ships and the salty smell of the Black Sea.

"In the proximity of the water, my heart felt closer to Jacob.

The summer with its warmth passed. The fall arrived with splashes of color over the landscape. Her love for him was as strong as the first day, but the image of his face began to blur in her mind. Almost six months had passed since the last time she saw him. In the first week of November, she received a letter from Jacob in which he announced his homecoming. As others before, that letter had taken such a long time to get to her hand, and left her with little time to prepare for the arrival of her beloved.

Miriam could not continue with her tale. She paused, lost in her memories.

"Esther, look at Mother Miriam's cheeks, they became pink with blushes, as if she were happy."

"Yes, Becca, she looks pretty as when father is here."

"I read the letter until I could repeat it word by word with my eyes closed," Miriam continued. "He wrote he was doing the journey by train. He planned to be in Odessa the fifteenth of that same November."

Esther got closer to the hearthstone that now had exploded

in colorful tongues of fire. Without noise, she took off her fur slippers and placed her feet close to the warm stone.

It was almost suppertime. Miriam attempted to leave the story for some other day, but deterred by both girls, she continued.

"I ran downstairs to tell Mother and Father the marvelous news, and to my surprise, Mother was happy. She shed a tear or two to show it. I was still talking to them when Mother got up from her armchair. Calling Alexia and Nanette, she began giving orders and instructions and the three of them left the parlor hastily, with Mother talking, and the two maids walking beside her, both assenting without words."

Again Miriam, with her eyes closed, was quiet, and her breath betrayed her fatigue. In silence, Esther and Rebecca got up from their places on the floor and tiptoed from the room. They knew they had time to take the tray with the rest of food back to the kitchen to Olga and be back before their mother awakened from her daydreams and noticed their absence.

Miriam remembered when she told her father, Boris Prusky. He was a gentleman. He had a good life and until then, no fears; but when he got up from his old leather armchair and embraced his daughter, tears ran down his cheeks. "Oh my, *shayna meidel*, I'm so happy for you," he said and held her tight.

She could not believe it. What displeasure she experienced when she looked into her father's eyes and realized he had lied. Maybe her parents expected another kind of husband for her, perhaps a businessman as her father? No matter their expectations, Jacob was her happiness. He was the love of her life forever.

Nanette was the best cook Miriam had known until she met Olga. She spent some time in the kitchen and learned the most elaborate French dishes and sauces from the fat woman. Miriam remembered that, two days before Jacob arrived, her mother and Nanette spent hours in the kitchen. They prepared delicious bonbons, caramels, and many preserves and marmalades to be served during his visit. They used the oven for hours to bake golden breads, perfect cookies and chocolate cakes.

"Mother, Jacob will stay only a week," she protested once.

"You two are making food to feed a fleet. He is coming alone. The rest of the crew will stay behind to guard the ship."

Miriam laughed as she removed a big basket, full of vegetables, from the chair before she could sit. Later, jokingly, Miriam told Nanette Jacob proposed to her because he wanted to continue eating the foods from her kitchen.

Her tales were stories in which only perfection was possible. She never told the girls her doubts or her fears about her own love story. That November letter had a strange effect on Miriam. She had the unsettled sensation of having drunk wine too fast. She was suffocated by a spinning spiral of feelings provoked by the inevitable arrival of Jacob. One minute she was completely in love with Jacob, minutes later, she was not sure if she cared for him at all. She blamed her emotions on her youth and inexperience in love matters. She decided that her love was no more than an infatuation provoked by that first night at the theater and the enchantment of St. Petersburg itself.

Her heart had an answer for all of her questions and doubts in the early morning of November 15, 1887. When Jacob appeared at the wagon's door before the train came to a full stop, wearing a dark gray suit, a bag on his hand, and a smile just for her, there were no more questions or doubts in her young heart. She knew she loved him.

They waited for Jacob's family to come from St. Petersburg to be present at their ceremony, but only young Sarah came. His parents argued it was too far and too short notice for preparations for such a trip. With the opposition of her parents, they were married. Her mother was disconsolate; Miriam was her only child and she had dreamed of her daughter having a long engagement with time to plan a formal wedding. Instead, Miriam married a man she hadn't known even a full year. Almost no guests were invited, and the part that disappointed Irina the most was the very simple ceremony with a still simpler reception.

In December, just before Hanukah on a cold but beautiful morning, a very happy Miriam married Jacob Vainer. Her mother cried through the whole ceremony. That day they gave each other their bodies and their love forever. They bonded their souls for eternity.

On January 15, 1888, Jacob left Miriam to join his ship. That was the first departure, the first farewell and the first time she felt completely alone. She walked with Jacob on the platform at the train station. One last time, Miriam and Jacob embraced. Then he climbed into one of the cars of the train that had begun to move, and waved to her. Miriam stayed in the same place, immobile, long after the train vanished to form an insignificant dot in the distance. Yuri waited for her in the carriage to take her back home.

The house, until that day noisy and full of life and happiness, seemed dark, cold and so empty. Miriam felt lost in so much space. She didn't know Olga completely, and she couldn't trust her feeling to a maid. She didn't want to run into the arms of her mother or father in search of support. She asked the universe to help her and give her the courage to be the wife of a seaman. Miriam prayed for a miracle to sustain her. On October 6, 1888, the miracle came in the form of a baby girl she named Esther. Jacob came home, yet he always went back to his other mistress, the goddess of sea, but until the day she died, Miriam never felt alone again.

CHAPTER III
A LONG VISIT

Odessa autumn of 1895

"Jacob, please come in with the girls, lunch is ready."

A young Miriam was at the kitchen window, her violet taffeta dress covered with a white apron. She looked radiant, her face painted with life. Her black hair, pulled back with a lavender ribbon, rested on her shoulders. She was happy, and smiled with delight. Her adored husband and daughters were at her reach.

"Esther. Rebecca, Mother is calling, let's go eat. I am hungry, too." Jacob raised his voice to be heard by the young players.

"But Father, I was winning," Esther protested. Disappointed, she left the racket on the garden bench and waited for Rebecca to walk around the net to join her.

It was already fall, but the yard was green and vast, and the old trees still laden with leaves shaded the badminton court from the warm sun.

Since the death of Irina Prusky, the Vainer family had moved into the maternal home. Boris Prusky, already an old man, couldn't live without the supervision and support of his daughter. For the next three years, and until his death, separation wouldn't be so unbearable for Miriam. She would have the company of her father, and her soul wouldn't be tormented by the absence of Jacob.

Jacob, who was at sea for many of his daughter's birthdays, promised Miriam to be at home for the little princess's seventh birthday. He had been absent for each important event in his daughter's life. He knew about the progress she made in life and education through letters he received from home. He regretted not knowing her, but he had chosen his dream when he was no older than his daughter. He had decided his own destiny years before Esther became a reality. He loved the sea more than anything else in this world, more than his wife or his daughter, more than his own life. Until his final moments he was never doubtful. His allegiance belonged to the Russian Navy and Tsar Nicholas.

Miriam was spared the anguish or the anticipated excitement of his arrival. Neither had she spent hours in vigil from the widows' walk before his ship anchored at the port of Odessa. He was not expected at home until the first week in October. However, it was just the middle of September when he was at the door on Balkovskaya Street with a brown suitcase in his hand, and the news that he had a full month of leave.

That September of 1895, the roses had not yet exhausted their blooms, and the marguerites were covered with white and yellow flowers. Jacob noticed the progress on the garden and knew that behind that prodigy was the hand of his wife. Under the direction of Miriam, the young Yuri and Olga cleaned and refurbished the abandoned conservatory on the southwest of the house. They bought Turkish rattan furniture and made green and yellow silk cushions for the sofas and armchairs. Esther and Rebecca loved the place and spent many hours there. At the end of fall and early winter they studied and did their homework in the conservatory. The sunlight in the glass house let them read without the help of candles or kerosene lamps. Yuri made the wooden pots. In them, Miriam planted the exotic orchids Jacob brought home from Ceylon on his previous visit a year earlier.

They had called at the port of Colombo before the fleet returned to Russia. He and some other officers had to wait for the rain to stop to leave the ship. It was close to evening when, after the deluge, they ventured into the city for a visit. The thick aroma from the tropical vegetation was suspended in the humid air they breathed. Hordes of hungry mosquitoes pierced their skins and clouds of black flies were everywhere, but long weeks at sea made the walk desirable. The lack of space and the activity in the crowded town was feverish. The sailors saw women carrying baskets and water jugs, dressed in long cotton skirts of vivid colors, and wore long scarves that covered their hair and part of their faces. Other women were on the side of the road, next to houses, cooking over braziers. Men behind wooden carts filled with brass and copper pots competed for the space in the narrow streets with rattan woven taxies pulled by men. On one of the streets they saw a caravan of elephants with their human cargo concealed by silvery curtains.

The group of officers, in their white uniforms, wandered through muddy roads. They were followed by curious children and beggars. With the last light of day, they stopped for a drink in an obscure bar. The establishment was run by a subject of the British Empire, Mr. Wallis, who had become rich quenching sailors' thirst. He hired native girls to serve the tables and entertain his customers. The place, popular with mariners, was two blocks from the port, and conveniently open day and night.

Jacob and his four friends were welcomed by Mr. Wallis, who gave them the first drink on the house. The man sent one of the servants to prepare a table with a tablecloth for the special guests. Entertained by Mr. Wallis, they drank many more rounds of Scotch whiskey. When the waitress came to direct them to the dining room, she found the sailors transformed into a happy and noisy group. Mr. Wallis' cook had prepared for the main course, lamb in a sauce with much hot curry, and other hot spices unknown to their palates. Their mouths were on fire, and they used a good amount of whiskey to extinguish it.

It was daylight when he awoke with a painful headache. The sweet smell of a cheap perfume nauseated him, and the bitter taste of whiskey and curry filled his throat. He had lost all sense of time, and didn't know where the other officers were. He couldn't remember at what point he left the bar or how he arrived next door to the brothel. A hot ray of morning sun intruding through a dusty window blinded him. His head throbbed heavily, his mouth suddenly dry, was in need of some water. He looked around and found himself next to a dark-skinned beauty with a tattoo of a flower on her belly and a red diamond on her forehead. She was indolently asleep, completely nude, uncovered, and cradled by multicolored cushions. Jacob felt the urgency to get out of that place.

The room was invaded by a bustling outside noise. He dressed, looked for his hat, which had fallen under a low chair, and held it under his arm. From his leather wallet, he took some money that he placed on a brass tray-table next to the bed, and pushed the wallet back in his jacket inside pocket.

Walking to the arched threshold, pressing close to the wall to avoid as much contact as possible with the greasy raffia braided curtain separating the room from the outside, he exited the room. He found himself in the crowded commotion of a local street market. There, among caged colorful birds, tiny monkeys chained to a pole, hundreds of burlap bags filled with teas and unknown herbs and spices, he discovered the magnificent orchids. Maybe because their beauty and fragility reminded him of Miriam, he bought many plants for her and kept them alive until he arrived home, ten months later.

Close to his thirty-ninth birthday, Jacob was tall and slender. A short blond beard covered part of his face, weathered by the constant exposure to salted seas and winds. The sun had tanned his skin and darkened his blue eyes. He was temperamental, and could become angry with undisciplined sailors, but his many years of command had taught him patience.

He shared the everyday routine with his fellow officers aboard ship, but Jacob, a reserved man, spent many hours alone in his quarters in the company of a good book. A passionate lover of classical music, he listened to his records on the phonograph he bought for himself in Germany. He preferred the quiet and solitude of his cabin, but could become gregarious after a few glasses of vodka. He lived his life fully and without regrets. He never claimed to be the best husband or father, but he knew he was a great sailor and a better officer.

At every port the entire crew awaited the arrival of the local postal authorities that delivered the mail bags, heavy with accumulated letters and many parcels. Jacob was a meticulous man and liked to keep all things in a certain order. The photographs he received were immediately placed in a large blue photo album. The letters from home were placed in two boxes. In a wooden cigar box of Havana cigars, he kept the empty envelopes. In a large mahogany box with green velvet inside, he placed the dated sheets. He continued to reread those same letters until the delivery of more correspondence in the next port. He could identify Miriam's handwriting with more assurance than her own body.

At the end of each day, Miriam wrote to her dearest Jacob and told him her most intimate thoughts. That was the only way she knew to let her husband participate in the family affairs. She was prolific in her letters. She told him with detail about the progress of Esther. Her first tooth, her first step, her first day at school. She gave him news about Rebecca, too, and the happiness the little girl brought to her heart. Often, Miriam mentioned the unfortunate events that forced Rebecca to be part of their family and stated repeatedly her decision to block any intent of Ishmael to claim Rebecca back.

With time, Miriam learned it was easier to communicate with her husband through letters. The political state of the country influenced him so deeply that in the last three years of their marriage, it was time for Jacob to go back to sea before they had fully re-established dialogue. She had to use love and tolerance to make the first few days of his visits bearable. The transition from his role as an officer aboard ship, to the one of a husband and father was difficult for him. They needed nights of intimacy to re-learn each other's touch. Only in those moments together, they were transported into a world without time. They renewed their old vows and promise, hidden from that outside, where years of separation could not invade their passion. She was complete only when she felt the proximity of his breath or the prison of his arms and knew that never would she be as close or love someone else as much as she loved him. Not even Esther.

However, events that would change their future continued to develop. Years of war and violence had shaken Asia. In 1895, Japan defeated China. Following extensive negotiation, Japan was pressured to make concessions over Port Arthur in Southern Manchuria and the Liaotung Peninsula. Actions that would benefit Russia and the plans of its Prime Minister Witte to further develop the Trans-Siberian Railroad. The political situation in Europe was harmonious. Nonetheless, some tension among the European countries could be perceived by an expert eye. Germany was in competition with the French Republic over the Tsar's favors. The Russian Navy was navigating every ocean of the world without restrictions. Jacob's fleet soon would leave from St. Petersburg for a trip to North America and southern South America.

"Where are you going next, Papa?"

"It will be a long trip this time, Princess, and a long absence."

CHAPTER IV
ABOUT DEATH AND DYING

Odessa June, 1905

"Mother, please open your mouth. The doctor wants you to take this medicine."

Miriam was shocked by the hand of her daughter. She felt weak, without the strength to move, not even her eyes. Some place in her dream, Jacob was about to go away alone. She had to go back to him. She had to join her husband.

Miriam refused to take any more remedies. She was tired. She just did not want to go on living. This was the last time, and she only swallowed the bitter potion to make Esther happy. Death struck with precision and took from her the most prized gift she had received for her seventeenth birthday, the Love of Her Life.

She was devastated. Certainly, she had Esther to live for, but with her husband, she was from that other time, the yesterday. Esther belonged to the awaited future, to the promise of the new century. She would have a life without war and devastation.

For years Miriam tried to understand and justify the reason why her country had chosen a path of destruction. Why would the Tsar of all Russia, for pride more than dignity, place his children in a disadvantaged duel with death? Why was he deaf to their cries and ignorant of their pain? Miriam remembered well that just the year before on February 4, 1904, Japan attacked Russia. In a surprise assault, the Japanese flotilla destroyed the Eastern Russian Fleet at Port Arthur. Followed by that first act of aggression, Japan declared war on Tsar Nicholas II. News about the events were too slow to arrive to calm her anxiety. The country was still in an economic recession, with unhealed wounds from the Boxer Rebellion. The newspaper said Witte tried unsuccessfully to convince Nicholas to have a peaceful settlement through diplomacy. In disagreement, the Interior Minister Pleve argued that a war was needed. Pleve said that to suffocate the imminent internal revolution they needed to be victorious in a "little" war.

Miriam concealed some of the events from Esther and Rebecca, but the inescapable reality was written not only in the news, but glued to the walls along the streets, in enormous black letters. They were given as pamphlets in the fruit and vegetable market. The discontent was among the women at the butcher shop where Olga bought the meat. She could hear the women talk while they waited to be served. They protested the high prices, the low salaries, and the voices were very loud shouting against the Tsar's irrational decisions. Political demonstrations on the streets were everywhere. The war with Japan increased the opposition to the Tsar in Russia's countrymen. New political movements arose. The liberal activists formed the organization called Union of Liberation. A few months later that same year, they joined forces with a larger group, The Socialist Revolutionary Party.

Miriam learned in the evening paper that Russia suffered heavy casualties in a succession of lost battles against Japan. On land, in the battle of Mukden, the paper said that between the months of February and March, 1905, Russia lost over 100,000 soldiers. She felt ashamed of her feelings. She was almost happy to think Jacob was a naval officer. To escape more casualties the Russian troops retreated to the north. By that time the Japanese had reached the end of their strength. They were not able to pursue the Russian Army and attempted to negotiate peace. Tsar Nicholas, ill advised, did not accept the Japanese offer, and waited for the Baltic Fleet attack on Japan. Jacob's ship formed part of the Baltic fleet. On May 27, 1905, his ship was sunk in the attempt to go across the Yellow Sea.

She read in the morning paper about the defeat of the Russian Navy. For almost two weeks she didn't eat or sleep, only prayed. The uncertainty and the lack of information consumed her soul, and she fell into a deep depression. The feared news, that she hoped never to hear, arrived on June 11, 1905. An official telegram informed Miriam that her husband had died.

"Esther, how can I accept his death without his body?" she screamed.

"Shhhh, Mama. Please, calm down, Mama."

Miriam cried disconsolately. She held the wrinkled telegram in her hands and collapsed into the armchair in the parlor. She was the epitome of desolation with her face wet with tears and her hair undone. She was so terribly sad, that Esther and Rebecca placed aside their own grief and hurried to console her.

Several weeks passed after the news about her father's death. Esther dedicated every moment of her day to improve her mother's health and sanity.

"Becca, what can we do to put a spark in Mama's heart?" she asked her cousin.

"My dear Esther, there isn't much we can do."

"She needs help, and I don't know how to help her." Esther was stopped by uncontained sobs. Her shoulders shook, and she clasped both hands in despair.

Rebecca walked to where Esther was seated. She kneeled next to her and thought for a long instant before she spoke. "You see, Mother Miriam has lost the will to live."

"I fear you are right, Becca."

"She began to die the day they brought the news about Uncle Jacob's death." Rebecca caressed Esther's face, and dried a tear from her cheek. "To want to live, you need to have a dream." Esther was about to interrupt her cousin but Rebecca placed a hand over her mouth. "Yes, I believe Mother Miriam has no more dreams to look forward to, only tragic realities."

The doorbell rang, halting their conversation. Without giving the chance for Olga to answer, Esther jumped up from the bedside chair, moving around Rebecca, and hurried downstairs. She opened the door, but nobody stood on the outside. Stepping out, she placed her hand over her eyes to protect them from the light of the blinding sun and looked around. The carriage that belonged to Dr. Feldman was stopped at the street just in front the house, but she couldn't see the doctor anywhere.

Dr. Feldman was still a young man, with childish blue eyes, sandy blond hair he combed to the back and a short beard he frequently scratched in puzzlement when he looked at Miriam. Esther always saw him dressed in a black suit, impeccable white shirt, stiff with starch that contrasted with the short black tie, glassy black shoes and a black tall hat. His clothes smelled like the lavender flowers they dried in the basement at the end of every summer. He used a gold chain that crossed his vest from pocket to pocket and a gold watch he checked quite often. Esther wasn't sure whether he really needed to check the time, or the ritual of taking the watch out, opening it, closing it and placing it back in the same pocket, all in silence, was used to ponder an answer when he was asked a difficult question.

"Dr. Feldman," Esther called out loud. "Dr. Feldman." She started to walk to the rose garden beside the house and found him bent over a rose bush.

He straightened when she called his name again. "Here Esther, I'm here." He pushed his glasses back on his nose and waved a hand.

"Admiring the roses, aren't you?"

"These roses are unusual. Where are they from?"

"From the United Kingdom. Not too long ago, Papa brought them for Mama."

"I haven't seen these colors or smelled this aroma before now. Most interesting."

"The one you were admiring is a young plant." She cut a rose, and offered it to the doctor. "The name of this rose is Reine de Violettes."

The doctor placed the rose on his jacket lapel, smelled it, and they started to walk back to the house. The silence was broken by Esther. "Where is your automobile, Doctor? I did not know you still used your carriage."

"Well, sometimes I use my old companion. Like everyone, my horse needs to exercise a little, so I take him when the ride is not too much effort for his age."

Esther frowned at the originality of the comparison. "…a horse with people," she thought.

"How is your mother today? Have you noticed any improvement in her health?"

He stopped, cleaned his feet on the entrance mat, and followed Esther into the house. Olga was at the door to receive the hat from the doctor. She placed it on the entrance hall table and disappeared. She would have time later to ask the doctor about Madam. They both continued their way upstairs to the bedroom where a languishing Miriam waited.

Rebecca rose and smiled at the doctor. In a coquettish gesture, she put a hand to her hair. Her knot was in need of help. "Mother Miriam is waking up," she whispered. Removing the doctor's bag from his hand, she placed it on top of the chest of drawers a few steps away from the bed where Miriam lay.

The doctor took out a stethoscope from the bag, turning to face Miriam. A shadow of defeat passed through his mind for an instant. He breathed deeply, and walked toward the bedside.

"Mrs. Vainer, can you hear me? I came to see you."

Miriam glanced up at him.

"How are you feeling today? With your permission, I will examine you now."

She did not answer, did not move, but with a slight insinuation of a smile on her discolored lips, waited with unattached indifference for the doctor to examine her. She didn't offer any resistance. She was a passive patient, but in the end it wasn't important what they put her through. She'd had enough of this life. She was ready to go.

Rebecca and Esther stood across from Dr. Feldman while he examined Miriam. He held her wrist with his left hand, and with his pocket watch in his other hand, he took her pulse. In complete silence he listened to her heart, looking inside her eyes with the help of a small flashlight. He asked Miriam to sit, and listened to her lungs. He helped her to lie down again. He moved away from the bed, unbuttoned the cuffs of his shirt and rolled up his sleeves.

Rebecca poured water from a porcelain pitcher into a basin, waited for the doctor to wash his hands and handed him an embroidered towel. Mechanically, Dr. Feldman dried his hands, placed the towel next to the pitcher, straightened his shirt and placed the medical instruments back into the small black leather bag.

He was baffled. His patient was technically healthy. The

doctor closed the bag and started out of the room. The tight muscles of his jaws showed his frustration when he walked with Esther into the parlor.

"Dr. Feldman, would you like some tea or maybe a cup of Turkish coffee?"

"A cup of tea will be fine, thank you, Rebecca."

He moved in his seat with unease. The proximity of Rebecca made him nervous.

Olga arrived with the tea service and placed it on the table. She asked the doctor if he had noticed any improvement in Miriam's health. She left the room alarmed, not just because of the words of the doctor, but the discouragement she saw in his eyes.

Esther served a cup of tea and passed it to Rebecca, then before she poured again asked, "Do you like some milk in your tea, Doctor?"

"Yes, please and two cubes of sugar, thank you." Dr. Feldman leaned forward to receive the tea cup. He sat back and drank his tea in silence

The formality was stiff to the extreme, but, of course, his visit was not a social call. They were there to talk about the health of Miriam.

Several more minutes of silence gave the doctor the time to choose words. "As you well know, I'm worried about your mother's life." A new pause, a sip of tea and he continued, "She doesn't seem to respond favorably to any of the treatments I have administered, and her health continues to deteriorate."

"When you arrived I was telling Rebecca my concerns, but now your pessimism scares much, Dr. Feldman," Esther stated in a frightened voice.

"We can't let Mother Miriam just slide away into unconsciousness. Can we?" Rebecca asked shakily.

The doctor paused. "There are two, maybe three possibilities if we consider hypnosis, but first we need to know how far you want to go with treatments for your mother. At least one of the treatments can be terribly painful, maybe traumatic," he added at the same time he cleaned his gold-rimmed spectacles that became fogged by the steam of the tea with his handkerchief.

"Please tell us, we'll do all we must to bring her back to health," Esther asserted with desperation.

"Dr. Feldman, tell us now what is on your mind." Rebecca said the last words with authority and a bit of irritation.

The doctor decided to put aside any reservations he had left, and told them he'd taken the liberty to consult the case of their mother with a colleague, since he thought he didn't need to ask Esther for permission. He took a moment of hesitation to look for the right words. It was a difficult task to explain a painful truth without inflicting pain.

"There are no more conventional treatments to try on her."

Rebecca interrupted him and asked, "Are you giving up? Is there nothing else to do for Mother Miriam?" The alarm made her voice tremble.

"Let me finish without interrupting me, please," the doctor asked in a kind tone. "There are, as I said before, three possibilities. The first one and the most pleasant of them, is to take your mother to one of the very modern and up-to-date health clinics. You can find excellent sanatoriums from here to Germany. However, you do not need to go too far. Fortunately there are some fine clinics east of Odessa, on the coast of the Black Sea. Those clinics are well recommended for their skilled body of professionals and dedication to their patients. The one I'm thinking about is quite close to Odessa. You can accompany, and stay with your mother in an apartment. That is, if you are reluctant to leave her there alone." He picked up the cup and drank more tea. Undecided to tell them the other treatment, he stammered and stopped his monologue.

"Don't vacillate, Dr. Feldman. We need to know every possible treatment, to make a better decision."

"You may have heard talk about hypnosis. Although there have been some *almost* miracle cures through its application, I do not believe your mother could benefit from it." He hesitated before mentioning the third possibility. "The other alternative," he stopped, breathed noisily and looked at both young women, "is very modern, dangerous, not well-developed or studied, and as a consequence, not well-known. I would say it is the last resort for many and I am including your mother in that many. It is called electroshock."

The two young women looked at each other. They had never heard or read of such a thing. Esther and Rebecca didn't know exactly what the doctor was talking about. However, if the electroshock treatment was painful, they would not choose it for Miriam.

Dr. Feldman looked for better words to use, to make his explanation clearer. Unsuccessfully, with each new word he used, they understood less, and both girls became increasingly apprehensive.

"The patient is treated once a day for a matter of seconds each time. The treatment consists of the passage of electricity to the body through some electrodes placed in strategic areas on the head. As I said before, it is a revolutionary way to treat depression, but there is no data to confirm its effectiveness." A heavy silence followed the last words of the doctor. Terrified and imagining horrific scenarios, neither Rebecca nor Esther could find the words to break that silence.

Finally Rebecca said, "This electroshock sounds a bit radical and quite dangerous, don't you think so, Doctor?"

"Well it is, Rebecca."

"Which one of these three methods do you recommend in the case of Mother Miriam?"

"I think it is for you to decide."

"I understand that, but you must have an idea about this. Can you tell us?" Rebecca demanded.

Esther was not able to articulate a word. The conversation was about her mother. Miriam's life was being determined in that precise moment, and she was not present to make the decision.

The doctor didn't give an answer to Rebecca. Instead, he said, "I will go now. I have to visit one other patient. I will be back tomorrow, early afternoon, to visit Mrs. Vainer and to meet with both of you." He stood up from the armchair, immediately imitated by the girls.

"Please don't leave the bag behind. You'll need it where you're going." Esther reached for the doctor's bag, forgotten on a side table.

"Thank you, dear, and do not worry so much. Tomorrow, together, we will find a solution and the right treatment for your mother."

Rebecca took his hat from the entrance table and looked in the mirror at his reflected image. *I like him. He is a handsome man*, she thought. She turned around and said to him with charm in her smile, "Here, Doctor, your hat." Then she opened the door for him and both girls saw him out.

They went back to the parlor and sat for a long time. They could not share their thoughts. They both were sorting through all the information given by the doctor. It was difficult to comprehend, and hard to accept, that whatever they decided would change not just their mother's life, but also theirs. Overnight they had had to become adults. For the first time they had the responsibility to act as their elders. A decision of such magnitude, could not be done in a hurry, and made them reluctant to choose. To decide the wrong treatment or to go for a radical one, as in the case of the electroshock, paralyzed them.

Esther was seated in the rocking chair in one of her favorite positions, her chin on her knees, her legs up, covered by the blue skirt and her arms wrapped around them. Her mother used to ask her to put her legs down and sit with her back straight. "As a lady." As much as she hated it before, Esther thought that if her mother died, she would miss hearing even that. She was so far away in search of an answer, she never heard, the first few words, when Rebecca began to talk. As always, she was the first to come up with a practical idea and to express it.

"I've been trying to place myself in Mother Miriam's mind to see and feel what she might have chosen as the best remedy for her illness."

"I know she would not pick a treatment that has not yet proved to be effective. She is a bit conservative in those matters," Esther said and the only thought in her mind were the electroshock, and the tortures of the inquisition.

"I believe Mother Miriam will be delighted to spend some time at the seashore."

"What makes you think that, Becca?"

"It will be a wonderful experience for her to be out of this house and pampered."

"Yes, you are right, Becca. I would love it myself."

"I'm sure it will be a welcome change for the three of us."

Esther stood up and went to the tall opened window. She

sighed and smiled, welcoming the summer breeze.

"We don't have to decide right now. It has been a long afternoon." Rebecca rose and joined Esther at the window. She put her arm around her younger cousin's shoulders. "We have time until tomorrow to decide."

"I'm confident Dr. Feldman will help us."

"I know he will, Esther. Considering she always loved open spaces, sun and fresh air, I believe Mother Miriam would enjoy a week or two in a health clinic."

The next day when Dr. Feldman arrived, they were ready and waiting for him with a smile and the decision. He was secretly happy to hear they both planned to accompany their mother. He would talk to Dr. Kaminski, the director of the clinic, and make all the necessary arrangements. He assured them that the personnel would be ready to receive Miriam and her two companions.

As soon as the doctor examined his patient and left the house, the girls began the plans for the trip. Rebecca asked Olga to take down three large suitcases from the attic and bring one to each bedroom. Suddenly the mood of the household had changed. It seemed filled with energy. All the windows were opened to the outdoor noises, and on impulse, Esther walked to the piano, stood in front of it, and with just one finger played notes to imitate the song a bird sang, perched on one of the old cedar trees. Rebecca, in her bedroom, tried on a dress in front of the mirror and jokingly referred to the trip, "Not quite the French Riviera, but very satisfying."

From the moment her father left, Rebecca decided to forget him and be part of her new family. She never mentioned him or her mother again. She kept them in that distant past. Determined and practical, when asked, she had the right answer. Small and slender, she had an easy smile and a pretty face. Unlike Esther, she was ready to become an adult. She learned from Olga the secrets of good food, and often joined the cook in the kitchen. At times, she helped Ana in the many chores around the house. She dreamed one day to have a husband, children and a home of her own.

It was a trip with a promise, a future to look forward to. They had no emotional relief since Jacob's death. They had experienced so much sorrow that the young women indulged in the illusion of the chance for happiness and healing. On Monday, July 3, 1905, with high hopes, Miriam, Esther and Rebecca left for the seashore for the rest of the month.

The weather in the outskirts of Odessa was perfect that summer. Dry, and cooled by the marine winds, and never too hot. The Black Sea town where the clinic was located was small and frozen in time. A fishermen's village. Only the main street was paved with big stones. A Byzantine church with white walls was on the north corner of the central square. Opposite the church, and on the south side of the square, was a fish, vegetable and fruit market. The life of the town gravitated around it. The houses were built over thousands of years of history. It was possible to see remains of ruins from the time when the Greeks and Turks were the inhabitants there. By contrast, the clinic was modern and elegant, with large spaces enclosed by glass walls. Rooms with enormous windows made the patients feel as free inside as outside. Terraces and patios with tables and colorful umbrellas were connected to the gardens by white Italian marble steps. The gardens were a masterpiece in themselves. Marble sculptures in a Greco-Roman style adorned the green hills. Lustrous granite benches lined the gravel paths. There was even a place that Miriam found, where she could hide from the rest of the world every afternoon. As soon as she finished her session with the psychiatrist, she hurried to the circular fountain with a small round white temple in the center. The temple had four columns and in the center, a statue of a Vestal. An endless stream of water poured out of a vessel she held on her shoulder. Miriam felt calmed by the sound of the splashing water.

Several tennis courts of red clay were available at all times for the intrepid who wanted to exercise an extra hour. So many people walked about and enjoyed the place. It was easy to forget it was a clinic for the ill and not an elegant vacation spot. Maybe that was the idea.

The doctors were very kind and acted as if nothing could irritate them, not even the most rebellious patient. Each patient had a nurse with him or her at all times. That same day, soon after they arrived in the clinic, a nurse was assigned to Miriam. That gave Esther and Rebecca a bit of freedom. They had time to read, walk in the park, play tennis, and swim in the outdoor swimming pool. They were young and soon placed aside their troubles. Once again a smile danced in their eyes.

As expected, the first days Miriam resisted the treatments. She didn't want to get out of bed, much less to go for a walk in the beautiful parks or exercise in the indoor warm water pool. Miss Petrovna, the nurse, asked Rebecca and Esther to go out to the gardens or maybe have a walk on the beach while she would talk to their mother. Nurse Petrovna sat next to the bed Miriam was on, and talked to her for hours. Miriam listened, cried at times, turned her back to the nurse and also smiled more than once. Esther and Rebecca were intrigued by the conversation. At dinner, when they asked Miriam, she smiled enigmatically and didn't utter a word. She never told them what the Nurse Petrovna and she talked about.

The ability and efficiency of the team of doctors, nurses and therapists produced miracles. Without noticeable demands, they made Miriam collaborate in her own recuperation. Esther and Rebecca were happy. They had the confirmation. The clinic was the right decision. It was the perfect place for their mother's rehabilitation. To see Miriam sit out on the veranda and speak a few words encouraged them. Even when the conversations were not significant, they were delighted with the small progress.

To avoid the impact the crowded dining room could have on the frail Miriam, they had dinner together on the terrace of her room for a few nights. As soon as Miriam felt stronger, they had their meals downstairs with the rest of the patients. They dressed for dinner. It was an elegant atmosphere and quite formal at dinnertime. As they arrived at the dining room, they were directed to their preplanned places. Esther and Rebecca, in their evening gowns, felt the gazes of admiration of the male guests.

Most of the tables in the dining room were occupied. At the table to their right was an elderly couple. The old lady told them as soon they met, that she and her husband were both in very good health. She attributed their well-being to their perseverance in using for years the month of July for detoxification of their bodies. They had no alcohol, tobacco, or animal meats for all those thirty-one days. That one was their second visit to the clinic of Dr. Kaminski. They were there in the summer of 1902. They loved the treatment offered for mental and physical cleansing, and were on a special diet of herbs, seaweeds, and vegetables. "…not even fish, much less caviar, that I miss very much," she said. "Too much salt."

Before breakfast the old couple went for long walks, and visited the large Turkish bath at the back of the clinic once a day, frequently before lunch. "You should try it," the woman told Miriam. "It cleanses all your pores and makes your skin younger and healthy."

Since the evening Miriam and the girls first had dinner in the dining room, a big round table kept Esther away from the conversation. Her eyes drifted aimlessly past the barriers offered by the crowded room, to arrive at the table with five diners. She could see the side of a circumspect large man with an abundant gray beard, next to whom was a thin woman with an angular face, shadowed always by the hats she wore. The couple was possibly ten years older than Miriam. At the same table was a wrinkled older lady no bigger than a child, and two handsome young men. The family was distinctive and severe in the manner each one of the members acted. The formality was extended to their clothes, which were dark and elegant but austere. They spoke Russian to the servers, but the few words they spoke among themselves were in another language. They did not smile much; looked almost angry.

"Becca, did you notice the foreigners?"

"How can you tell them apart from the rest of the people around us?"

"Hmm, of course I can. Such different people, they seem bored."

"I'm sorry, Esther. They look just like people to me."

Esther would find out a few days later their name was Perlman and they were originally from Poland. They had moved to Odessa eighteen years earlier in search of a dryer climate for their son. They were in the grain export business. The family, including the grandmother, would spend most of the summer there. Each of the last ten, they had visited the clinic to seek treatments for their younger son. He had been sick since the age of seven with rheumatism in his legs and arms.

That explains the wheelchair, she thought. Sometimes the illness made walking or using his hands very painful. Esther wanted to stop and talk to the family, but there was not much room for socializing at dinnertime. Miriam was extremely tired, and soon after the meal every night, Rebecca and Esther accompanied her to her room.

The schedule for the patients started early in the morning. At seven o'clock, Nurse Petrovna gave Miriam an injection of vitamin B complex. Petrovna helped her to dress, made certain she drank an enormous glass of milk, and by 7:30, nurse and patient were downstairs on the women's exercise floor. They worked out with clubs for exactly twenty minutes. Miriam rested for five minutes, and Nurse Petrovna gave her a cold shower, called there, the Swedish Bath Massage. Petrovna held a wide hose that spit out iced water with incredible force. Miriam had to brace herself with the wall hand bar just to avoid being knocked down. Miriam was so cold after that part of the treatment, her teeth chattered, and her lips remained blue until she was completely dressed. She had not recovered her appetite, but breakfast at nine o'clock was a welcome rest. She was tired from the previous ordeal, and wouldn't make the effort to walk to the central table for food. Nurse Petrovna surprised her, when the first morning, she arrived at the table with two plates filled to the rim with breakfast foods.

In the center of the room was a large round table replete with the bounty taken from the generous sea. The mortified Miriam said the barely cooked pink shrimps with heads and whiskers stared at her. She didn't dare eat them. Soon enough, Nurse Petrovna learned the way her patient felt about the small crustaceans, and ceased to serve them to her. There were other exquisite dishes she could serve. Miriam had no objection to eating smoked herring or pickled fish eggs. With pleasure, she ate some poached red salmon and especially loved the breads, which the wise Nurse Petrovna quickly realized. On a smaller rectangular table were the freshest golden breads with the aroma of just taken from the oven. The nurse prepared from that table a small plate with breads, cheeses, and butter, which she took from a crystal bowl placed on a larger bowl with crushed ice. That was too much food, but, Miriam knew better than to protest, and she ate it all in silence.

From the breakfast room, Nurse Petrovna took Miriam to the women's solarium. Once again, she took off all of Miriam's clothes, even her corset and underwear. The nurse made her lie for five minutes on her back, and then ten more minutes on her stomach. "The nurse makes me flip over like a latke," she protested to Esther. The rest of the morning was used for enjoyment, as the nurse called it. Miriam could read, walk in the garden, or talk to other people until lunchtime.

The afternoon program was more pleasurable. Miriam liked the exercises. They were in a warmed pool. For her, the least favorites of the afternoons were the sauna and the massages. Her skin resented the dry heat, and was irritated by the powder for the massages. She detested the hour she had to endure with Dr. Rosenthal, the psychoanalyst. The doctor made her face her phantoms.

The active day caused Miriam to take frequent naps, and a long one in the afternoon to recuperate from the exhaustion. She had to go early to bed at night to be ready for a fresh start the next morning. However, when she learned there was a concert at the outdoor theater every Saturday evening, fatigue didn't stop her. That first Saturday they attended a string quartet recital. Miriam took every minute of that evening as a present. The black hat with the three tea-colored roses, the new pale yellow dress she wore, the walk to the theater, the girls' bubbly talk and their laughter. The night and the brilliancy of the stars didn't escape her notice, and she was aware of the breeze and the smell of salt from the sea. She chatted with what Rebecca and Esther thought was excitement. After a bravo at the end of the concert, with the last notes of a Brahms string quartet still vibrating in the air, Miriam clapped with enthusiasm. Unnoticed, life was returning to the old familiar way.

Dr. Feldman became a quotidian visitor of the three women. He was pleased to know the clinic was a perfect suggestion for Miriam. He met daily with the other doctors, and was delighted to learn about her progress, and the gradual improvement of her will to live. Dr. Feldman encouraged but did not pity her. When she complained about the sun, he asked her to continue to sunbathe no less than ten minutes a day. That was a revolutionary approach to treat the body. Except for the peasant women who were exposed to the extreme cold of winter and to the suffocating heat and suns of mid-summer, powdery white skin was synonymous with beauty. Ladies kept away from the sun.

At the clinic, Dr. Feldman found a way to be free of obligations at lunchtime, and joined the three women at the table. Miriam was terribly tired from her morning treatment. As soon they finished lunch, she desperately needed to rest. Before she was put to bed by Nurse Petrovna for an afternoon nap, Dr. Feldman asked Miriam for permission to take Rebecca and Esther for a walk or a carriage ride in the countryside.

It was obvious to Esther, Dr. Feldman showed a special inclination for her cousin. She was sure the doctor would prefer to walk with Rebecca alone, and invented a good reason for not joining them each time. The truth was, Esther would rather stay behind and look for something to read in the clinic library. It was a marvelous library and had a great selection of contemporary writers. She found more than one book she had yet to read by Anton Chekhov. Esther loved his short stories and plays. That day when she stepped into the library, she noticed a young man in his wheelchair. He had a book on his lap, but he was not reading it. He just looked through the closed window at that unreachable vast park. The noise of her steps made him turn his head. When he met Esther's eyes, he recognized her as his curious dining room neighbor. They smiled at each other. Without a second thought, Esther walked to where he was.

"Hello, what you are reading?"

"The Bishop," he said and showed her the book cover.

"Oh! You like Anton Chekhov, then," Esther said, and sat next to him.

"He is one of my favorites," he answered.

"Mine too. I read that book not long ago."

He was, or appeared to be, as young as Esther, pale and fragile. His eyes and his skin looked bluer in the daylight, and seemed vulnerable in his wheelchair. She learned they shared a passion for reading. From afar, his older brother observed them. Throughout that first meeting he never came closer. The new friends continued to talk until Esther recognized the familiar figures of Rebecca and Dr. Feldman in the distance. She left the library with the promise to meet again the next afternoon, to keep each other company and talk some more about books.

Esther ran to tell Rebecca. "His name is Albert Perlman, and his older brother is Gustav." She took her cousin by the arm, and adjusted her excitement to Rebecca's slower pace. "And do you know they live less than eight blocks from our house in Odessa?"

That evening at dinner Esther and Albert waved to each other as friends. Gustav moved his head in a formal bow and several times he tried unsuccessfully to engage Esther's evasive eyes.

Through the rest of their stay the friendship between Esther and Albert grew stronger. They continued to meet at the library in the afternoons. Before the Vainer family left the clinic, Esther and Albert exchanged addresses and decided to meet again once he and his family were back in Odessa.

CHAPTER V
BACK TO ODESSA

Odessa 1905, the end of the summer

With every new day, Miriam had recovered and healed one new piece of her soul, shattered with the death of Jacob. By the end of July, she was still weak, but indeed, her health was much improved, and she was allowed to go back home to Odessa. That Friday morning, Miriam met with Dr. Kaminski. Rebecca and Esther were asked to be present. The director of the clinic made sure the two girls understood that the health of their mother was not yet fully recovered. To regain complete health, she had to continue at home with a prescribed treatment similar to the one she went through at the clinic. She would be under Dr. Feldman's supervision.

The chief doctor gave Miriam a white paper with a long list of directions to follow, and a box, as big as a shoebox, filled with small brown bottles containing herbal teas, vitamins and homeopathic remedies. She should continue to take those medicines for two more months, she was informed. Those were the same remedies Nurse Petrovna made her take every day. Dr. Kaminski also informed her about a plan suggested by the team of doctors who had looked after her for the previous three weeks. He passed an envelope with the instructions and recommendations for Dr. Feldman to follow. After a brief casual conversation, Dr. Kaminski accompanied them to the door. With a head gesture and a conventional smile, he said goodbye to the three women.

Miriam's face was aglow with enthusiasm. She could barely wait. She would be back home in a few more hours. She had to get ready and spent part of the afternoon busy with the departure plans.

For Esther, to pack was an unbearably laborious task. "I can't imagine the reason that made me put all these clothes in my suitcase. I haven't used most of them and now they don't quite fit back into it anymore," she lamented, as she sat on the bed defeated with trying. "How could I ever place all this chazeray in just one suitcase?"

"What you mean, my dear, is that you can't do your suitcase without Olga's help. Isn't that right?"

"Well, Becca, you know me, I'm not good at folding."

"Yes, I know you well. You are lazy."

"I hate this packing business! Will you please help me, Becca?"

Esther learned how to use her angelic smile and a helpless tone of voice effectively to avoid most responsibilities. The youngest in her family, she was a pampered seventeen year old. Pampered so that even Rebecca surrendered to her pleas. She would flame with irritation when someone mentioned that she was the feminine portrait of her father arguing, "…but I have my mother's wavy dark hair." She thought Miriam was a beautiful woman. Nobody but Rebecca knew how much Esther resented the perennial absence of her father and the languid resignation of her mother. Only her older cousin could read those rebellious moods reflected in her deep blue eyes. For hours at the time, her interest in art kept her in her small studio behind the kitchen. She would much rather work with her oils and brushes on a canvas than to help with the household chores. She loved acting, and was always ready to improvise a play in front of her family. Like Rebecca, she also had an unshared dream. She hoped one day to be a renowned artist, and perform Chekhov's plays in all the Russian theaters.

Once Rebecca had placed her own clothes in her bag, she helped Esther to fold and place everything back into her cousin's suitcase. They laughed and talked with vivacity about the past weeks, Esther's new friend Albert, his handsome brother Gustav, and the dear Dr. Feldman. It was late when they finally finished packing.

The two girls ran to the quarters of their mother, knocked at the door and entered the silent room. The bed was unused, and the suitcase lay open on a wooden support next to the night-table. The room was empty.

With apprehension, they called Miriam's name and received no answer. The large French windows were wide open, and they ran to the terrace where they found her. She was unable to notice their presence, absorbed in the spectacle of a purple sunset. Behind her, the two girls couldn't escape the romantic sight and waited until the sky was darkened by the night to break the enchanted moment to ask her to go with them downstairs for dinner.

The girls hoped that after the meal, they could go to the music room. A piano recital was announced for that night and Esther didn't want to miss it. Dinner was pleasant, but the extra emotions of the day had made Miriam tired. They were surprised by their mother's decision. After dessert she suggested that the girls should go to the music room without her. She desperately needed to rest. Esther protested for a moment, but accepted the idea rapidly.

They accompanied Miriam to her room and rushed to the concert hall. This was the first time that Gustav Perlman had the opportunity to be next to Esther. Attentive, he helped her to her seat. He used his charm at every possible opportunity, using his smile of impeccable teeth and seductive talk on an invulnerable Esther.

The next morning, after breakfast and goodbyes were said to everybody, the maids placed the baggage in the clinic bus, and were driven to the train station. They did not look back, all too happy to turn their heads to the past. They had abandoned sorrow and death. They left the institution with a promise of life in their future.

The trip home seemed easier and faster. Rebecca and Miriam were surprised by the presence of Dr. Feldman at the station. Many people got in, but nobody else left the train, only she and the girls. She didn't have the stamina to question the reason for his presence there. She was tired and anxious to get to the house and gladly accepted to be driven home.

As soon as Dr. Feldman helped Olga take the luggage out of the car and in the house, he asked for the letter they'd sent him from the clinic. He was on his way to see some other patients, but reminded Miriam to rest after lunch, and promised to be back in the late afternoon to visit her.

She was so delighted to be back in her home at Balkovskaya Street, she didn't mention her fatigue. She took off her straw hat and handed it to Olga, looked at her image reflected in the mirror on top of the console. "A pale and thin unknown old lady," she said in such a low voice that no one but she could hear it.

Slowly she walked to the stairs with the presentiment she was about to begin a new chapter of her life. Before she continued her way up, she turned around and asked Olga, "Would you please make a teapot and bring it to my quarters? I'm dying for one of your cups of tea."

Rebecca tried to hold her arm, but she refused, shaking her off. She could do it without anyone's help. She turned back and slowly but determinedly, started the first familiar step.

It was almost evening when Esther wakened her. "Mother, Dr. Feldman is here to see you."

"The doctor? What time is it?"

She placed some more pillows behind her mother's back before she answered. "He's downstairs talking to Rebecca, but he is coming up. Don't you think he shows an interest in her?"

Miriam did not answer. She'd been married at that age. It was time for Rebecca to fall in love and marry while she was still young and desirable.

The rest of the summer passed and Miriam, supervised by Dr. Feldman, continued the treatment. She hadn't wished to walk as much, and without the strong figure of Nurse Petrovna around to demand it, she had no intention to exercise at all. Autumn wasn't her favorite season since it always depressed her to see Nature's death, and that year, more than ever before, a veil of melancholy enveloped her.

Albert Perlman had visited Esther repeatedly since he and his family arrived back from the clinic the first week in September. They became good friends and used their time together to discuss books and politics.

Esther inherited her mother's passion for politics. "Life did not hold still while we were gone from Odessa, Albert. Have you noticed? Many people are unhappy with the Tsar."

"I know, Esther. When I go with Gustav to my father's business, often I hear the workers talking while they are sacking grain to be shipped."

"They haven't forgotten the Bloody Sunday of St. Petersburg Square, have they, Albert?"

"I'm afraid we haven't seen the end of it, Esther. Signals of discontent are in all the levels of Russian society."

"Have you read anything about a man call Leon Trotsky? Look." She showed Albert a sheet of paper with an inscription and foot prints on it. "The streets were covered with them. I picked up this pamphlet on the sidewalk the other day coming from the market with Olga. I brought it home to show to you."

Those were times of national turmoil. In St. Petersburg, in the very beginning of the year 1905, a strike started at the locomotive plant. Father Georgiy Gapon was a Christian Orthodox priest and head of a union sponsored by the police. He deflected the workers from their revolutionary frame of mind, and convinced the demonstrators to present a petition to the authority, instead of revolt. In the petition, among other demands, they asked to end the war with Japan, to grant civil rights and a shorter workday for the workers.

Father Gapon led thousands of the workers in a peaceful march to present the petition to the Tsar. January 9, 1905, the scared troops under the command of Grand Duke Vladimir Alexandrovich, a relative of the Tsar, opened fire and massacred several hundred unarmed workers. That day was to be known in history as Bloody Sunday. The massacre united the people. Strikes in protest rose across Russia. In June of 1905, the Union of Unions was formed and Paul Miliukov was elected president of the confederation. He was helped by the charismatic Leon Trotsky, who began to gain popularity and acceptance with the workers. In Odessa the unrest hadn't passed unrecognized, and on June 14 of that same year, a strike started by sailors, ended in a mutiny aboard the battle cruiser Potemkin.

Esther was in the city in June, but maybe because she was worried about her mother's health, paid no attention to the incident in the Potemkin. She had no time to read or think of politics then. Things had changed and those weeks in the clinic helped, not just her mother's health, but brought the whole house back to the old rhythms.

Every time Albert visited Esther, he was accompanied by Gustav. He used the condition of his younger brother to force his presence in each visit. "You don't need any handicap to aggravate the problem," Gustav said once in a superior tone of voice. "Driving those new cars is dangerous. It is a good thing for Albert to have a chauffeur."

That was not the complete truth. Certainly Gustav was not interested in the discussion of politics with a woman. In his opinion, those were men's matters. Nevertheless, he enjoyed Esther's company immensely. He used any possible excuse to be around her. He could sit quietly in a corner of her parlor for hours. He would sip many cups of tea, listen to music or just observe her gracious movements. Gustav never had gotten into serious amorous relations with women. His good looks, manners and economical position had made him a very desirable bachelor. Until then, and he was already twenty-five, he had defended his freedom with tenacity. He was the first born in his family. Unlike Albert, who inherited his mother's delicate features, he was tall and had dark wavy hair, green eyes, a thin moustache and a conqueror's smile. Women found him irresistible. Esther, on the other hand, never paid too much attention to Gustav or flirted with him. To her, he was only the brother of her dear friend, Albert. Disconcerted by her distinct behavior toward him, Gustav never felt the need to guard his feelings from Esther until it was too late.

Miriam was suspicious. Ignorant of Albert's intentions, she had some personal dislike and opposition to the frequent visitor. She didn't think it possible to have just a friendship between people of different sexes. She didn't believe that intellectual interest was the force driving Albert's attention. She was afraid to analyze her dislike for him, but it was obvious his illness had something to do with it. In her selective mind perfection was a must, with no space for defects. She couldn't force herself to see the education and brilliancy, or Albert's perfect manners. Neither had she wanted to notice the sadness of his pale blue eyes or the tenderness in his smile. Miriam was able to see solely the constriction of the brown wooden wheelchair that so often carried him.

From the first visit of the brothers in September, when Gustav brought Miriam flowers and French chocolates, she became enchanted with him. There was a perfect and handsome suitor. Furthermore, she was pleased with his visits. Intimately she believed Gustav was the ideal candidate and the perfect husband for Esther. Miriam entertained the idea of her daughter married into a good and wealthy Jewish family. "I like the young man, and I hope she chooses him when the time comes. I hope she would decide that Gustav is the right man for her," Miriam confessed to Olga one afternoon.

Indulgent of her mother's lucubration, Esther thought of marriage as the infringement of a woman's personal freedom, and she had no plans for marriage any time soon. Miriam could tell her secret worries to Olga, who listened patiently. "Before we become concerned about Esther's possibilities, we may need to see Rebecca married. I think Dr. Feldman will make a perfect husband for her, don't you?"

"Oh, madam, they look so beautiful together, they do make a perfect couple." Olga straightened her back from the cutting board, cleaned her hands on her apron, and smiled enough to show her white large teeth.

Dr. Feldman had a very busy life. His time was tightly divided. At dawn and before breakfast, he exercised for twenty-five minutes and took a bath. By 7:10 am he was at the hospital to see patients, a job that took most of the morning hours. At one o'clock sharp, after a light lunch, he was in his office. There he would see the sick and some not-so-sick but bored ladies who hoped to capture his attention. He reserved the evenings to visit some of his patients at their homes. There was not much time left for the doctor to share a future with a woman. He believed it was impossible to aspire to an amorous relationship with Rebecca. At the end of each day, he felt he did not have enough time left to dedicate to her, but Joseph Feldman never had the will to stop his desire.

Earlier in July that year, he arranged with a colleague to do his work in the city while he was twice a week at the rehabilitation clinic where Miriam was a patient. He began to take some extra time to stay for lunch and walk in the idyllic gardens with Rebecca. In August, when she was back in Odessa, they continued with the habitual long walks in the parks carpeted with fall leaves. He was a passionate lover of Italian opera. Puccini was possibly his favorite composer, but he could not affirm it because he cried while listening to La Traviata. Unexpectedly, during a walk, he would suddenly stop and sing a romantic aria from La Bohème, or Madame Butterfly, to her. The emotions Rebecca had awakened in the heart of Joseph were not sufficient to overcome his timidity, however. Until that moment, he never imprisoned her hands in his or got close enough to kiss her. Rebecca liked him very much and enjoyed his company but was very intrigued with his attitude. Often she debated the reason for his visits, wondering if he was interested in her as a woman, or if he had become, as Albert, another dear friend of the family.

A week earlier, soon after Joseph left, Rebecca decided she would not see him again and would never go with him for a walk for the rest of her life. She was almost twenty and would not waste one more minute of her time, or her shoe sole in those walks with him. It was time for her to find a husband.

Not all marriages were as romantic as the marriage of Mother Miriam and Uncle Jacob. They fell in love from the first moment they saw each other. She heard many times before she heard it from Olga that once the husband was found, love would follow. Rebecca thought she'd found a possible husband in Joseph, but she wasn't sure he cared for her. Unfortunately, his behavior disconcerted her so frequently, she was confused. Each time she gave up on him, he arrived with a special gift for her and showed so much interest she became hopeful once more.

Almost a month after they arrived back from the clinic, he came to the house with an exotic Papa Gallo from the Amazon forest. The bird was in a silvery cage. Joseph bought it from a sailor from a Brazilian ship that was anchored at port. The man had been in a fight and appeared in the hospital drunk. His clothes were soaked in blood from a wound on his forehead. The sailor who carried the caged bird in his hand, left it on the floor while the doctor stitched his head. The Brazilian was out of the room when Joseph called him, showed him the forgotten cage, and asked if he would sell the animal.

"I thought the bird was beautiful and rare. Until now I have only seen them in zoology books." Joseph knew the sailor intentions were to sell the Papa Gallo and use the money for more liqueur. "I was sure you'd like it. Have you seen such a vibrant color in feathers before?" He placed the cage at eye level to show her the Papa Gallo with the multi-color plumage.

"Of course I have, Joseph, but only in ladies concert hats," Rebecca laughed and said, "You must agree with me that the feathers look prettier on the bird."

"The sailor called her Rita. Now you have to find a name for it."

"Rita is a woman's name, isn't that right? Maybe it was the name of the sailor's girlfriend." She moved her head aside to see Joseph on the other side of the cage, then asked one more question. "Don't you think the poor bird is confused enough having a new owner?" Rebecca wouldn't change her name either; she would keep her beautiful name. She took the cage from Joseph's hand and walked with it into the parlor.

"Rita, welcome to this house of women."

"I knew you'd like the bird."

"Would you like a cup of chocolate, Joseph?" Then she hurried to close the big window. "It is getting chilly here."

Long arrows of migrant wild geese were on flight to the southwest over the Black Sea. The birds' abandonment of their nesting lands was the primeval indication winter was inevitably close. Olga already had received the supply of firewood for the fireplaces. She also asked for the coal for the stove and braziers to be delivered that same afternoon. She'd taken the heavy curtains out of storage and placed them on the clothes line to air to erase the smell left by months locked in a trunk with moth balls.

In the kitchen, rows of jars with preserved fruits and vegetables were piled on the counter. They had to be taken to the storage room in the basement, but Olga waited for Ana to help her to carry them down. Still on the stove was a big pot with wild berries being preserved. The day before, Rebecca and Esther picked the blackberries in the countryside. Olga had placed strings of mushrooms, eggplants, peppers and tomatoes to dry close to the kitchen fireplace. The smell of sage, rosemary, and lavender hung to dry from the ceiling beams competed with berries to perfume the whole house. Until the past spring Miriam had looked after some of the garden plants and they had grown and matured under her hand. Since the death of Jacob, she had lost the desire to be outdoors, and she asked Esther to take care and prune the rose bushes that afternoon.

Esther was not a born gardener. She lacked the patience and the interest required and complained out loud of her dislike of the feel of the soil on her hands. "I can't find any pleasure in digging in the dirt," she said to her mother. "I have a full history chapter and an English lesson to study for this afternoon before Mr. Glazunov arrives." She always found a good reason and a way out of the garden chores.

"Don't you think I should ask Yuri to prune them?" Esther thought her idea was brilliant, and the right way to avoid any contact with the plants. She took off her leather gloves. "He will do a better job, don't you agree?"

She pushed to her feet, cleaned her apron that was dirty with soil and twigs, placed the gloves and the pruning clippers in the basket and started on her way to the window. Esther extended her hand across the window to reach the hand of her mother and with alarm asked Miriam, "Are you all right? Your hand feels terribly cold. Are you catching something?" She touched Miriam's forehead with her lips.

Alarmed, she rushed into the house. The breeze brought in the smell of the dried leaves. The room felt humid and cold. Esther closed the parlor window, and knelt next to her mother. Miriam looked more pale and frail than ever. With a loving gesture, she reclined her head on her mother's lap. It was then she felt her mother quiver.

"I think you are catching something, Mama."

"Oh no, darling, the room is cold, that's all."

"Would you like a cup of hot tea?"

"That would be lovely, Esther, thank you."

"Let me take you to your room first."

Esther stood up and held both her mother's hands. Miriam had to be helped up. Her legs did not respond to her commands.

Esther put her arm around her mother's waist, and walked with her upstairs. When they arrived at the top step, Miriam breathed with a whistling noise. Once in her room, Esther helped her to sit in a recliner, put a muffler over her legs, and covered her shoulders with her blue shawl.

Olga arrived in the bedroom prepared. She had a brazier with red coals, and placed it close to the bed. With efficiency, she lit the fireplace fire. The room warmed in minutes, then and not before, they helped Miriam to get in bed. Miriam was so cold, her body shivered uncontrollably, yet she burned with fever. Before being asked, the worried maid rushed to the kitchen and brought back a hot water bottle that she placed under Miriam's feet. Ignorant of the new development, Rebecca arrived in the bedroom to find Miriam in her bed, very still, with her eyes closed. As she sat on the foot of her bed, Esther pulled a tendril of her hair between her fingers lying close to her forehead and twirled it while she gazed at her mother. Olga, immobile, stood beside her. Rebecca was the only one of the three women to remain calm, and she knew what needed to be done.

"Mother Miriam is very sick. You must come at once," she wrote in the note she sent to Joseph by Mikhail, the older son of Yuri.

The doctor had to restrain his impulse to answer Rebecca's call immediately. There were some very sick patients in his office he had to see, before he could rush to the house in Balkovskaya Street. The influenza cases he had seen in the last week were out of the ordinary. In his expert opinion, they marked the early stages of an epidemic. There wasn't much he could do for his patients other than to make them comfortable, keep the fever down, and wait for the body to heal itself. There was no known medicine that could cure influenza. He was preoccupied with the fact that several of his patients at the hospital had died. In most of those cases, malnutrition had played an important role. The patients who used the hospital were the very poor or the destitute.

He parked the car in front of the house and hurried inside. Before he could knock on the door, Olga opened it, took his hat and said, "It is Miss Miriam." She asked him to follow her upstairs.

The room was still and very silent. Joseph stopped at the door to let his eyes become accustomed to the darkness, walked to the chest of drawers and placed his black bag on top before he took two long steps putting him in front of the heavy curtains. Under the stupified gaze of the three women, he pulled the curtains aside and opened the window. "Mrs. Vainer needs to breathe clean air." With a deep frown denoting his concern, Joseph took a stethoscope out of the black bag. He moved close to the bed, adjusted his glasses and examined her for just a few minutes. Still without a sound and with a very somber face, he washed his hand, picked up his bag and left the room. Both girls followed him out. Neither Esther nor Rebecca was prepared to hear what he told them. Miriam had pneumonia, and he didn't know any effective remedy to treat it. They needed to keep the fever down, keep the room aired, wait, and hope.

Olga bathed Miriam in infusions of medicinal herbs that she had picked in the early fall, and made her drink a potion made from spider webs. Yuri traveled by horse to the Dnestr River southwest of Odessa to cut branches from some willow trees that grew at the edge of the water there. He expected the trees would still have some leaves left. Ana, Yuri's wife, boiled the leaves and the pieces of branches of the willows and made a tea that Miriam drank. They knew the willow had medicinal power and would keep her fever down and numb her body aches. Joseph consulted with one of the professors at the hospital, and two of his colleagues, and administrated some medicines recently discovered. Esther and Rebecca followed all the directions the doctors prescribed.

On November 29, however, at the early morning hour of 3:40 am, as Olga would affirm later that was the time of the morning that Death comes every day to Earth to claim most of his victims. Miriam died.

Olga was a Christian Orthodox as many other Russian people in those days, but she celebrated not just the Orthodox Church holidays but the Jewish too. She loved the latkes and the blintzes they did for Hanukah. She had worked for so many years in that Jewish home, she knew the Jewish ways. She had learned their rituals and traditions almost as well as the Orthodox ones. With uncontainable sobs of sadness that made her blow her nose noisily, she walked through the house and covered the mirrors with black cloth.

Yuri walked to the Synagogue to talk to Rabbi Zimmerman. There was so much snow on the ground, it was too difficult to use the sulky, and his horse was still exhausted from the long ride the day before. The good Ana was at the door to receive the people who rushed to the house as soon they heard the sad news. Each one brought some special dish. There was so much food in the kitchen.

That early morning the pale winter sun tried unsuccessfully to break through the heavy clouds. The day awakened gray. Inside, the house was warm and the fires were lit in the fireplaces, but Esther, sitting on the floor of her room, never felt so cold.

CHAPTER VI
A NEW DAY

Odessa, November, 1905

"Come with me to the door," Olga said to Esther. "There are no more potatoes left in the basket, I need to buy some. I can hear Borikof calling."

Life was reflected in everyday happenings. In the deafening shout of Borikof to announce his presence. He was one of the street vendors who passed by every early morning. He pushed his wheeled cart full of fragrant fruits and vegetables, and had a happy word and toothless smile for each of his customers.

Life was in the indecipherable blackened face of Mr. Gelatian, the Armenian man who sold coal from a horse-pulled wagon. He had shouted for such a long time, his voice had abandoned him. He always had a smile, while he talked in a whisper. The banging noise made by the buckets hanging from the back axle announced the arrival of the wagon. It was impossible not to notice the children who walked in front of the house on their way to or from school. Their laughter was a loud obvious burst of innocent happiness.

Life was all around Esther, but she was blinded to it. Her eyes were still fixated on the past. She had never before experienced such a feeling of loss. Her mother had died too young, and before she could pass on the family history. Esther felt deprived of her origins. She had a strange sensation, as if she were suspended in the air with no roots to ground her. She saw herself as one more victim of the political unrest. She blamed the Russo-Japanese war and the surrounding circumstances for the death of her parents. She was so terribly angry about becoming an orphan. On more than one occasion, she found an excuse not to meet with Albert. It was not as enjoyable as it once was. She had lost interest in any discussion of politics. She looked for a reason to refuse his invitation to a recital of piano music, and she resisted with intensity when Albert tried to convince her to go with him and Gustav to the opening of an exhibition of French art from the Impressionist School.

Suddenly, Esther awakened to a new current of thought. She began to read books about the occult and spent hours in the kitchen with Olga, where she learned secrets of the spiritual world. The plump woman was an expert on the matters of spirit and psychic phenomena. Often, they shared a cup of sage tea while she listened to Olga's tales of ghosts and supernatural occurrences. Esther became completely absorbed by the possibility of life after death. She had an incessant curiosity and asked many questions about the people with mediumistic ability.

"They could communicate with those who have passed," Olga told her one evening. "They are the bridge between both worlds."

The idea that she might find a way to talk with her parents, or for them to talk to her, grew stronger in Esther's mind. Spirituality displaced any other interest that had filled her life until then. Her time was consumed by this new obsession.

Rebecca mourned her loss in a more earthy way. For days she cried over the death of Miriam in the privacy of her room. Miriam was the only mother she could remember, and her death made Rebecca terribly sad, but she knew her younger cousin needed her support. She had to be stronger than ever, so she put on a practical façade and overcame her sorrow. Rebecca worried about the unexpected way Esther had began to alter her life.

"It is very dark here, darling, you need more light," Rebecca stated. She lit both the gas chandelier and the kerosene lamp on the side table.

"It was enough with the light from the flames." Esther sat

on the furry rug in front of the fireplace, with her body bent forward. Her face and her book were dangerously close to the glaze.

"If you get any closer to those embers you'll burn your nose. What are you reading?"

"Life Beyond Death," she answered. "Have you read it?

Unlike Esther, Rebecca had always been a bit superstitious. She did not like to see a mocking bird in the morning, she would never walk under a ladder, and if a black cat crossed her path, she would change direction and find another way. She had believed in the spiritual word since she was very young. Esther used to laugh at Rebecca's eccentricities. Now it was Esther who had forgotten her books and passion for politics and vehemently embraced the occult. Rebecca didn't think it was bad to discover a new way to enrich what she already had learned. It was good to accept death as a passage and a continuation. It became a problem when Esther wouldn't leave room for anything else. She was, in Rebecca's opinion, completely absorbed by that magical world. Rebecca sighed with resignation. She counted on her cousin's strength of character to eventually surpass grief and bring her back to her senses. After all, she thought, the human spirit sometimes needs to escape to another dimension to look for the way out of such sorrow.

Meanwhile, Rebecca had another immediate preoccupation. Since her aunt passed, she couldn't help but wonder about her father and his whereabouts. If he was alive, he should be informed of the death of his only sister. On an impulse she walked to her desk and sat down. She wavered for a moment. Finally, she found the courage, and took out a small, black Chinese lacquered box placed inside a decade before. Hypnotized by it, she rested the box on the desk, clasped her hands together and stared at the shiny cube for the longest time. She had never forgotten the box or its contents, but until that instant, she had never felt the need to see them again. Her heart pounded with such force, it deafened her. Every fiber of her body trembled when she extended a hand to lift the top. Slowly, she took out a long gold chain with a locket. Her mother had placed the jewel around her neck the day she died. Inside the locket was a picture of both her parents when they were very young. Rebecca put the chain aside and took the only picture she had of her father from the box. It was taken before they arrived in Odessa, the same year he disappeared. Young and handsome, he was tall in white summer clothes and held a hard straw hat. The smile she remembered was captured in the photograph.

He was a deserter. He had deprived Rebecca of a father and until that instant, the child in her hated him. She looked at his image and was amazed to realize her love for him was still intact. Such a discovery unearthed a torrent of turbulent emotions and made her feel vulnerable.

The question remained unanswered. How could she find her father after more than fifteen years of silence? She knew of no way to reach him, had no address to write to him. Since the day Ishmael left, Miriam had avoided mentioning his name in Rebecca's presence, and she took to her death an unforgivable secret. She had never told Rebecca about the letters she had received from her brother. Her correspondence with him was secret. She covered every possible trace so well, that nobody in the family ever had a clue. Ishmael sent the letters to Rabbi Zimmerman. The old man, with his infinite kindness, understood and respected Miriam's request for confidentiality. The rabbi never demanded an explanation from either of them. He became the intermediary who delivered Ishmael's letters to Miriam and sent hers to Ishmael.

A long year of silence followed the disappearance of Ishmael. The first timid letter Miriam received from him had the postage of some small town in Hungary. With each new letter she learned a bit more of the bohemian life her brother had chosen. She forced him to stay away until she could one day tell Rebecca. She promised him she would later explain to his daughter about the letters and about her father, but the perfect opportunity never arose.

The creak of the wood on the last step of the stairs brought Rebecca back from her thoughts. "Someone has come upstairs," she said to herself. Hurriedly, she placed the chain and the picture in the black lacquered box, closed the top, and put it back in the drawer just in time. After a knock at the door, and before she had time to get up, Esther entered the room. She held what appeared to be a card.

"Oh! I thought you were dusting your room. I guess I intruded on your work at the desk. Sorry."

"It's all right, Esther. Come in, I've finished."

"Look, Rebecca, Mr. Resnik has sent us a letter." She showed the message to her cousin, and asked, "Would you like me to read it to you?" Before Rebecca could answer, she said, "Well, you can read it later, but it says that he would like to meet with us at our convenience."

"Good. He was on my list of things to do for this week. I can scratch it now."

"Apparently he has some information from Mama he promised to pass on to us."

"I wonder what this lawyer wants to tell us." Rebecca got up, reached for the letter and read it. She looked at Esther, alarmed. "Do you think he will tell us we have financial troubles? Do you think we're penniless?"

"It can't be too terrible; he has not hurried to see us until now." Esther sat on the foot of the bed. "We'll go Thursday and we'll know." She changed the subject with a picturesque smile. "I also came to tell you that your doctor is waiting for you in the parlor."

Rebecca was surprised. She wasn't prepared for Joseph or his unannounced visit. She sat at her vanity and looked at her reflected image. She put some color on her lips, tried to repair her hair, stood, and left the room without another look. She hung her apron on the balustrade, and while she rushed to meet him, she adjusted the collar of her blouse. She breathed deeply to calm her heart before she entered the parlor. Joseph was at the window and turned when he heard Rebecca's steps. Throughout Miriam's illness he had always found a reason to go by the house. Later, after her death, Joseph continued his assiduous visits, but he had no excuses and had to announce his calls days or hours in advance.

"Joseph, what a surprise!"

In two long steps he was next to Rebecca and reached for her hand. "I apologize for calling on you unannounced, but I am leaving this afternoon for Moscow and I could not go without letting you know."

He told her of his intentions the same morning he had received a telegram from one of his relatives. His father was in poor health. The winter started early that year in Moscow, and the weather had been especially bad. It had snowed endlessly. Such inclemency had a terrible physical and emotional effect on old people. Apparently, his father was a little bit sick but very depressed, and longed to see him. Joseph had made arrangements for a doctor, a colleague of his, to take care of his practice until his return. He planned to be back in Odessa in no more than ten days. Rebecca accompanied him to the door. She opened it, and he started his way to the car. Just a few steps from the gate, he stopped abruptly and vacillated, as if he had forgotten something in the house. He turned around and in an instant, was back at the door.

Joseph took Rebecca in his arms, kissed her with passion, and whispered, "I love you. Wait for me." With the same rapidity and characteristic long steps, he was at the gate and in his car, waving to an astonished Rebecca until the hedge obstructed her view.

From the other side of the entrance hall at the foot of the stairs, Esther called Rebecca's name several times before Rebecca regained her composure, closed the door, and was able to answer.

The following Thursday in the early afternoon, Esther and Rebecca took a taxi to go to the business district in downtown Odessa. They had to convince the carriage driver not to wait for them while they went for some tea and pastries. The times were difficult. The less expensive public transportation had taken many passengers away from him.

From the tea house, Esther and Rebecca visited a new bookstore, and went into a hat shop that had the most extravagant but beautiful hats. There were no more places to hide to delay their feared encounter. With resignation, they walked through the paved stone streets to the lawyer's office. They were received by a secretary and immediately the young man asked them to have a seat in the baroque waiting room just across from the office of Mr. Resnik.

In a very polite tone, the secretary told them they had to wait. The lawyer was with the previous client who had been in for quite some time. "I believe it'll be just a few more minutes."

Esther selected a magazine with a beautiful photograph on the cover. It was a picture of the pyramids and the Nile River in the foreground that attracted her attention. "What an exotic land." She showed the cover to Rebecca. "That is a place I'd love to visit, if we have enough money, of course."

"Are you delirious? That kind of trip costs a fortune."

"It is so much in fashion. Everybody is going to Egypt these days."

In the same magazine, she read an article about the progress in the development of the Orient Express. The train service had arrived in Constantinople and the temptation to travel abroad was in crescendo. She had never been any place out of Russia. Finally, the secretary signaled the wait was over, and Esther left the magazine on the table.

Forty-five minutes had passed from the time they arrived until the door of the office of the lawyer opened. A woman with a perennial smile came out, wearing a big hat with an enormous blue, fluffy feather. It matched her voluptuous roundness. She was in front of Mr. Resnik who remained inside the office. He held the door open and smiled back at the woman. He had in his hand a handkerchief which he passed repeatedly over his moustache, lips, and bald head. Esther and Rebecca glanced at each other and had to make an effort to avoid laughing out loud.

Rebecca murmured under her breath, "He will go to any length to keep his clients happy."

Mr. Resnik was not handsome by any means. He was a short man with a big belly, proof of his taste for good food and wine. He was very well dressed. In summer or winter, he wore suits of the same dark gray or blue color. He had very small feet, even for his size. His hands were always too warm and sweaty. From early times, when Esther went to his office with her parents, she had avoided touching or shaking hands with him. She had made fun of him many times, but recognized that as a lawyer, he was sharp. Besides, he had a rare virtue for his class … he was honest and trustworthy. He had been their lawyer for as long as she could remember.

Mr. Resnik invited them in. The office was as baroque as the waiting room. It smelled of liquor, cigar smoke, and the previous client's expensive perfume. The lawyer didn't sit at his desk, instead showing the girls to a sitting area with two green leather armchairs separated by a black wooden side table with an ornate porcelain lamp on it. Across from them was a small green leather sofa and on the corner, a tall lamp with a green glass shade.

"Electricity is a marvelous invention, isn't it?" The lawyer smiled when he pulled a chain and the opaque green glass of the lamp became translucent with light.

There were no preambles. He waited for Esther and Rebecca to sit down and went straight to business. "I am sure you would like to know the reason you are here."

Both girls squirmed with apprehension, but neither of them spoke nor nodded.

"As I mentioned to you in my letter, there are two matters of most acute importance to discuss." He reached for a folder and some papers from a long table behind the sofa. He opened the folder and looked for something inside. With annoyance, he reached for the papers and rapidly turned the pages, which were held together by a big clip. Bothered by the fact he couldn't find the documents he sought, he left the folder and the papers on the sofa, walked to the corner of his desk and pressed a bell to call his secretary. Followed by a timid knocking, the door opened to show only the beardless face of the young man. He looked around to locate his boss, before the rest of his body entered the room. In complete silence he approached the back of the sofa, stood next the lawyer, and waited for orders.

"I can't find the bundle of letters that were in the Vainer-Prusky file. I'm sure they were left with the Prusky papers. Please bring them to me, Andrew."

As soon as the lawyer finished his order, the silent secretary left the room. Andrew was the opposite of his employer. He was extremely thin with curly and bushy dark hair, and was at least a head taller than Mr. Resnik. His clothes were not expensive or new, but they were well kept. Esther would later learn that he studied law. He had limited funds to spend even in food, since almost all the money he made at work was used to pay the university and to buy the required books. He hoped to finish his studies and become a lawyer that next year. He had no family in Odessa, and had to rent a room in the attic of a brothel. It was the cheapest place he could find and the only one he could afford. Some of the prostitutes pitied him and gave him a bowl of hot soup in the evenings. He paid back their kindness with his knowledge of jurisprudence, and helped them to solve the problems they had with the law from time to time. A few minutes later, but after he had knocked at the door, Andrew reappeared with what looked like love letters held together with a dark blue ribbon. Rebecca and Esther were totally ignorant of the existence of such letters. They moved in their seats, puzzled. Illicit or illegitimate were words that came to their minds. If not, why did those letters have to be guarded by a lawyer?

The curiosity overcame Rebecca, who impatiently asked Mr. Resnik, "Could you please tell us who the letters are from?"

"Well, let me tell you first that every time your mother received one of these letters, and as soon as it was read, she gave it to me for safe keeping. I am about to unveil a family secret that has been hidden from both of you for good reasons, I think. It was to be told later. Your mother wanted to wait until you were the right age to understand."

"Please be concise and clear," Esther instructed.

"Your parents thought you were too young to be told. The premature deaths of your mother and father have changed many things. They, instead of I, were planning one day to have this conversation with you. Fate decided otherwise."

Parsimoniously, he pulled one end of the blue ribbon, and the bow loosened. He pulled an envelope from the top of the bundle, opened it, took the letter out and started to unfold it. Esther had arrived at the end of her short patience. Rebecca, calmer, leaned forward with anticipation.

"Believe me, ladies, this is difficult for me too. I apologize if I cause you any more pain. You both have had plenty of suffering."

"Can you please get straight to the matter, Mr. Resnik?" Esther nearly screamed.

"Unfortunately, with their passing, now it is my duty to talk to you about this most delicate situation that concerns both of you but will touch Rebecca intimately." He smiled at Rebecca and adjusted the gold-rimmed glasses that slid down his nose.

He placed the paper closer to the light and began to read:

Moscow, 7 July, 1905

"Dear Miriam, I was worried. Not hearing from you for such a long time troubled me deeply. My anxiety diminished this morning when I received your letter. It is the first letter from you in more than two months.

I understand your grief and my heart is saddened by your sorrow. Believe me, I know how devastating it is to lose someone you love. When Sofia and the baby died, I thought I would go mad. The pain was unbearable. For a long time I was convinced I was damned, never to regain sanity, but I was wrong. Sofia's beloved image which had accompanied me, and was so vividly engraved in my mind for years after her death, began to fade. Slowly her eyes, her smile, her soft skin blurred, falling into the mist of the past. My memory of her, so real in the beginning, was transformed into light and was not enough to let me see her. I had to reach for a photograph. The pain that was suffocating me the morning she died which I thought would kill me too, with time became bearable. I know time will help you in the same way. You will never forget his existence, and his love or the happiness he brought into your life, but the pain you feel today will slowly, diminish. His image will blur in your mind, and your heart will survive.

"I am planning to be in Odessa before Passover, but as you may have heard, the political situation here in Moscow is very grave and it is sometimes dangerous just to walk in the streets. Nonetheless, I need to visit you. Maybe together we will find a way to talk to Rebecca.

"I trust that when this letter reaches you, it will be of some comfort to your pain.

"My dearest sister, you are in my prayers and in my heart.
Ishmael

As soon as Mr. Resnik read the last paragraph, and before he could began to explain, Rebecca reached for a small lace handkerchief in her purse. She stood as if catapulted from the green armchair and rushed to the window behind the desk. Her eyes, veiled with tears, were fixed on the wet cobblestones of the street. Outside, the winter afternoon continued to develop uneventfully. The rain had stopped, but dark clouds were pushed by an insistent Arctic wind, and the sidewalks were deserted.

It was impossible to imagine her father alive. The words had such a strange sound. Through the years, to justify his disappearance and excuse his silence, she had imagined him paralyzed, sick and bedridden, or dead from a tragic accident. In her mind, and until she erased him from her memory, he was killed millions of times.

"My father is alive," she repeated again and again, in a whisper.

Rebecca felt torn by strong emotions. She fought to regain control of herself and repress her indiscreet sobs. She was not sure of her own feelings, and did not understand her tears. Should she be happy with the news that her father was alive and had a job some place in Russia? Why was she angry then? Could she ever forgive him? He had robbed her of his presence for fifteen years. Resentment and indignation filled her heart and left no space for love.

Esther overcame the astonishment the news caused and ran to console Rebecca. She held her cousin tightly. "Please don't cry, Becca. It's not that ominous."

"How could they lie to me, Esther?"

"We'll come to understand the reasons Uncle Ishmael had. It's going to be all right. I promise you."

She had to find words to comfort Rebecca, and be careful not to let her thoughts come out of her mouth. Her mind was blackened with anger and intolerance. Esther's outlook on life, as her father's, was pragmatic. True to her beliefs, she never hesitated when asked for her opinion. She was analytical, and weighed each situation without allowing emotions to play a role in her decisions. To find her own position in politics, she read and studied all the political currents available in the country at that moment. She was completely against the Tsar's unjust regime. On the other side of the spectrum, she could not stand the lack of structure and the chaos of the Anarchist doctrine, nor the violence they manifested in their acts. She considered herself a liberal thinker, maybe a socialist. She could talk politics or discuss philosophy for hours. Never had she run out of argument, and she found the right words for each situation. However, she had an irrational reaction to the news about her uncle. Until that afternoon, she had never before experienced such an outrage. Fury had blocked her mind; the words that were about to escape her lips were foul and the language vulgar and perverse. Esther made an effort to keep her mouth shut and console Rebecca.

To judge from the number of letters in the lawyer's file, her mother and her uncle had written to each other for a long time, possibly years. The answer to that, never to be asked to her mother, would be demanded from her uncle. Why had they kept it a secret? What reason could they have had to deprive Rebecca of his love? What reason is there to separate a daughter from her father, or for a father to abandon his child?

Impatiently, Mr. Resnik checked the time on his pocket watch. The meeting had taken longer than anticipated. The small man coughed to clear his throat, and call the attention of his clients back to him. "Would you like to have a cup of tea, my dear? We have more business to discuss, but, I think it would be all right if we leave it for a later time." Without giving them the opportunity to respond, he called Andrew and asked him to make an appointment for the following week. Mr. Resnik looked once more at Rebecca's pale face and told the secretary, "Andrew, bring some tea for the ladies, please."

Distraught and exhausted with the news received from the lawyer, they canceled their plans for the rest of that afternoon in downtown Odessa. They had had enough excitement for one day, and asked Andrew to call a taxi for them. Humiliated by the secret unveiled by the lawyer, they felt they were ignorant victims in the conspiracy web fabricated by their family. They drove home holding hands, as when they were frightened little girls. Each needed the support and courage given by the other.

Olga impatiently waited for them, and, as she had so many other times, before they could touch the front doorknob, the door opened and the old maid's imposing figure appeared and filled most of the opening. She moved aside to let the girls enter.

"Clean your feet well. It is muddy out there, and I don't want that dirt in the house."

Olga loved them as if they were her own and tolerated all their capriciousness, but she had to be firm. Since their parents passed, she was the only mature adult in the household. Obediently, Rebecca cleaned her short boots on the mat and walked into the house.

Esther, a bit lazy, took her shoes off, and handed them to Olga, then kissed her noisily on the cheek and asked, "Did you bake something delicious today? After the horrid visit with the lawyer, I'm dying for a cup of your hot chocolate with whipped cream on top, the kind you used to make for me when I was a child."

Olga kept silent. She was not surprised by the somber result of the visit to the lawyer's office. As she had with other secrets, Miriam had shared that one with her too.

"Maybe a piece of a very sweet cake with much icing on top would be the perfect complement," Esther said, as she walked into the kitchen followed by Olga. "We'll prepare some chocolate for Rebecca too. I know it will comfort her."

The next day, Friday evening, Andrew, Mr. Resnik's secretary, came to the house. It was an unexpected visit. Olga directed him to the small music room where Rebecca and Esther had taken refuge. They were interpreting a piece from one of Max Bruch's "Concertos for Violin." Rebecca accompanied Esther on the piano. Andrews's presence was unnoticed by the girls, who were involved in their interpretation. When they stopped, Andrew clapped vigorously, and exclaimed "Bravo, Bravo!" as he entered the room. When he saw the terror reflected on the faces of both girls, he reassured them that everything was all right. Sensitive to the fact that the event in his office had unsettled them, Mr. Resnik sent his secretary to make sure they were well. Andrew had with him the complete bundle of letters. It was the lawyer's thought, that reading all the letters could unveil the reason they were kept in the dark for all those years.

Even after he had been in the warmth of the house for several minutes, Andrew looked cold and hungry. His nose was red and his lips were purple. He was not adequately clothed for the inclemency of winter.

Esther noticed his short jacket and the summery pants, and

felt very sorry for the poor young man. “Andrew, we are about to have supper. Would you like to join us?” Before he could refuse Esther said, “Olga, Andrew will stay for dinner.”

He and Rebecca were engaged in conversation when Esther used their distraction to disappear without being noticed. She came back to the music room with both arms full of her father’s clothes. “See if you can wear them. They are beautiful clothes.”

“Miss Esther, I cannot possibly accept such generosity.”

“Of course you can, you must. My father would be happy to know they didn’t go to waste. You need them, Andrew. So they are put to good use.”

The three enjoyed the impromptu evening. Two deep plates of hot stew, a generous serving of cake and a cup of tea brought the color back to Andrew’s cheeks. After dinner they talked for hours about politics, books, theater and classical music. Andrew was about to leave. He had on a heavy overcoat, fur hat, gloves, and a bundle of clothes over his arm, when he asked Esther, “Do you like Chopin?

“Oh yes. He is one of my favorite composers.”

“Good. Next time I visit you, I will play some Chopin nocturnes for both of you.”

CHAPTER VII
ISHMAEL

Odessa December, 1905

"Quite an unexpected change, Esther. I enjoyed Andrew. He's so nice."

"Isn't he, Becca? And he plays Chopin. Such a romantic!"

"He is obviously tired. Have you noticed the dark circles under his eyes?"

"The poor thing has no time to rest."

They would soon send him an invitation for an early supper, and Olga would give him a substantial meal, the kind that would keep him warmed for days after. They would play the piano together. He could interpret Chopin, as he had mentioned the previous evening. From the moment they met, Esther felt sorry for Andrew. She admired his perseverance, and looked for discreet ways to help him. Obvious assistance would make him feel like a charity case. Andrew had a difficult life. He could only study at night, as his days were filled with working at the law office. Mr. Resnik was an astute hawk when it came to business, and that quality had made the lawyer rich, but a tyrant who demanded efficiency and perfection from his associates, however, he used little of his accumulated fortune to pay their salaries. They made barely enough to survive.

"You like him very much, don't you, Esther?"

"I do. I think he is more sensitive than the other young men I know."

"I have the impression we'll be seeing dear Mr. Andrew on Sunday afternoons."

"Well, he'll be a good addition. He is well educated, and has elegant manners. I know Albert would like him as well."

"You are right, dear. I think he is nice and has a bright future."

"Yes, eventually, he'll be a lawyer."

"Hmm, a lawyer friend of the family is always a good thing."

Rebecca did not say out loud what she thought, since she was afraid to upset her cousin, but if Mother Miriam were alive, she would never approve of Andrew, a goy, frequenting the family or becoming a friend of Esther's.

"Fathers and mothers are the background history of their children. A man without a family could hide his past and many secrets that may not be discovered until it is too late," Miriam once stated while she talked to the girls. The words made an impact on the mind of young Rebecca, and she would remember them forever.

Maybe Andrew had no family in Odessa, but most certainly, he was born into one, and had one someplace in Russia, Rebecca thought. She knew Esther well, and she was not worried. Soon her cousin would find some imperfections in all that virtue. She was convinced that even when Esther was interested in love as a romantic event, she was not too eager yet to commit to anyone in marriage.

Rebecca had a more urgent worry and an immense moral dilemma to resolve. She could not see the way to the truth. Her emotions were blinding her. She was too angry to understand her elders' conduct. Why had her father ignored her existence for all those years? How could Aunt Miriam keep that unforgivable secret? Rebecca believed all the mystery could be brought to light if the letters were read, but she also understood in doing so, she would violate and enter into their most private thoughts. Now that her Aunt Miriam and her Uncle Jacob had died, only her father held the key to the truth. She would compromise to find a solution for the equation that tormented her. She would not read the letters. They belonged to the past and to the dead. She would write to her father and urge him to explain his behavior and his motives, if there were any. She had to go to

Mr. Resnick's office and demand that he give her the address in Moscow where she could write to her father.

A week later, on a Thursday, Rebecca and Esther visited the lawyer again. They had an appointment scheduled for two-thirty in the afternoon. This time they went straight to the office. Visiting shops and bookstores could wait, and it was too early for high tea.

Andrew received them with a friendly smile, and showed them to the baroque waiting room. "I am afraid it will be at least fifteen more minutes," he said, as he turned his head to check the round clock across from his desk in the other room. "The client that is in with Mr. Resnik has been there for no more than half an hour," he winked an eye and whispered in a confidential tone.

The fat woman with the Musketeer hat and big bosom crossed the mind of the two young women, and they smiled with complicity. A while later, the door opened, and a small, middle-aged woman, wearing too much make-up and an expensive astrakhan fur coat, came out of the office. Rebecca and Esther could not restrain their laughter.

"This Mr. Resnik." Esther smothered her voice as she covered most of her face with a magazine she was reading. Rebecca lowered her head to conceal her smile. She pretended to look for something in her purse.

Several more minutes passed before they left the waiting room. The office was cold, and they found the lawyer closing the windows when Andrew showed them in. Lipstick stains covered his bald head and one of the cuffs of his white starched shirt. He tried to hide the tell-tale marks by pulling down the sleeve of his jacket.

The meeting with Mr. Resnik was short and very informative. The lawyer explained with simplicity the good news about their financial situation. Without a doubt, they had more than enough money to last them the rest of their lives. When Rebecca demanded her father's address from Mr. Resnick, he grudgingly gave it to her. She couldn't help but wonder why the lawyer had to guard the past with such stubbornness. A few minutes of polite conversation ended the meeting. The short man walked them to the door, and once more reassured the young women he would be forever at their service.

"Yes, Mr. Resnik, I certainly know what you mean," Rebecca answered him in a tone with a touch of sarcasm in it, remembering the fat and the little women, and with a big smile she told him, "We'll call on you, certainly we will."

On their way out, Esther stopped at the secretary's desk. She invited Andrew to come to the house that Sunday afternoon. "Two other friends will be there, please come." It was the first time since her mother had died that Esther would see Albert and Gustav.

The winter cold made them walk briskly to the Viennese tea house, The Blue Danube. The owners were two brothers who had immigrated to Russia. People said they left Austria in 1896 when they were called to duty to serve their country. They had a reason; they were the only two left alive in their family of ten. All of their brothers were soldiers and died while serving under the Austro-Hungarian Empire. They could fight no more wars. They were bakers, not soldiers.

For months, the two men had traveled by foot at night and hid when the sun came up. One day, they arrived in Odessa, and started their own business. They claimed to have the best cakes and comfitures in all of Odessa. The bakery was very successful, and on the very first day of 1900, they opened the tea house. Among their specialties were the most delicious Viennese coffee served with a swirl of whipped cream on top, a thick and rich dark hot chocolate, and a variety of teas—including a special blend of Jasmine tea brought back from the Orient especially for them.

Esther and Rebecca removed their overcoats and hung them on top of many others on the metal clothes tree at the entrance. Behind the counter was one of the brothers, busy at work. He greeted customers as they arrived and thanked those who were about to leave as he took their money at the cash register. As soon as Rebecca and Esther walked into the salon, they were received by waltz music interpreted by a small group of musicians. The ensemble played on a platform in the very back of the salon. The place was always full, and people often waited in line to be seated. Fortunately, that day, there were a few empty tables, and they chose a small one under a window. A young waitress who wore an Austrian Alpine costume took their order and rapidly disappeared.

Her hands were still cold, and Esther rubbed them against each other with energy. She was the first to speak. "Obviously, the waitress eats the cakes of the house." She alluded to the roundness of the server. Rebecca smiled in silence.

"It is cold, isn't it?" She changed the subject rapidly, as she frequently did. "I thought it would take much longer to finish with all the business about our finances. It wasn't bad, was it?"

The waitress interrupted the conversation, left the tea service and the cakes, and discreetly disappeared. Esther hurried to serve the tea.

"Oh, thank God! We can breathe easier now that we know we are not indigents."

"It will make our life easier, Becca, won't it?"

"Maybe now we can plan a small trip to Greece or Italy." Rebecca had always wanted to see the Parthenon and the Roman Forum. "I'm sure it can be an enlightening experience to walk on the Via Apia."

"That is a marvelous idea, but before we go, we need to take care of more immediate affairs, don't you think?"

"My dear, your persistence in ending your phrases with a question irritates me. Tell me what is on your mind."

"I will. I would like to write to your father, my uncle," she corrected herself. "It's my obligation, not yours, to contact him and inform him of my mother's death." Esther expected some form of resistance from her cousin. Instead, she only received silence, making the forgotten surroundings more evident. The noises of porcelain cups, silver cutlery, conversation and the orchestra became a roar.

That evening after supper, Esther went to her room and opened her secretary, an old oak piece inherited from her grandmother, Irina Prusky. She sat in front of the blank paper for several minutes. She needed to calm down. She could hear her heart pounding forcefully in her ears.

Finding the right words was not easy. She began to write the date and a word or two many times. She threw several sheets of paper with no more than a sentence on them into the waste basket and dipped the dry pen in the black ink numerous times before the letter was written.

Dear Sir,

It is very difficult for me to write to you after all these years. You must know I was led to believe you were dead. Learning otherwise through Mr. Resnik does not make the occasion happier or the writing of this letter easier. You are a stranger to me and to your own daughter by your own choosing. With this letter, I do not intend to judge your behavior or reinitiate our link to you.

I could have written to you sooner, but as you may understand, not knowing of your existence until last week made it impossible for me to do so.

It causes me infinite pain to have to inform you that on the 29th of November, my beloved mother, your sister, passed away.

It is my sincere hope this letter reaches you.

Esther Vainer

Esther took a deep breath and rested the pen on the holder. With mechanical movements, she folded the paper and placed it inside an envelope. Then she dug in her purse, looking for the address she was given by Mr. Resnik. She addressed the envelope: Ulitsa Petrovka 17, Moscow.

"What in God's name is he doing in Moscow?" she asked, and then answered herself, "possibly hiding from his own phantoms?"

However, it was late, and it was not up to her to analyze the life of Ishmael. Perhaps the future would bring an answer to her questions. She left her room thinking about asking Yuri to take the letter to the post office, but decided to do it in the morning.

Olga waited for Esther in the kitchen. She had to tell her about Mr. Pissani, an Italian medium who had amazed Russians with his predictions and communications with the dead. He had arrived in Odessa the week before. The cook was in the fish market when she overheard the two women in front of her talking about the unbelievable mental powers of the clairvoyant.

While the romantic side of Esther entertained the idea of communicating with her parents through the medium, the earthbound Esther thought it over and soon came to the conclusion that the ephemeral chimera was no more than another illusion. She wanted to believe the many people who said they were helped by Mr. Pissani. They had, indeed, heard from their dead.

"It could be a fantastic experience," she told Olga.

Attracted by the mystery of the unknown, she decided it would not hurt to attend one of Mr. Pissani's sessions. It made her excited to think it was possible, but Esther was too tired. The visit with the lawyer, though it went well, had given her a headache, and the effort it took to write the letter to her uncle left her emotionally drained. She couldn't listen to one more word. She had to go to bed, it was late. She asked Olga if they could continue the conversation in the morning.

On the way to her bedroom, Esther's imagination could not stop. Absorbed by that spiritual world, she continued to daydream. The possibility of failure was big. The worst scenario would be that the medium would not be able to contact or communicate with spirits on the other side. In that case, the theory of existence of life after death would not be proven, and her hope of communicating with her parents would remain unfulfilled. The uncertainty made Esther shiver from head to toe.

The kitchen, warmed by the fireplace, was the preferred room for breakfast. Esther and Rebecca had yet to finish their cocoa when Yuri's head appeared through the translucent glass of the kitchen's back door. He knocked, opened the door and took off his muddy boots before he came in. The night before, Olga had asked him to be there first thing the next morning to pick up a letter from Miss Esther to be taken to the post office.

Yuri had worked for the grandparents Prusky since before Miriam visited St. Petersburg. He showed up at the door of Grandmother Irina, hungry and cold. She didn't have the heart to send away an eleven-year-old orphan. Madam Prusky fed him and offered him a job in the stable. Peter, the old stable master, taught him how to look after the horses and the carriages. With the years, and after Peter died, his job responsibilities increased. He was the one who repaired, mended, or fixed most things in the household. A marvelous gardener, in winter and summer, he took care of the vast yard. With the help of his oldest son, he continued to look after the horses and the carriages. He was married to Ana, and had two children, Mikhail and Ivan. They all lived in the back of the property in a small house adjacent to the carriage house.

It was cold outside. Esther offered Yuri a cup of hot cocoa. He thanked her. "I had breakfast already, Esther."

She placed the letter in his weathered, open hand. "The letter has to be on its way today, Yuri." She accompanied the man on his way out. She waited for Yuri to put his boots on, and closed the door behind him. She turned to face a disconcerted Rebecca.

"Cousin, what did you do?" It was the first time in a very long time Rebecca had called Esther cousin. She only called Esther by the blood link rather than her name when she was angry or upset. The last time Esther remembered being called cousin was the day she accidentally stained the pretty pink dress of Rebecca's favorite porcelain baby doll with chocolate.

"Well, I was about to tell you. I wrote to Uncle Ishmael last night."

Rebecca opened her mouth to initiate a protest, but was stopped by the loving voice of Esther, "Darling, you'll write to him, I know. You'll do it later, when you are ready."

"Before I write to him, I need to know what I want to say, Esther."

"When the time comes, so will the words, without you even thinking of them."

"I'm not sure he wants to hear from me." Her voice was broken by a sudden sob. "I have so many questions." She wondered what he was like after so many years. Would he look old? How close was his image to the one in the photograph with the straw hat? Where did he work, was he a teacher as before? Why was he in Moscow, so far from Odessa?

"Shhhh, Becca, calm down, you are hurting yourself unnecessarily."

"I have trouble defining my own emotions. I don't know if I hate or love him."

"Of course you don't hate him, sweetheart, but you are running ahead of yourself."

"Imagine, Esther, I don't understand my feelings for my father."

"Time will bring you answers to each one of your questions and peace to your heart."

"Does he love me?" There was much Rebecca didn't know about her father. However, nothing would prepare her for his unexpected visit and the moment they would meet again two months later in early 1905.

The day Ishmael left Miriam's house he had determined to end his life. He was so saddened by the death of his wife, Sofia, and his infant son, he did not want to go on living. It was not worth the effort, happiness had escaped him. He could see only darkness on the other side of the tunnel. When he abandoned Rebecca, he believed he had chosen the best for her. "She will be in better hands with my sister." He was no longer a good father. He had nothing to give his daughter, not even love. He was empty. Without a big drama, he would end it all by slowly sliding into obscurity.

His plan could have succeeded if he hadn't encountered dogs from a circus caravan on the way out of Odessa. The animals were happy, free from the chains that had made them prisoners for weeks. Just before each function, Demetrius, the owner, restrained the dogs. It was the only possible solution. Otherwise, they would bark and scare the people who visited the circus. They acted like puppies, ran in front of the horses, chased rabbits, and the shadows of the twilight.

The animals were muddy and wet when they stopped to smell Ishmael. Proud of their discovery, they barked so loudly the lead wagon was alerted by the racket and stopped just before it ran over the bulky shadow. The driver of the wagon, still in his red-tailed Master of Ceremony jacket, saw what looked like a man on the road. Rapidly, he reached behind the long wooden seat for a brown horn, which was gilded on one end and adorned with colored ribbons and a brown leather strap. He took a deep breath and filled his lungs with the humid air, lifted the brass mouthpiece, placed it on his lips and blew with such force that his cheeks swelled. A monotone musical note escaped from the horn. The sound lingered in the misty air long after the caravan had come to a complete halt.

The drivers from the other wagons imitated the leader. They jumped down and took lighted lanterns from the wagons, walked down the uneven road toward where the dogs and their master stood. They saw the thin and elongated barrier that lay on the road, blocking their path.

CHAPTER VIII
LIFE IN THE CIRCUS

Odessa, October, 1890

"What seems to be the problem, Demetrius?" asked a young man dressed in clown clothes. "I was half asleep when I heard the horn blaring. I stopped just before crashing into Ariana's wagon."

"I don't know yet, Mario. I need more light to see."

The man's eyes were not that good anymore, and he had to wait for the other lanterns to arrive. He kneeled to take a closer look. With the last vestiges of light of that autumn evening, the man could see the silhouette of the dogs. They were still, but their tails pointed at the wagons and they sniffed and barked at the dark bulk. The man whistled to the dogs, and obediently, the animals sat and panted as they waited for their master's next command.

"Here, take my lantern," instructed Mario.

The unconscious Ishmael didn't hear the note that made the caravan come to a halt, or the commotion that surrounded him. He was completely drunk from vodka and drugged with laudanum. As planned, he was submerged into a deep abyss.

The man called Demetrius approached the prone body and called the dogs that had barked, sniffed and poked the immobile bundle on the road. The bulk was not a dead animal, as he first thought, but a man, and he was alive. When Demetrius picked Ishmael up, his body was as limp as a rag doll. The older man carried him to the back of the wagon with no visible difficulty.

He placed Ishmael on the wet grass at the side of the road. The darkness and the lanterns made the costumed figures seem macabre. Inquisitive about the unconscious man, they circled Ishmael.

Demetrius opened the back of his wagon, pulled down a wooden ladder, and made room between his circus apparatus and his clothes. Then, he unrolled a long cushion in the narrow corridor he created.

He had to move past the curious to walk into the circle to tell them, "Go back to your posts. We'll restart the march as soon as I put this man inside my wagon."

Ishmael was in the same position in which he'd left him. Without effort, the big man climbed the five steps and deposited the inert body on the narrow mattress. Then he went back to his position of leader on the front wagon. Before he sat, he blew the long horn once more to signal the restart of their eternal exodus. The dogs in front of their owner's wagon ran, barked and played happily once more. Oblivious to what had just happened, the mind of Ishmael was absent, surrounded by nothingness.

The intelligible uproar of music and commotion produced by multitudes awakened him. He opened his eyes to see a big red and purple featherless bird with a yellow beak and blue, round eyes lying next to him. The papier-mâché animal seemed like a toy made for a giant child. His brain couldn't decipher what his eyes showed him, and he had no recollection of such a place. Only one thing pierced the confusion and was clear. He was alive.

His first thoughts were of Rebecca. He was sorry for the pain he caused her, but he did what he thought was best for his daughter. He would not go back. Her life with him in it belonged to the past. Ishmael attempted to move and felt terribly sick. He raised his head from the cushion to find he was confined inside some kind of wooden wagon.

"A gypsy wagon," he thought.

His muscles hurt and would not respond to his orders to move. He made a titanic effort and pushed to his knees. The world was spinning around him. He was shaken by uncontrollable spasms. Perspiration dripped from his forehead temporarily blinding him. He crawled to the open door, moved the curtain aside, and started down the first step. Dizziness and a persistent ringing in his ears made him stop to gasp for air. A sharp pain in his stomach made him shout out. Nausea convulsed his body, and filled his mouth with a bitter liquid. Once more, he lost consciousness and fell into soft darkness. Ishmael was later told it took him more than two weeks to regain control of his senses.

Boris Prusky, Ishmael's father, was the fourth generation of businessmen in his family, and had aspired for his son to follow the tradition. Against his father's will, but with his mother's blessings, he went to St Petersburg. At the age of twenty, he was the first in the family to graduate from a university. To complete his happiness, that same year, his wife, Sofia, gave birth to his daughter, Rebecca.

Ishmael was reserved, kind and sensitive. He was an intellectual, but had his theory about exercising. "Everybody must exercise once a day. It is good for you," he told Sofia the day they met at a fencing tournament. He competed in fencing and was the champion of his class for three consecutive years. "Physical activity is the perfect complement for an active mind," he used to tell his students. He devoted his life to his wife and daughter and ancient history with the same love and passion.

The name of the big man in red who had saved his life was Demetrius Shoent. He was a young fifty-one-year-old subject of the Austro-Hungarian Empire. Like his parents before him, he was born in the circus. When Demetrius was in his early twenties, he inherited the circus when first his father, then his mother, died from a cholera epidemic. He had no wife to look after, and no children that he was aware of. Although he was a happy man, he lamented the lack of descendents. Since the first day of entering his fifties, the sadness of having no one to pass the circus to haunted him.

The older man took care of Ishmael, a stranger, as if he were one of his own. For days, he prepared and made Ishmael drink what he called an ancient magical elixir. A mix of medicinal leafy grasses picked in the mountains of north Turkey. After the grasses dried in the sun, he hung them from a wire in his wagon. Demetrius boiled the herbs for an hour before the infusion was ready, and it had to be drunk immediately afterward.

"You have to drink it hot," Demetrius said. "It makes you sweat, and eliminates all the poisoning drugs you still have in your body. It'll clear your mind, too." A very loud outburst of laughter moved the big man's stomach.

Weeks went by before Ishmael could separate reality from fabricated fantasies and nightmares. His feverish mind tormented him with ghostly shadows from his life. Repeatedly, he had the vision of the iridescent figure of little Rebecca, suspended inside a glowing light, accusing him of abandonment. She cried in desolation, but nobody was there to comfort her.

One sunny winter morning at dawn, Ishmael awoke. He was a different man, thin, with a long beard, hungry, and in need of a bath. Only his sad green eyes had not changed. From that day on, he erased the past. The circus became his life, and Demetrius a fatherly figure. He was twenty-five when he was reborn into his new circus identity. The first month following his frustrated suicide attempt, he was frail and didn't do much. He avoided contact with the circus people. He was content to just feed the animals—they could not talk or ask questions. With time, his resentments softened, and his attitude toward his circus family changed.

One day before the function began, he helped inside the tent. Since then, he had placed and picked up the props and apparatus used by the performers in the two ring arenas. He learned their artistic abilities and particular needs. Months later, when he was physically and emotionally recuperated, he became one of the attractions at the circus.

He was not much of a performer, but in the intervals between the matinee and evening, he was part of the entertainment. With Ariana assisting, he demonstrated his ability with swords and sabres. The crowd liked his act and applauded furiously. He had obliterated the image of Rebecca from his mind, and buried his past in Odessa.

Twice in the next six years, the circus and Ishmael visited Budapest, the birth place of Demetrius. After the dogs found Ishmael half dead in the late fall of 1890, the circus left Odessa, and took a south road that bordered the Black Sea. The caravan stopped for days at a time in towns on the road, and over a month later they arrived at the mouth of the Danube River.

The circus stayed for a week in a small town called Galati at the edge of the river. That was the first time Ishmael got out of the wagon to help with the chores and to pay for his food with work. With the young son of the Flying Angels, a trapeze couple, and two of the clowns, he made several trips to the river, taking the performing animals to drink. They bathed and brushed the palomino horses to have them ready for the performance. The last trip was with the two elephants and their one-year-old female baby, two camels, and the horses which pulled the wagons. While the elephants cavorted in the river, he and the others youngsters filled big leather bladders and casks to place on the backs of the elephants and horses.

He never used the camels. "They have a nasty disposition," he once said to Demetrius.

Several trips to the river and much effort were required to carry the water back to the camp for the consumption of the rest of the animals and the human members of the group. In the evenings, he was exhausted and didn't have the will to see the show. He didn't even want to waste his gaze on the immensity of the dark sky.

Several months passed before he felt as strong as he once did. By then, the caravan was already past the Transylvanian Alps. They were in the Austro-Hungarian Empire and stopped in the town of Orsova in the spring. After he went to the Danube for water, as every day before, he felt strong enough to help the others raise the circus tent. From that moment on, as they followed the silvery serpentine meanders of the Danube to Demetrius' beloved Budapest, Ishmael helped with most of the jobs in the circus. Every time an act was missing a performer, he would take his place. Nonetheless, he made a very bad clown, bears and tigers scared him, the circus had already enough acrobats and he thought he didn't have the flair or the elegance of the trapeze people. He didn't scare easily, but he lacked the audacity and that bit of madness which was needed to become one of the Flying Angels. Besides, at twenty-five, he was too old to start a career as a performer. He was defeated by the fact that he continued to be a professor of Ancient History and a former student of antiquities. He never could be one of the saltimbanqui.

Demetrius understood his adopted son's hesitation, and with great practicality, put him to work behind a desk. Ishmael began to manage the circus money and all business affairs, from the tickets to bookkeeping. He paid the salaries before the circus moved to the next town, but always waited until the tent was down and the wagons were ready to go. Quite often, somebody tired of the vagabond life, and maybe after he had fallen in love with one of the local beauties, left the circus. They started roots and family in some unknown small town. For each one that left, another one was ready to enjoy the romance and mystery of the circus life.

For years, that was the only job and life the wounded Ishmael had. In the springs and summers he with the circus following the Danube and the coast of the Black Sea. At the end of the autumns and winters, to escape the weather they moved east and south and crossed the Bosforus into the Turkish Empire. The circus took their entertainment from Constantinople to many of the southern towns bathed by the Mediterranean. Some other winters, when the political situation made it less desirable for the circus to visit Turkey, they stayed on the west side of the Mediterranean Sea and continued their way south in search of warmer weather and the transparent air of Greece.

With each new stop, Ishmael forgot one more piece of his other life and started to believe in himself and in the future of his new universe. He considered Demetrius and the people of the circus his adopted family. He never could forget Rebecca, but the chain that had kept him moored to his past slowly opened its link. He cut his hair, and shaved the beard covering most of his face and emotions. He kept a moustache, as he had before the circus, which was not big enough to cover his smile. He bought a new style of clothing, and boots instead of formal shoes. His memories, once nightmares, were vague images. Ishmael moved to a land of brighter dreams.

Demetrius was a good-natured man, but had very strong emotions. He loved good drink, good food and not so good women in that exact order. He could laugh with the same easiness that he cried. He could break a rib in a bear hug if he was happy, but, if he was mad, he could fight until blood would run from the nose of his adversary. The previous summer, when the circus visited his beloved country, he had some run-ins with the law. The spectacle had just finished when all hell broke loose. Most of the people who went to see the show that afternoon had left. The problem began when three men demanded their money back from Ishmael. They had too much aquavit, a Scandanavian distilled liquor, and they were completely drunk. Convinced that what they had seen in the show was rubbish, they became disorderly. The troublemakers began to break some of the seats of the circus, then hit two of the jugglers who tried to stop the rioters from damaging the benches.

"What seems to be the problem, Ishmael?" Demetrius asked.

"These men are out of control. They are too stoned."

"Let's see if I can change that." Demetrius pulled up the sleeves of his shirt while trying to talk them out of the problem. One of the men, possibly too intoxicated to hear, hit him on the head with a piece of the broken wood. Demetrius realized that words were not going to solve the quarrel. He used a more persuasive way. Force. The blood from his forehead ran down his face and neck, soaking into the white cotton shirt. He was so angered by the attack he rammed them like a wounded bull. One of the men lay on the grass, and later ended up in a hospital.

"Don't you two cowards run away!" he shouted. "Come back and fight as men."

The next morning, imperial soldiers brought a signed paper. A magistrate ordered the circus to be closed for the rest of that summer. The same document ordered them to leave town. They were no longer welcome. Demetrius was so outraged and red in the face, everyone thought he could have an apoplexy attack and die, but he did not. He swore that for the next five years he would not put one foot in that ingrate country and the circus left Budapest. He was a man of his word and he always kept his promises. He never went back to his native country, dying at the age of fifty-nine, crushed by the weight of the wagon he had intended to repair.

Being pushed out of Budapest changed Demetrius. From that moment on, he didn't laugh as loud or drink as much, but he cried a bit more. They were urged by necessity to find another profitable source of revenue for the circus. They had come east, and after following the river for several days, as they had many times before, the caravan turned north to make camp at the mouth of the Danube River on the dazzling white sands of the Black Sea. Ishmael examined the maps and magazines as he planned a new route for the circus. That evening after supper around the campfire, he approached Demetrius and the rest of the troupe.

"It is my opinion we have walked the old places for the last time," said he told them. "I can see the prints of our wheels engraved in the stones of the road we have traveled. Don't you think it is time for us to make a change?"

The silence was broken only by the cheerful noise of the fire, the distant background of the night animals and the soft sea waves dying on the beach.

"We must make use of the good weather to venture into the center of the Russian country with our wonderful show."

"Are you suggesting we go north?" Mario, the clown, asked.

"Yes, my friend, I am." Ishmael's voice and his usual soft spoken tone convinced the group to venture into a harsher country.

The incident in Budapest changed the mood, not just for Demetrius, but for most of the members of the circus. Many of them were born in the circus and knew only the life of a nomad. Never before that time had their circus been expelled or banned. They felt offended and saddened by the experience. Changing the route renewed their hope and helped the troupe to open their eyes to the dream of a different horizon.

In Russia, Demetrius and the circus never went any further east or north than the city of Odessa. They were welcome, and the business bloomed for the month they were there. The cosmopolitan population of immigrants and sailors from around the world converged in Odessa. They brought good money with them, and were willing to pay to see the spectacle offered by the circus.

Being in one place for a long time was well received by the circus family. The men enjoyed being still for a change; they liked the break from the hazard of picking up camp and moving elsewhere. Some of the women checked into a hotel for a day or two, and pampered themselves with the easy life of hot baths and soft beds.

The first time Ishmael went back to Odessa in the fall of 1891, he never dared contact Miriam or his daughter. He had to relinquish his desire to hold Rebecca. He had to look at her from a distance. It was not until the next year when the circus visited Odessa again that he contacted his sister. On the way back south, every year, Demetrius and his circus continued their visits to Odessa in the autumn, and Ishmael continued to meet with Miriam.

For a while the circus integrants' lacked the courage to go into the "snow country," as they referred to most of the Russian territory that had six months of winter snow. The idea of getting caught in a snow storm with the wagons and the animals disturbed Demetrius. Ishmael insisted in his argument that there were three beautiful months of summer in which the north was a ravishing cornucopia of deep woods and ample fauna to be hunted for food. They ignored the fact that in many cases, hunting was prohibited without official authorization.

During the summer of 1892, the circus went as far north as the city of Kiev. The circus was so successful that Ishmael, proud of his decision, conceived an ambitious plan for the next year. They would start the route north earlier, and would arrive in Moscow by the month of July.

The spring of 1896 had just started when Demetrius and Ishmael learned that the coronation of Nicholas II would take place in Moscow on May 14. Since they wanted the circus to be part of that historical moment, they started the caravan north bound for Moscow. The wagons followed the Dnieper River and stopped in Kiev, as the year before. After two weeks, with the animals rested, they took the west bank of the River Desna, with plenty of time to arrive in Moscow for the coronation. Unfortunately, a blustering snow storm slowed them to a halt in the town of Bryank. Demetrius, Ishmael and the rest of the circus family never made it to the crowning ceremonies of the new

Tsar. They read in the newspaper that on the 14th of May, during the festivities for the coronation of Nicholas II, while the crowd waited for the procession to pass, more than a thousand people were crushed in a panic stampede. That year, Moscow was saddened by the tragedy. Demetrius turned the caravan back south before the end of the summer, and stayed in Odessa a full extra month.

Ishmael again would have time to see his sister and learn more about his daughter. His plan to take the circus to Moscow was postponed and would not be accomplished until July of the next year, when the romantic experience of Ishmael and the circus would tragically come to an abrupt end. Demetrius died on the afternoon of July 6, 1897, on the outskirts of Moscow, after a fatal accident. With his chest crushed, but still conscious, he asked to be placed inside the main circus tent.

"The spirits of my parents are there waiting for me." Ishmael wanted to take him to a hospital, but the older man refused. "I will die in my circus, among my friends and my animals. I want to smell the circus, not ether and alcohol that can't be drunk," he protested.

Everyone was present. No more than a foot away, the troupe of Chinese acrobats stood in a single line at his side. They had just finished practicing when the accident happened. Mario and the other five clowns, the Flying Angels with their children, Ariana and her mother Riana, the bearded woman, kneeled on the other side of Demetrius. Next to Riana was Argos, the lion tamer.

The rest of the circus family continued to arrive. They could not believe what their eyes showed them. Demetrius could not die; he was invincible. Ishmael, who could not contain his sobs, sat on the arena and held up Demetrius' head. The old man breathed with noticeable difficulty, and each time the air filled his lungs, the pain made him gasp. Demetrius' voice was a whisper, but he insisted on talking. "Let me speak now," he demanded.

Ishmael got closer to him to hear what he had to say. It came as no surprise that he left the circus to his adopted son. That night, the circus performance was canceled. The men built a platform with firewood. The women bathed Demetrius and dressed him in his best clothes and red jacket. With the help of the men, they placed Demetrius on top of the pile of wood. In a pagan ceremony, they drank, danced, and prayed through the night, and just before dawn, they lit the fire. That day, after the last embers were extinguished, the men collected the ashes and placed them in a large urn. Demetrius' ashes would be left to rest in the wind of every town where the circus stopped, from Russia to his beloved Budapest.

A week after Demetrius' death, the circus began the two daily afternoon performances with major success. All the seats were sold and the money people spent on the side attractions was abundant. Business was better than ever, but after his savior was gone, Ishmael had no interest in remaining in the circus. He passed the obligation to keep the circus alive to the Flying Angels. They deserved to inherit the circus more than he. The circus was their life.

Shaken by the tragedy, but liberated by it, Ishmael once again changed the course of his life. He would stay in Moscow. He applied for a teaching position with the university and looked for a place to live. For the next eight years, during the summer vacations, he went back to Odessa to visit Miriam every year until her death. He honored his sister's wish that he not interfere with Rebecca's upbringing. As much as he loved Rebecca, he was afraid to take care of his daughter by himself. The first year as a professor, he made very little money. He knew that at that time, he could not offer Rebecca the stability that Miriam did.

"Rebecca will be happier with them," he repeated to himself. "She has a good mother in Miriam, and a little sister in Esther. She does not need me anymore."

In time, he began to believe it.

CHAPTER IX
THE MESSAGE

Odessa, January, 1906

"Oh, Becca, I'm so happy with the news I could dance!" Esther said. With her dirty hands, she picked up her skirt and turned in a circle.

"What happened, Esther?"

"Don't you know? Let me tell you, Olga got an invitation for us."

Madame Peschanaya, the medium, would hold a reception in her home and Mr. Pissani would be the guest of honor. With him, the three women would participate in a session of foretelling the future and trans-medium communication.

"I imagine you would like to go too, wouldn't you?" Esther cleaned her hands on a kitchen towel and opened the oven door. When she took out a golden cake, a delicious aroma invaded the kitchen and made Rita flap her wings to ask for food.

"Are you asking me if I'll go to see a psychic?"

"Yes, my dear Becca, Mr. Pissani."

"I wouldn't miss one of his prognostications for all the gold in the world."

"It'll be next Friday. I'm so exited, I can hardly wait, and do you know what else? We'll have a chance to see the inside of Madam Peschanaya's mansion."

"I have no curiosity or desire to be inside that house," Rebecca remarked.

"I do, Becca. It seems so somber from the outside, I love to see the rest of it."

"Just the thought of being there raises the hackles on the back of my neck."

"Did you know that she and Mr. Pissani are good friends?" Esther placed the cake on a platter and left it on the table. "Don't go anywhere, wait for me. I'll be back in a minute. I'm going to the basement for a jar of strawberry preserves for the cake."

The cook of Madam Peschanaya's household was a friend of Olga's. They frequently talked when they met at the market. Through the cook, she learned that Mr. Pissani was Italian, not Spanish, as most everybody thought. At the butcher's, while they waited in line, she told Olga her employer had met Mr. Pissani in St. Petersburg twenty years earlier when he visited Russia for the first time. On that occasion, both of them were young and green in the arts of prognostication and psychic phenomena. They attended a conference given by a Russian theosophist, Madame Elena Petrovna Blavatskaya. They both followed her philosophy and admired her mediumistic qualities. Her theories of the mystical insight into the divine nature were well known, and her name was associated with the history and development of the extra sensorial. Her book Isis Unveiled, published in 1877, was a source of inspiration and was studied by spiritualists for many years after her death in 1891.

The cook said, "Mr. Pissani has the same kind of mediumistic ability that Madam Blavatskaya had."

She had heard her madam praise his abilities and affirmed that, with the years, Mr. Pissani's powerful visions of both the past and the future had increased considerably. He had amazed the crowds of many countries and earned his deserved reputation.

Madam Peschanaya herself was not without merit. She loved astrology and considered it to be a science. She predicted the future in the tea leaves left in the cup after a person had drunk the amber liquid. She had demonstrated that she was quite good at those arts, but her true method for foreseeing the future was through card reading. She was also an expert in Chiromancy, but her notability came through predictions of political events with such a length and veracity that convinced even the nonbelievers. She described in detail some events of the Russian-Japanese war, and her clairvoyant ability went as far as to mention the intervention of President Theodore Roosevelt of the United States of America in the matter. He had indeed convened a peace conference. The meeting happened in September of that same year, as she had foreseen. The predictions Madam Peschanaya produced stupefied her admirers and followers.

The possibility of such an extravagant meeting had brought excitement into the lives of the three women as had no other topic of conversation. Their infatuation with the supernatural was obsessive, and their expectations increased with the proximity of the séance. The hope placed in the assembly and the foreseen future left no space for them to live in the present.

Esther had guests on Sunday. Albert and Gustav were coming for tea, and if Andrew finished his studies at the school library, he would come too. He was aware of the difficulties he could encounter on every step of the way to the zenith of his career. To become a doctor of jurisprudence would demand from him an effort no less than superhuman. He knew that the higher education he aimed to achieve was reserved for the upper classes, but he was ambitious and prepared for the fight.

Esther didn't like to cook, and with Olga preparing every meal, she had the perfect excuse to stay out of the kitchen, but she adored making desserts and comfitures. She had prepared some chocolate bonbons and baked the cake she had planned to serve Sunday. She sliced the cake in two layers, filled it with some of the strawberries they had picked and preserved that early fall. She covered it with a rich Chantilly cream. She had just begun to decorate it when the racket Rita made disturbed her again.

From the wooden stand which Yuri made for her, Rita walked up and down, whistled and repeated "good, good" and whistled again. The bird continued to make noises and flap her wings, and didn't stop until Rebecca got a carrot from a basket, cut a piece and gave it to her.

"I know why Joseph did not keep the Papa Gallo," Esther informed her. "Your bird is sometimes too noisy. The only way to keep her silent is by stuffing her beak."

She put the last final touches on the cake on the table in front of her. She had a metal bowl with whipped cream in one hand and a long spatula in the other, which she shook in the air menacingly with the look of a killer in her eyes. "You are impossible." She stood as she laughed at the bird. "I'll bring a big and mean cat into the kitchen if you don't shut up."

"Olga is spoiling her," Rebecca replied as an excuse. "Every time she is in the kitchen preparing any kind of food, she gives a piece of it to Rita. Now she just expects food from the cook, whoever she is."

A loud explosion interrupted the conversation; it made the kitchen shake and the glass in the windows vibrate as if a bolt of lightening had struck the house. They later learned it was a bomb that had detonated. An anarchist had placed the explosive inside an office near the fruit and vegetable market. The building was more than ten blocks away from their home on Balkovskaya Street, but the intensity of the blast shook the foundation of the house.

In 1905, the terrorist attacks had become an everyday occurrence throughout Russia. It was said the attacks were specifically aimed at killing government officials. People objected to the way they were governed by the Tsar and his appointees. The grandiose excesses of the imperial family upset the population and caused unrest. The discontent increased in the cities. Unemployment among the lower classes and the peasants had continued to grow. People had become poorer, and hunger was an everyday reality.

Workers rebelled against injustice with demonstrations and organized strikes. Day and night it was possible to find protesters and violence everywhere. The political situation in the city of Odessa was no exception. Menacing crowds of agitators were found too often. The order on the streets was disturbed. Esther and Rebecca felt surrounded by that rage and avoided going out of the house. They stopped their daily walks at the park, and their freedom was compromised.

"I think this is a good time to plan a vacation in the southwest of Europe or North Africa," Rebecca said.

"I don't think winter makes for good traveling weather."

"Greece or Italy would be a more tranquil place than here, Esther."

The menace of a revolution continued to influence Esther, who found plenty of excuses, such as too much snow and danger in the crossing of the mountains into the European countries. She reflected for a moment and suggested planning a trip for spring.

"If we are brave enough, we can cross the Atlantic to visit Aunt Sarah in New York."

It would be a fantastic trip and a great vacation for them. The idea, mentioned by Esther, was received with enthusiasm by her cousin.

"If we're going to America, we should start learning some English. Yiddish and French won't be sufficient there," Rebecca commented, carried away by the prospect. She envisioned the trip as a fantasy more than a possible reality.

That Sunday, Andrew was the first to arrive at the house. The inherited new clothes he wore made him look more handsome and quite attuned with the occasion. As she had expected, immediately after Esther introduced him to Albert and Gustav, the three acted as if they had been friends forever. They talked politics, as always. The theme of religion was introduced and welcomed as a refreshing change. Andrew was Christian Russian Orthodox and was unacquainted with other religions. They compared the Christian and Judaic philosophies. They talked about Ravel and his piano music, Jeux d'eau à la Villa d'Este.

"Do you know that Ravel composed it in 1902 and dedicated the piece to Fauré?" Andrew asked.

"Oh, yes, I do." Gustav affirmed. "I think the music was inspired by the fountains and the water cascades of the Italian Villa d'Este." He explained that they had visited Tivoli the previous year in May.

"What a place. I'll never forget it,"

Albert remembered and sighed.

"Later we took Albert to a clinic in Naples."

In the south of Italy, there were several rehabilitation clinics that used thermal waters for therapeutic purposes. Albert experienced an almost claustrophobic sensation when technicians submerged him up to his neck in mud that was prepared with volcanic black ashes and herbs. Those heavy baths, rich in sulfur and smelled like rotten eggs, were advised for his illness and prepared specifically for him.

"The doctor assured us the treatment is very good for curing rheumatism, as in my brother's case," Gustav said.

Andrew looked at Albert with increased interest. He didn't seem an invalid. To the law student, he looked young, beautiful and very intelligent, but not handicapped.

The afternoon brought joy to Esther and Rebecca and made the recent family displeasures less worrisome. After tea and Esther's cake, Andrew played the piano to the enjoyment of the hostesses. Gustav stood, walked to the piano, and asked Andrew to interpret a Schubert's lieder. Gustav sang with a beautiful voice that delighted his surprised audience. At the end, after the ecstasies and a moment of silence, the enchantment was broken by enthusiastic applause.

"Isn't that an absolute surprise?" Esther whispered to Rebecca. "When he sings, he looks almost human. I liked the change, don't you?" Esther, suddenly more communicative, told the young men their plans to make a trip to America.

"Do you speak the language?" Gustav asked.

"No yet, but we will." Rebecca answered.

"You can't visit a country without speaking the language." Esther said. "The limitations would confine you. It'd make you prisoner of your own ignorance."

"I can teach you English, if you like. Once you know it, you would be free again," Gustav said.

Esther and Rebecca looked forward to an escape from the violence that surrounded them. They knew that April was a wonderful month in New York. Esther had yet to write to her aunt, but they could begin to learn English right away.

Separated a bit from the others, Albert spent most of the afternoon engaged in conversation with Andrew. They had affinity in their characters, similar tastes in classical music and theater, and shared the same kind of political ideas. They were still in an animated conversation when it was time to leave. Gustav saw the advantage in the situation, and tried many of his seduction techniques on Esther. The conqueror's smile and the velvety voice were tricks that had given him much success with ladies before. He was sure he was in love with Esther. He hoped his feelings would be reciprocated, even if he had to work hard to gain her affection.

It became obvious to him that she wasn't impressed with

his flirtations. To awaken her interest, he needed to find a more sophisticated approach. More opportunities would arise if he taught them English and visited with Esther at least once a week. Before the two brothers left that evening, Gustav was too insistent and anxious to help them with the new language and made it impossible for the young women to refuse his offer. Esther and Rebecca exchanged glances of complicity and understood. They thanked him and accepted.

Later that night, over a cup of hot chocolate, Rebecca asked, "Is it just my imagination, or did I really see the icy look you had on your face beginning to melt when you talked to Gustav?"

"I have to agree with you. He doesn't irritate me as much."

"He acts so charming around you. How can you resist him?"

"My dear, the day I meet the love of my life, I'll know it instantly, and I can assure you, he is not the one." Esther could easily deceive Rebecca.

However, she couldn't deny to herself that she liked Gustav a lot more that she was prepared to accept.

How awfully nice for Gustav to offer to help them with English, Rebecca thought. Since Gustav would not do anything less than perfect, she was sure they had found the ideal teacher.

"Let's not begin the classes tomorrow," Rebecca proposed. "Let's wait until next Monday." Her mind was too involved in the spiritual world, and she complained about not having any space left to indulge in the mundane matters until then.

Believing the meeting with Mr. Pissani would bring them transcendent results, Esther, Rebecca and even Olga spent the rest of the week prisoners of the hours and minutes separating them from Friday's meeting at Madame Peschanaya's house.

At six o'clock that evening, the three women were ready, each absorbed in her own thoughts. Esther was in the parlor. Rebecca found her with her back tense and straight, her face pale, her lips tight, and her hand distracted in a handkerchief.

"The taxi is not here yet," she said to Rebecca.

Olga arrived in the room dressed in a dark gray suit and a red Alpine hat with a brown pheasant feather. Without paying attention to the young women, she walked to the big window and repeated Esther's words. "The taxi is not here yet. We can't be late."

She looked at the wall clock and impatiently walked back to the door. "If the session starts before we are there, they won't let us interrupt, and they will make us wait outside."

The sanguine face of Olga contrasted with the paleness of Esther's. They expected so much from this meeting, but what? Rebecca was the only calm one. She knew that nothing bad they could foresee and tell her, could exceed the displeasure and pain that Mr. Resnik's news had already brought her.

"The taxi is here," Olga shouted and held the front door open with one hand and the key in the other. She didn't trust the girls; she had to lock the door herself. When she arrived at the car, she had to sit next to the driver. There wasn't sufficient space in the back for her.

The house was not far away. In earlier times, they could have walked the distance, but the political instability and the winter evening gave them enough justification for the ride. In less than ten minutes they were on Bogatova Street at the front of a mansion built in a baroque rococo style. The door knocker, in the shape of the head of a dog, felt very heavy in Esther's trembling hand. She let it slip and it hit the door just once. The loud, but dark, noise scared her. A young woman in a black uniform opened the door and showed them to a large, well-illuminated room filled with dark, elegant but heavy furniture. A bubbly mood prevailed in the group of the people who had arrived before them. The extroverted personalities of both Esther and Rebecca vanished. Intimidated by the unexpectedly strange-looking crowd, they tried to hide behind Olga as they had done when they were young.

A larger group around a man was indicative of the presence of Mr. Pissani. With curiosity, Esther made an effort to pinpoint him in the crowd. She saw him from a distance and worked her way through the crowd to get closer to him. He paused in mid-conversation. He looked at Esther for the longest second and smiled at her. That was the first time their eyes met. Surprisingly, he was nothing like she had imagined. In fact, he was a very earthy, inconspicuous being. He was a balding old man with a crown of white, curly hair that gave him an awkward, monk-like appearance. He was tall and had a prominent, round abdomen. Two things impressed Esther in that first glance: his deep brown eyes that looked simultaneously fiery and tender, and his huge hands with their thick fingers, which resembled those of a hard-working peasant. He appeared to be a simple and ordinary man, much like anybody's grandfather, not an authority in the Trans-medium world and possessor of great mental power.

Anticipating the start of a fantastic evening, the noisy group quieted down considerably when they noticed the maid in black had came back into the room. With a strong voice that projected clearly to those in the back row, she directed them to follow her to another area of the house, but on the same floor. In this smaller chamber, there was a soft penumbra, lighted by just a few candles. In the center of the space and under an unused chandelier, sat a round table surrounded by nine chairs. Chairs and tables also lined the walls of the room. A tall window was open, and a cold breeze moved the curtains. Feeling threatened by the atmosphere, Esther and Rebecca instinctively held hands.

Madam Peschanaya reminded them of the vivid display of a male peacock when she entered the room. Her purple dress was as elaborate as the architecture of her house and very expensive. She wore gold bracelets set with precious stone on both arms, and rings on almost every one of her fingers. Her most exotic adornment was a heavy jeweled necklace. A long purple gaze shawl covered her bare shoulders. The weightless chiffon fabric flowed as if suspended in the air when she walked toward the table. She was followed by Mr. Pissani and his modesty.

Before they sat down, Mr. Pissani asked some people to join him at the table. "To increase and maintain high energy and vibration," he explained. To the amazement of the three women, he walked straight to Esther, and extended a hand which seemed bigger in proximity with hers. He took her by the arm and told her in Russian with a heavy Italian accent, "You will sit by me, yes? I would like that." He didn't wait for an answer, and began to walk with her by his side.

A candle was lit in the center of the table, and he asked all those who sat around it to hold hands. The silence was absolute and everyone in the group waited for Mr. Pissani to start some sort of recitation or prayer, or even to speak in tongues to invoke his familiar spirits. To unsettle the audience's expectations, he sat still with his eyes closed, wearing a very peaceful expression on his face and an almost imperceptible smile. The minutes passed. The deafening tick-tock of a clock in another room unnerved some attendees and made them move uncomfortably in their seats.

At a signal from Madam Peschanaya, an assistant placed a pencil and a sheet of white paper in front of Mr. Pissani. With his eyes completely closed, the trans-medium began to write. As soon as the sheet of paper was filled, the assistant appeared from behind, and without disturbing the scribe, removed it and replaced it with a new one. At the same time, the man arranged the written papers in some order on the long table just behind him.

Over half an hour passed before Mr. Pissani finished writing. He murmured something, as if he were in conversation with someone. He moved his head several times, and agreed with that same being. Then he opened his eyes and the assistant handed him a handkerchief, which he used to dry the tiny drops of perspiration on his forehead.

Esther was so disappointed, she could have cried. She looked for Rebecca and Olga seated across the room from her. The old woman had her eyes closed and seemed to be asleep, and her cousin's eyes were lost in the elaborate design of the Persian rug. Both of them appeared to be bored and distracted. Some coughs and the creaking of the wood chairs were the only signs of movement.

The end of the session was marked when Madame Peschanaya rose from her chair. "Before you leave the room, walk by the table next to the wall. There are some messages for each one of you. Be careful not to disturb the order in which the papers are arranged, and please be sure to get only the one that has been sent for you."

Esther was detained by Mr. Pissani when she attempted to leave the circle. He took both her hands between his and told her to wait, as he had something to tell her. He looked with focused attention at each of her palms, and to Esther's astonishment, he said, "You are thinking of taking a trip and a trip you will take, but bring your dear things and the photographs of your dead parents with you. You are not coming back to Russia." He smiled at her enigmatically, and with characteristic Italian charm, he kissed her hand and moved aside to engage in conversation with a group that awaited him.

Shaken by the revelations, Esther moved on to Rebecca and Olga, who waited for her at the long table. They were in the search of the messages left by the spirits for them.

"This one must be yours, it is the only one not for wives, sons, or husbands," Rebecca said.

She walked with Esther to retrieve a sheet of paper with a few sentences written on it. Esther picked the paper up from the table and read.

Let the dead sleep and their spirits will rise. They are the past, but you do not put them to rest, you make them part of your present. Do not forget them, keep them in your heart and you will not walk alone. You have to look to the future. There is where you will see your life. Do not feel sorrow, your future is exciting and beautiful and it starts now.

CHAPTER X
AN UNEXPECTED VISITOR

Odessa, still winter, 1906

"Will you ever tell me about your message, Esther?"

"But, Becca, I don't have anything to tell you."

"What on earth did he tell you and why are you so secretive about it?"

For several weeks after the experience at Madam Peschanaya's mansion, Esther was haunted by images of desertion and abandonment. Mr. Pissani's voice echoed as a litany in her ears. The words sounded as clear as they had the moment he spoke them to her. She wanted to remember his words forever, so she sat at her desk and wrote them down on a sheet of paper. Before she folded the paper to hide it in her purse, she read it again.

He was definitely wrong, she thought. She would never leave her home. She was born there. Her life and history were imprisoned inside those walls. It was well known the Italian medium had predicted the future with great accuracy. Maybe, just maybe, this was one of those rare occasions in which he was wrong.

Without much effort, Esther began to convince herself that Mr. Pissani must have made a mistake in his prediction of the future. To keep from being paralyzed by terror, she had to forge a plan to stop all possibilities of abandoning Odessa before they even began. It occurred to her that the simplest solution was to stay within the limits of the city, and never, until her death, venture any farther than those boundaries. The idea was absurd. She refused to be a prisoner of her own destiny. Defiantly, she rebelled against the prediction.

"Look at you, so reticent to share it with me," Rebecca said.

"Here it is." Esther held out the sheet of paper she picked up from the long table at the spiritualistic session to Rebecca. There was nothing on it that needed to be kept a secret. "I did not share it with you until now because the message made me sad." She waited for Rebecca to take the paper.

"I don't have to read it, Esther. It's all right."

The message didn't contain news of a romantic future or a great fortune for Esther. "It just talks about my parents and my past." Rebecca never opened the prediction, and Esther placed it back inside her purse beside the one she'd written.

"Of course," Rebecca said. "We can't believe word for word what a spiritual message said. Much less sit and wait for it to happen."

"Oy Vey!" exclaimed Esther, "I thought I was the non-believer."

Rebecca secretly wished with all her heart that the message would be right, word for word. She wanted to get married, have children and a reasonably happy life, but later. Before finding a husband and get married, she believed they should make the much desired trip to America. She hoped it would help Esther forget her fears.

The spring was less than three months away, leaving little time to prepare for such a journey. "Esther, dear, I've been thinking, and I'd love to take that trip to America that we talked about the other day. It would be splendid to visit another country, and it will keep us away from this turmoil."

"Becca, maybe it's too soon to make such a long journey."

Rebecca protested with a touch of irritation in her voice "I don't understand it. Seems to me you have lost interest in our plans to visit other countries, is it so?"

"Not exactly. We still can go later."

"I'm enthusiastic about your idea to go to America, and I want to go visit your aunt now."

Esther never mentioned to Rebecca or Olga what Mr. Pissani had predicted for her when he read the lines on her hands. She had a hard enough time forcing herself to forget and reorganizing her life with new limits on her boundaries. She would never confess her fear of the future to others.

"We have time, Becca."

"Nonsense, we must take the trip while we are young and free," Rebecca insisted. The present time was as good as any other. It was neither that far, nor that hard of a journey. Besides, as Rebecca put it, "We can break the trip into small parts, so it won't seem so long."

Soon, Esther ran out of arguments against the trip. She knew Russia was her country, her home. She would never choose to live anywhere else. Nothing or nobody would keep her away, and she never would leave forever. She would write to her Aunt, Sarah Vainer, who in keeping with American tradition, had dropped her maiden name and taken her husband's last name. She was Sarah Bernstein now. That evening, once dinner was over and she had spent some time in the kitchen chatting with Olga, she wrote to Sarah to tell her of their intentions. She needed to know if spring was a good time for Sarah to receive them.

After breakfast the next morning, Rebecca quietly got up and left the kitchen while Esther helped Olga clear the table. She came back a few minutes later with a pad of white paper and a pencil. "I think we have to make a list of things we'll need." She began to write down a plan.

First, they had to decide the best way to get to America. It was inevitable they'd have to cross the Atlantic Ocean, and there was no other way to do that than by ship. The question was where to board that ship. There were many possibilities.

Olga interjected and wondered aloud why they didn't just take a ship from Odessa. "We'll take you from home directly to the port," she told the girls.

Rebecca had the fanciful idea of going by ship from Odessa to Constantinople and spending a few days in the exotic city. "Wouldn't it be grand to have time to visit the palace of Suliman, the Magnificent and St. Sofia?"

They imagined themselves walking through the mysterious bazaars, shopping at one of the rug and metal markets and buying presents to take to America. Esther, caught in the web of Rebecca's plans, mentioned that she had heard there was a market where the Turkish people sold only objects made from gold. "Hundreds of small jewelry shops in the same place," she stated.

They could visit Turkey for a week, and from Constantinople, take the Orient Express to Paris. That was such an extravagant possibility. They were terribly tempted, but thought it may be a little too expensive for them. Another attractive idea was to visit Europe and the northern part of Africa, then sail the Mediterranean Sea to Spain or Portugal. From there they could board a transatlantic ship and cross the ocean to America. Esther suggested a visit to Egypt and the pyramids. The fantasy took them far afield. With the open wings of their imagination, they flew far away, to remote and enchanted places. Esther forgot the menace of her future. A new dream was born in the heart of the eighteen-year-old woman, and a smile danced on her lips, replacing her worried frown. Esther sat at her secretary and sent a note to Gustav. They must start English lessons at once.

Gustav received the note with absolute delight and answered Esther that same morning. They would begin the classes the next afternoon. It was not quite two o'clock when Gustav was at their front door, ready to teach.

Esther took extra care when she combed her wavy hair up in a chignon. Its dark hazelnut color contrasted with the white transparency of her skin. She put a touch of color on her lips and smiled. She liked the image she saw reflected in the mirror. "I'm very pretty," she thought. "Maybe I can become Mrs. Perlman and never leave Russia." At that moment, Esther had a very specific agenda in mind—to marry Gustav.

Gustav brought an English book and a pad of paper with him. For two uninterrupted hours, they studied the rudiments of the English language that first day. Before they broke for tea, he gave them some exercises to do.

"Is it too much to ask you to have these exercises ready for our class on Wednesday?" he asked.

He was so pleased to be in the house with just the two girls by himself. He would have come to the house every afternoon if asked. He had no competition from the intelligent Albert or the handsome Andrew. The burst of jealousy disappeared as fast as it had surfaced. Andrew was a Christian, and Gustav knew the poor fellow had no chance with a nice Jewish girl. Gustav could perceive a change in the way Esther accepted his gallantries, and he was sure she liked him a bit. Soon after they had tea, he took his book and papers from the dining room table and left, but not before he kissed Esther on the hand.

She had to control and overcome the almost irresistible impulse to take her hand away from him. Maybe with time she would become accustomed to his touch, but right then she didn't like it. When his hand caught hers, it felt sweaty. Esther hoped that what her mother had affirmed and she heard many times, would happen to her. "You don't have to love your future husband. Love comes later, after you marry him."

Esther had never fallen in love. While her intellect gave her reason to accept Gustav as a possible husband, the lack of love made her reluctant to enter the fascinating circle he astutely created for her. She would resist Gustav and his deceitful behavior. She even dreamed that he allured her with kindness and presents into an obscure trap.

Esther obstinately guarded her freedom. Since she was fifteen, with Rebecca, they had volunteered two mornings a week at the Christian Orphanage of St. Mathew.

"Those are not Jewish children," her mother told her once.

"They are just orphans in need, Mama," she replied.

They read and played with the children, and every Christmas season, they helped the children construct a big Father Christmas. She wanted to continue attending oil painting and ceramics classes with Mr. Pulaski. She had much to learn from the old maestro before she could create art on her own.

Esther assumed Gustav would take her away from all those things she loved. More than once Olga had told her she continued to escape young suitors because the real one had not yet crossed her path. Maybe she was right.

The wise old woman frequently added with a certain touch of boastfulness in her voice, "With each of the men in my life, I knew they were the 'one' before they became my lovers."

Esther and Rebecca laughed each time they heard it, and

imagined how someone could have been her lover. In their eyes she was too fat and old; they didn't see her as attractive.

"The class went very well. I don't think it will be too difficult to learn English. Tomorrow, we have to go buy some books so we can continue to study," Rebecca said.

Esther did not answer; she was disappointed in Gustav. She had already found a flaw in him. With all the money he had, she thought it would've been very elegant for him to buy the books they needed for their lessons. Since his attempt to conquer was so evident, he could've made the gesture just to please her.

"My dear cousin, are you hearing me?" Rebecca raised her voice when she spoke. "You seem far away."

"I was thinking of the last time we do something without knowing it is the last. Do you ever think of the last time you had dinner with your mother and father?" She remembered the last time she went to the port with her mother to bid farewell to her father. Esther became quiet for an instant, took a deep breath and continued, "If I only knew that time was to be the last, maybe I could have said more, held his hand longer, kissed him one more time. However, we don't know when that last time will be, do we?"

"Esther, you are scaring me. I know you well. You are hiding something, tell me what it is."

Esther did not want to tell Rebecca about Mr. Pissani's prediction. She was about to tell a lie, but somebody knocked at the front door and saved her. She got up from the armchair and hurried to answer the door.

A delivery boy had brought a long white box and an envelope for her. The youth made her sign a receipt and left before she could go in to get some coins for a tip. In the box, there was no card, only an exquisite sheaf of yellow tea roses. "Oh look, Becca, they are so beautiful!" Before she opened the envelope she recognized Gustav's handwriting. "What now?" she wondered.

"You won't know what it says unless you open that envelope, dear."

Without enthusiasm, Esther read the note, then laughed. Gustav had invited them for tea. "He's counting on us to accept;

his invitation is for tomorrow afternoon at 3:30. He will pick us up and take us to the Blue Danube, or any other tea house we desire. I wonder if he'll pay for the two of us or just me."

The tone of voice Esther used when she talked of the man she inwardly planned to marry was too sarcastic and made Rebecca laugh. She immediately wrote to let him know they accepted the invitation and asked Yuri's older son, Mikhail, to deliver it to the office at the factory. He could use his new bicycle to take the note to Gustav.

The morning found Esther in her small art studio in the back of the house. The place was cramped with canvases, easels, tables, and ceramic pots. The shelves were filled to capacity with books, and everything in the room had a perennial smell of oil paint. When she was troubled or wanted to hide from the menace of the world around her, she always took refuge inside those protective walls.

Red coals glowed from the brazier in the middle of the room. The air was warm and impregnated with the smell of the turpentine she used to clean her brushes. Esther was absent, immersed in one of her artistic compositions. A few weeks earlier, in her art history book, she had finished the chapter about French Impressionists and thought it was a fascinating style.

"This pretty new style, defined by the artist as the play between color and light, has as much happy rhythm as a Mozart symphony," Mr. Pulaski, her art teacher told her.

Up close, the work looked almost grotesque and unshaped. One had to stand at a distance to appreciate it. The concept baffled her. Until then, it was the opposite of what she had studied.

Her interpretation was not as dramatic as those examples shown by her teacher, but she attempted to emulate the impressionistic style. She was painting a still-life. The model was on a side table next to the small window. A piece of white cloth, a modest tin plate with two onions, a wooden board with a piece of dark bread on it and a tall green glass bottle completed the composition. She stepped back a few feet to appreciate her masterpiece and thought, *Ne c'est pas mal.* It's not a painting to be accepted at the French Salon, but I like it.

She was so absorbed in her work, the time vanished between her brushes, tubes of paint and her canvas. Rebecca loved to draw with charcoal and quite often joined Esther in the studio. She had spent several hours in the back room with her cousin that morning. She abandoned her drawing, complaining that her eyes were tired, and she needed fresh air.

Olga disliked the smell of that place altogether, and almost never went there for a visit. When she wanted to see their work, she asked the girls to line up their art pieces against the kitchen counter. Esther hadn't expected anyone to disturb her, and the door opened so rapidly that it startled her.

"Do you know what time it is? You may need to clean your brushes and cover your oil palette right now. We'll be late for tea if you don't hurry."

"It is not that grave. Gustav can wait a few minutes until I'm ready. He'd better learn to respect my work from the very beginning of our relationship, if we are to have one. Don't you agree?"

Esther looked at the small clock on the wall opposite the door. It was almost three. She placed the brushes in a can with solvent and hoped they wouldn't be ruined when she came back later that evening to clean them. "Too much soaking," she said. She'd take care of them once she returned from tea.

She ran into the house and began to take her clothes off on the way. Rebecca picked them up behind her. By the time she arrived at the top of the stairs, she was nude and ready to jump in the bath Olga had prepared for her. Ten minutes later she was seated in front of her vanity, wrapped in a green towel. She had finished combing her hair when doubt and panic enveloped her thoughts. She questioned whether her pursuit of Gustav for a husband was a wise idea. Maybe marrying Gustav would force the prediction of Mr. Pissani into reality. What if he had to go to live in another country forever? She would be forced to accompany him. She should not consider marriage as the only option to keep her in Odessa.

"The solution is to avoid all amorous relationships and be alone for the rest of my life." She laughed at such an ugly and boring possibility.

Esther placed some color on her cheeks and lips. She had lost some weight lately, but was still beautiful. From her closet, she selected a pale pink suit, a gray embroidered blouse and a gray hat. She opened her jewelry box and took out a string of pearls and pearl earrings. She was about to wear a ring, but noticed her fingers were already adorned with blue oil paint.

"I'll keep my gloves on until I come back home." She picked out a pair of gray gloves and a clasp purse, put her hat on, and she was ready to go for tea. She had minutes to spare as it was not yet 3:30. She rushed to the parlor where her cousin waited and sat with her.

A messenger knocked at the door with another box and another note.

"We may not go out for tea this afternoon," Esther said in an acid tone, with an unopened envelope and a square box of chocolate bonbons in her hands.

She was wrong and had misjudged Gustav. He had been detained by unresolved matters in a business meeting, but was confident he would be free before teatime. In his place, he had sent the note through the messenger from the factory. A chauffeured car was parked at the curb, waiting to take them to the Blue Danube, where he would meet them. When they arrived at the teahouse, Gustav, with all his elegance, was at the door. He had flowers, not just for Esther, but also for Rebecca.

"I think I'll like this courtship very much, and I would love being your chaperone every time you go out with Gustav," Rebecca whispered in her cousin's ear.

As a relentless businessman who knew how to harvest every opportunity, Gustav used all his wiles to charm his conquest. With the innocent invitation for tea, he opened a door into their lives. From that day, until the moment the two young women left to go on their trip to America, the house on Balkovskaya Street was perfumed with exotic aromas from the most unusual flowers he could find in the town's florist shops. Gustav even extended his generosity to Olga. Quite often, she received some of her favorite chocolates. He became a bit more possessive with Esther, and on more than one occasion, he unsuccessfully attempted to stop some of her Sunday afternoon meetings with Albert, Andrew, and the dear Doctor Feldman.

Joseph returned from Moscow later than he had anticipated, but he was back into his routine in Odessa. Once again, the hospital patients took much of his time. His father's health continued to deteriorate until the end of December. Without hope and with no more remedies to administer to him, Joseph expected the old man to die. But suddenly, and without apparent reason, the illness disappeared with the same rapidity with which it had started.

Since his father was under the care of a colleague, Joseph no longer had a reason to remain in Moscow. A week after his inexplicable recuperation, Joseph left his father to return to his almost abandoned practice in Odessa. He had to put his affairs back into order, and his visits to Rebecca were short and sporadic. She was delighted to have him back, and at that time, the notes they wrote to each other every day were sufficient for her.

When mid-January came about, the winter softened, became old and weak. The sun showed its luminosity more often, and the days were less windy. Once again, it was possible to go to the country for a walk.

In late autumn, Olga always picked mushrooms for the rest of the year. They all accompanied her to her secret place in the forest, and made a day trip and a picnic of the event. She found the perfect place among the luxurious foliage of the most ancient blue spruces and cedars. The thick canopy of immense trees blocked the sun. The rich, humid soil was a fertile womb for a vegetal universe, where the biggest and best quality mushrooms were produced. The previous fall, sadness had impeded Olga, and she could not gather the harvest.

Aware of the influence the old maid had over both young women, Gustav used all his persuasive ability to win her favor. He fawned over her with attentions and presents. He knew that was the first step in gaining the heart of the woman with whom he was so much in love.

The Sunday Gustav invited Esther and Rebecca to one of his elaborate picnics in the country, he had the clever idea of including Olga in the invitation. He promised to drive her to the hidden forest, and the three of them would accompany her. They would help her search for the legendary mushrooms. Sunday, to the surprise of the three women, he arrived to pick them up in a big carriage pulled by two enormous black horses.

Olga pushed both girls and Gustav out of the house, she was ready to go. At the carriage, the driver stepped down to help the ladies get in. Rebecca and Olga sat behind the driver, and Esther and Gustav in the opposite seat. With a large lap robe, he covered their legs to protect them from the chill of the morning, and ordered the driver to commence the trip. It was nearly noon when they stopped for lunch.

The driver, George, ran to the back of the carriage and took out a large trunk, a folded table and folded canvas chairs. He searched for an ideal place with lots of shade to protect the ladies from the sun and gusts of wind. Laboriously, he set up the table. On it, he placed an embroidered white tablecloth. George went back to the trunk for a large basket. He refused Olga's offer to help him, and flashed her a smile with his big teeth, yellowed from years of smoking a pipe.

The driver took one last trip to the carriage, and brought back another folded table and a dark, lacquered wooden box that contained a phonograph and records. He cranked the Victrola, put on a record, and the music of a waltz competed with the concert offered by the strings of the wind and the song of the birds of the countryside. For an instant he danced with an invisible partner, but went back to his chores and plucked some crystal glasses and a bottle of white wine from the basket. He began to dance again while from the top pocket of his jacket, he pulled out a corkscrew and used it to open the bottle. He stopped again and filled the glasses. On the table, George placed a small basket replete with crackers and toasted bread, a crystal plate with caviar, a wooden board with a variety of cheeses and another basket with exotic fruits from the tropics.

Gustav and Esther walked a few yards to a ravine formed by the primeval erosion of a silvery river that ran through it. The ferns and grasses near the water were exuberant in their perennial green, but the tall trees, shivered cold in their nudity.

Rebecca followed them, and wished Joseph were there by her side. She was not happy with the chaperoning business. The day was a little bit cool, but perfect. The bleak landscape hadn't yet began to awaken from the winter sleep and contrasted with the green and dark pine forest nearby. When they went back for lunch, they found Olga in animated conversation with George.

"That old George, he loves women." Gustav whispered and smiled.

As much as Olga loves men, Esther thought.

The food was light and delicious and they ate, enjoyed the sunlight, the smell of grass and the conversation. Sadness was replaced with the perfect harmony of the moment. Immediately after the music and lunch paraphernalia was placed back in the carriage, they were ready to go find the mushrooms. This time, instead of joining the others, Olga effortlessly jumped up and sat next to her new friend, George, on the driver's seat. She had to give him directions to the forest.

They had traveled for no more than a mile when the soft strains of carnival music join them. Esther and Rebecca eagerly asked Olga if they could visit the carnival, and Olga consented. Instead of picking mushrooms, they spent the rest of the afternoon at the carnival. They enjoyed watching three black bears dance to the tempo of an accordion played by a little peasant girl. Esther and Rebecca, who disliked imperfections, felt sorry for the bearded woman, they didn't stop to look at her.

The cotton candy and hot chestnuts were delicious, and Esther and Rebecca ate too much of both. They sat next to each other on the carousel, which had forever been Esther's favorite ride. Olga and George, maybe tired, sat under a tree, and kept each other company. Esther, Rebecca, and Gustav went through the glass labyrinth and had trouble finding their way out. When they finally found the exit, they made their way to the carriage, where George and Olga awaited them.

Exhausted from the long day, they returned to Odessa in the cold twilight of that wintry Sunday. The carriage stopped at the house on Balkovskaya Street, and Gustav accompanied the three women to the front door. A menacing glance from Olga deterred his attempt to come in the house with them. He kissed Esther on both cheeks, said goodbye, and left.

For the first time in months, Esther felt happy. She had forgotten the predictions of Mr. Pissani. Life was beautiful, and on that day, she could have sworn she loved Gustav a little. Her happiness would last until the next morning.

The partially opened curtains allowed an indiscreet ray of sunlight to penetrate the room, awakening Esther from her slumber. She opened her eyes to see Olga leaning over her with a cup of tea in one hand and an envelope in the other. Esther sat up on the bed, anticipating a disaster. "What happened?"

"I don't know. I'm not clairvoyant and I won't know until you open the envelope and read the note inside." Olga switched from sarcastic to seriousness and said, "Wake up first and have some tea. You'll need it."

The envelope had been delivered by a young man, the gardener of the Perlman family. The note was from Madam Perlman. She informed the Vainer family that she wished to visit them at four o'clock that afternoon.

"Obviously, she is coming for tea, Olga," Esther said, in an incredulous tone of voice. Then she dropped the card on the bed and raised her arms in a comical gesture of resignation.

Olga rose from the chair, which continued to rock, as if moved by an invisible being. She ran downstairs and repeated on her way down, "Oh my God, Oh my God!" She ran through the back yard and all the way to the carriage house. She knocked on Yuri's closed door. When Ana opened, Olga told her in desperation about the visitor and asked for her help.

For the rest of the morning, both women were busy. They cleaned, moved furniture around, rearranged flowers in the vases, and baked cakes and chocolate éclairs, Olga's culinary specialty. She only baked them when she had to impress someone. Once they finished with the house, Ana polished the silver with extreme care, and Olga cleaned the Chinese porcelain tea set Jacob had given Miriam years earlier.

"So much fuss over an uninvited visitor we don't even know," Esther protested. "Why do you care so much about what she thinks? She should have waited for an invitation."

"Don't be too hard on Madam Perlman. She'll be your mother-in-law one day. Besides, she may be nice," Rebecca replied with humor. She remembered Mrs. Perlman's arrogant face from dinnertime at the clinic.

When Madam Perlman arrived, Esther and Rebecca were in the parlor. From the window, Esther saw the car pull up. Once the car was parked, the chauffeur ran around to open the door for Madam Perlman. Esther had to repress the urge to go to the front door, open it, and see the woman in. Instead, she waited for the guest to ring the bell and for Ana to direct her to the parlor. When she finally entered the room, a very determined Esther got up to receive her.

"Madam Perlman," she said, "to what do we owe the honor of your unexpected visit?" Without waiting for an answer she asked, "Do your children know you are here?"

They certainly had no idea their mother was there. They also didn't know she was terribly interested in meeting the woman who had taken both her sons away from her. Madame Perlman arrived at the house with a preconceived notion. She thought to find a femme fatale, but instead, she found a beautiful, intelligent, and well-mannered young woman. Against her own will, she liked Esther very much.

Prior to the meeting, Esther didn't have a preconceived dislike for Madam Perlman, but the nature of the visit had caused her to have a slight animosity toward the older woman.

CHAPTER XI
FAMILY

Odessa, still winter, 1906

"Did you send Albert an invitation for Sunday?" Rebecca teased. "I'm sure Gustav would drive him, just so he could be close to you."

"I'd love to see Albert," Esther answered. "I haven't heard from him in weeks."

"He is not sick, is he?"

"No, no more than always, but Gustav told me Albert meets with Andrew quite often."

"That explains it."

"Gustav told me his parents don't approve that friendship."

"Do you think the social differences are part of the problem?"

"I don't know. Gustav wasn't clear about it when I asked him. In fact, his answer was quite evasive. I still don't know why they dislike Andrew."

"Dearest Esther, should I remind you that on Monday, you sent an invitation to Andrew?"

"I'd like to see Andrew, too, on Sunday. Nothing wrong about that, is there?"

Rebecca paused, blew the charcoal dust from her drawing, and placed the board with her dreamy landscape against the table. "Are you trying to irritate Madam Perlman, or simply making it possible for our two friends to meet freely?"

Esther did not respond. *Did they like each other too much,* she wondered? She didn't know why Mr. and Mrs. Perlman opposed the relationship, and she didn't understand the ambiguity of Gustav's answer. Was it a matter of religion, social class, or something else? Esther didn't feel guilty.

Andrew and Albert didn't meet only at her house. Albert had repeatedly told her he and his friend, Andrew, went to the theater and concerts together. She wasn't the least bit worried about irritating Madam Perlman; in fact, she perversely enjoyed it.

Madam Perlman with her ill curiosity had changed the happy mood between Esther and Gustav, and their relationship wasn't quite as open as it had been before the surprise appearance. Esther put up a shield of indifference as protection, and distanced herself from the man. She never told him or Albert of their mother's visit and her arrogant behavior.

With stubborn perseverance, Gustav continued to visit Esther. He brought her flowers and chocolates and invited her to the theater, ballet and concerts. Since Esther was in mourning over the death of her parents, she used it as the perfect excuse. She declined each of his invitations. Madam Perlman, with her overbearing and contemptuous conduct, had dried up Esther's illusion of becoming Gustav's bride before it flourished.

Prior to the mother's visit, Esther had seen the romantic and unconventional demonstrations of love in Gustav as extravagant. Since that afternoon and forever after, Esther perceived them as decadent excesses. Madam Perlman would never know how much she had hurt the future and the possibility of happiness for her own son. From that moment on, Esther questioned whether or not Gustav was a good choice for a husband. She kept her mind busy, and refused to ponder a problem for which she had no concrete answer. She placed her energy into studying English and diligently embraced the preparations for the trip to America. The letter Esther anxiously awaited had finally arrived. It was a long letter full of advices and recommendations from both her aunt and uncle.

When her Aunt Sarah received the news from Esther, she was so moved she had to ask her husband, Frank, to read it out loud for her. The tears blocked her vision. She was absolutely delighted with the idea of their visit. So was Frank.

They didn't have children of their own and viewed the arrival of the two girls as a blessing. Her aunt insisted they visit for at least six months. There was so much her aunt wanted to show them and share with them, and, as Sara wrote, "So many wonderful things to see and so much to do in this accelerating country." She had to show them her favorite place in New York. "Central Park is so completely beautiful in the spring. You both must see it in its brilliancy."

Frank, an opera lover, asked them to stay until the end of the fall. He wanted to take them to the opening of the Opera season and the New York Symphony. He suggested they start the trip no later than April 15, so they could be in America by the first part of May. "With these modern ships, it is impossible for something to go wrong. Crossing the Atlantic is a comfortable experience and will only take a short time," he wrote.

The lack of information had paralyzed them. Esther could again write to her aunt, but it would take too long to receive a reply. As they considered alternative routes, they couldn't completely agree on their itinerary, but they did agree on the departure date. Esther and Rebecca jointly marked the tenth of April as the beginning of their journey. The weather in April was sometimes rainy, but it was always good. Usually, there were no high winds or storms at that time of year.

When Esther asked Gustav for his opinion, he said, "It's the perfect time of the year for crossing the Atlantic."

The debate was over, and since they had little preparation time left for the trip, they hurried to get ready.

Odessa was a mercantile emporium. For centuries, the strategic position of the city had made it the beginning and the end of many lines of trade. It was easy to find delicate Chinese silk, linens, and cottons from India, Turkish leather, and the most elegant French and Italian lingerie in the downtown district shops.

Before tragedy struck their home, Esther and Rebecca used to enjoy the downtown shops. Again, they found themselves excited by the frivolous chore of buying new clothes. For once, they ignored danger presented by the political unrest and the chaos on the streets, and they ventured into the center of the city. They needed a new wardrobe for the trip, and they had to buy some fabrics and take them to Madame Petrovky, the seamstress.

Madame Petrovky had a small shop not too far from the law office of Mr. Resnik. For the last thirty years, she had made dresses for the Prusky family, starting with Grandmother Irina. The seamstress still worked, but she was getting old and her eyes and hands tired with little effort. Two of Madame Petrovky's daughters had worked with her for years and knew the business well. They took charge and handled most of the confections.

Esther and Rebecca needed some clothes for the spring and summer, as well as some traveling dresses, blouses and practical skirts. "So many days on the ship requires some planning for the wardrobe," Esther told her cousin.

"I have to be at Madam Petrovky's this afternoon at two o'clock; I have an appointment to try on some of the clothes she is making for me and pick up some blouses that she has finished. Her note said the blue suit is also ready. Would you like to come with me?"

"Only if you promise me we'll be back by four o'clock. Joseph is coming for a cup of tea and a short visit."

"Your doctor is always in a hurry, isn't he?"

"He has to go back to the hospital. Since Moscow, he's behind schedule and has some catching up to do."

Joseph was attentive but evasive when in Rebecca's presence. Since before he left for Moscow, when he kissed her, Rebecca had not seen another sign of his love. Perhaps it was because they did not have an opportunity to be alone. Rebecca had not yet told him of their plans to travel to America. The right moment for discussing the trip had not presented itself, but she expected to have the chance that afternoon. She prayed for Joseph to arrive on time, to have a cup of tea and stay long enough to have that conversation.

The lack of work in Odessa and its surrounding area brought hunger and infirmities. The most vulnerable, children and old people, died. At the hospital, many patients were gravely ill and in much need of help. There were never enough doctors to take care of all of them.

Joseph told Rebecca once, "One day the medicine in this

country will be free. Everyone will have access to the kind of attention that today only a few can afford."

Dear Joseph, Rebecca thought, he was so passionate when the matter was not personal. She had fallen in love with a kind and caring doctor, but she had given her heart to a man who didn't know it. He never talked about himself, his past or his family. He was so private. She wondered about him, but felt she had no right to ask.

Doctor Levin, their family doctor, retired. He passed the practice to the shy, young doctor, and introduced him to his patients. She had met Joseph the day Dr. Levine brought him over to meet Aunt Miriam.

Joseph Feldman was thirty-two years old and single. He had come to the city three years and four months earlier. He bought a big house, too big for him, close to the hospital where he was working. He lived alone.

Rebecca learned through Olga that he had an old maid. She looked after the house and Joseph's clothes. One more person was in the household, a young man, the gardener and handy man. He took care of almost everything else, including the old horse that pulled the carriage.

Until he went to live in Odessa, Joseph never moved from the paternal home. He was born, studied and worked in Moscow, where his father lived. His mother had died when he was too young to remember her. Using his father's memory and a faded sepia photograph, he continued to reinvent his mother features, to keep her image alive in his mind. He had no brothers or sisters. Unbeknownst to Rebecca, Joseph was a widower. Since the two most important women in his life had died, he made a promise to himself: "Never fall in love again, there is too much tearing pain." He felt he was the victim of a wicked destiny. He had made that pledge before he met the irresistible Rebecca Prusky. In the beginning, he easily ignored his feelings for her. They were too insignificant to disrupt his celibate, safe, routine. However, destiny smiled at him again and opened the door to happiness.

The sunny month of July, the countryside and those long afternoon walks on the clinic grounds in the company of Rebecca, played a prank on his unguarded heart. Joseph forgot to shield his emotions. He stopped resisting her charm and surrendered to the new feeling that invaded every cell of his body. His scientist's mind did not investigate. He didn't know how to analyze his inebriating love for her. He accepted that he was completely in love with Rebecca, but he wasn't able to overcome his old fears. He knew his mother's and wife's accidents were just that, accidents. He loved Rebecca and he wanted to keep her alive forever. He didn't want to destroy her with his bad luck. Defeated by his love and need for her, he decided not to anticipate the future. He came to terms with his past and the reality of his present, and with renewed hope, he entrusted fate to work in their favor and weave a path of light for tomorrow.

At four o'clock, Rebecca was in the parlor with a steamy teapot, some small sandwiches and chocolate cookies. It had rained for over an hour, and Joseph had yet to arrive. Rebecca and Esther got wet on their way back home from the seamstress. Esther had gone straight to her bedroom, and hadn't come down since. In the fireplace, the fire danced, wood cracked and hundreds of tiny stars escaped. Rebecca didn't have time to change her wet clothes, but took her shoes off and placed her feet on the stone hearth. The marble was warm and a comforting sensation invaded her. She sat on the floor and rested her back against the side of the sofa. She felt drowsy, closed her eyes and drifted to a place of eternal spring and happiness.

She awoke with a smile on her lips. The daylight had given way to a gray evening. Outside the rain continued to softly fall. The clock's bell marked half past five and Joseph still had not arrived. She knew she would need to become accustomed to his delays if she expected to share her life with a doctor. She would have to make some changes in her own life and learn how to be more patient and understanding.

The tea was cold in the teapot. She relinquished her warm place in front of the fire, stood, and took the tray with the tea service. She should have kept the tea in the samovar, she thought. Barefooted, she started her way to the kitchen when the front door bell rang. Joseph looked fatigued when she opened the door. Rebecca did not need to ask, she knew it had been a trying day for him.

"Oh dear, you look beaten," she said. "Come with me to the kitchen; I'll make you a good cup of cocoa. It'll warm you up. Are you hungry?"

"No, thank you, Rebecca, I'm not. I'm sad and tired." He was silent for minutes before he continued, "I'm so sorry you waited for me all this time. I had no way to let you know I would be late." He walked to one of the chairs that were around the kitchen table and sat.

Rita didn't whistle or flap her wings; she seemed to understand the gravity of the moment. She closed her eyes and went to sleep on her wooden stand.

"She died," he cried. "I tried so hard to save her, and she died."

"Joseph, what you are talking about? Who died?"

"I kept her alive for as long as I could: I expected a miracle. But she had too much poison in her system, and in the end she died."

Rebecca had no idea what Joseph was talking about, but though it made no sense to her, she did not ask. She silently prepared the hot cocoa. She walked back to the table with two cups and placed one in front of Joseph. She sat next to him. She warmed her hand on the hot surface of her cup and waited.

Rebecca had intended to talk to Joseph about the trip to America that evening, but the moment he arrived, the circumstances changed. She anticipated a tale of horrid proportions, and held back her news about the trip. She sipped her cocoa, and in complete silence, placed the cup on the table. It was time to listen, but waiting was not one of Rebecca's virtues. "Please tell me what happened," she urged Joseph.

That morning, just before noon, a man had carried a young woman into the hospital. Joseph thought she was about the same age as Rebecca. The man, a neighbor of the victim, had found the girl lying unconscious close to the front gate of her house. At first glance, the man thought she was dead. The neighbor passed the gate and kneeled beside the inert body. When he looked more closely, he realized she was still breathing. Without delay, he put her in his sulky and rushed her to the hospital.

"I fought for her life until I was exhausted," Joseph said.

"For many anguishing hours, I tried to save her. At moments, I believed I was winning the battle, but she had lost the will to live." The young woman never regained consciousness, and without a sound, she died. "I didn't even know her name."

"Do you know how or why it happened?" Rebecca asked

"Yes, I later found out that she was the only survivor in her family."

When an anarchist's bomb exploded earlier that month in the factory where they all worked, her parents were killed. She escaped unharmed and couldn't understand why destiny spared her. Guilt and loneliness made it terribly painful to go on living without her parents.

"She decided to end her unhappiness by ending her own life."

"Dear God, what a tragedy."

"Today, more than I have at any other time, I want to believe there is an afterlife. I want to believe that somewhere in the celestial universe, that girl is smiling again and has been reunited with her family." Joseph paused. Without enthusiasm he sipped some of the hot cocoa that Rebecca had prepared for him. "Ivana," he said.

"Was that her name?"

"Yes, I finally learned her name, Ivana Ivanovna."

"What a horrendous way to end a life, in a lonely hospital bed. The poor girl." Rebecca mopped tears from her eyes.

"My darling Rebecca, I had other plans for our meeting today." Joseph said. He had gone to the house on Balkovskaya Street to talk to her about his life before Odessa. He was ready to tell her of the traumatic events of his past, and how they continued to affect him. "The circumstances have changed; the death of that girl has affected me deeply."

"Maybe we can pretend today did not happen." Rebecca reached for Joseph's hand.

"Yes, maybe we can meet for tea some other time and make of that tomorrow what we had anticipated for today." After one more sip of the unwanted cocoa, Joseph found the courage to say, "I have a secret I have to share with you."

Joseph rose from his chair, walked the distance that separated them and extended his hand to help Rebecca to her feet.

He intended to kiss her, but Esther burst into the kitchen and stopped the kiss from being more than just a delicious thought.

When she realized her cousin and Joseph were in a romantic prelude, she tried to retreat, but it was too late; they had seen her. She used her talent as an actress to pretend not to notice their closeness, and she acted as if she hadn't intruded on their intimacy. She smiled and came into the kitchen. "Joseph, how nice that you came to visit us." She walked to the samovar. "I'm freezing. I came for a glass of hot tea. Would you care for one?"

"Thank you, Esther, but no. It has been a very long day for me, and I was just leaving," Joseph said with embarrassment.

"I'll see Joseph to the door, dear. I'll have some tea with you when I come back." Rebecca rested her hand on his arm, and together they walked to the door. With the promise to visit her next afternoon, Joseph touched her lips with his and left before she could kiss him back..

CHAPTER XII
FATHERLY LOVE

Odessa, end of winter, 1906

"Oh Esther, I love him so much. He is wonderful," Rebecca said as soon as she returned to the kitchen.

"I didn't mean to interrupt your romantic moment. I didn't know, I'm sorry," Esther said, and smiled apologetically.

"It's all right, dear, don't worry. Joseph was leaving anyway."

Esther, who had finished her cup of tea, got up. On her way to the sink, she asked Rebecca, "Have you seen the letter I left for you on your secretary?"

"No, what letter are you talking about?"

"I took it to your room. You may want to read it soon, it's from Moscow."

She only knew one person who lived in Moscow, two, if she counted Joseph's father, but the old man had no reason to write to her. Rebecca hurried upstairs. The anxiety made breathing difficult, and she had to stop to inhale deeply when she arrived at the second floor. Her hand didn't want to let go of the banister. Petrified, she entered her bedroom, closed the door behind her and rested her back against its wood. It took minutes before she worked up the courage to move over to her desk, push the chair aside to get closer and pick up the letter from the top of the secretary.

The room was dark and she had to bring the envelope closer to her eyes to read it. It was indeed addressed to her. She turned it around and read the return address on top of the reddish, unbroken seal. Her knees shook and weren't able to support her weight. She placed the letter on top of the desk and slowly sat down. Her eyes were fixated on the letters written on the envelope. She didn't respond when Esther called her from the foot of the stairs. She didn't notice when Esther knocked at her door, opened it and entered the room. The large, white envelope hypnotized her.

Esther startled Rebecca when she asked her, "Well, are you going to open it? Aren't you curious to know who sent it, or what it says?"

"I'm terrified. I know who sent it. I read it on the envelope. It is my father. I didn't open it because I don't know if I'm ready to read it yet."

Esther looked at the date on the stamped envelope and said, "For goodness sake, this letter was sent to you in the middle of December, all those news are old."

"Imagine, Esther, it took more than two months for it to get from Moscow to Odessa."

"I think you'd better open it at once." Esther advised. "It may contain something of importance, something you may need to know right now. If not, why would Uncle Ishmael write to you now?" Esther changed her tone of voice and knelt in front of Rebecca with a theatrical attitude that made Rebecca laugh. In a prima donna tone, she added, "Please be brave and open the letter, don't make me spend one more minute in ignorance."

Hidden under her comic melodrama was real concern. Esther couldn't think of one good reason or bad excuse for her Uncle Ishmael's renewed interest in their well being. The letter was puzzling and mysterious and made Esther very nervous. She anticipated bad news. The muscles of her neck tensed, but with effort, she controlled her anxiety and didn't show Rebecca her apprehension. Instead, she walked to the window, moved the curtain aside with a mechanical action, and looked into the darkness of the night. She waited for Rebecca to finish reading the letter before asking, "Well, Becca, are we in the middle of a crisis? What do we do now?"

"Oh, Esther, this is a critical moment for me." She corrected herself. "For us. My father is coming to Odessa for a visit."

"What? Your father here in Odessa? When, Becca?"

"He does not give an exact date, but I believe it will be soon. Probably sooner than I would like. I need time to get used to the idea."

"I wonder what he wants." They couldn't think clearly, it was late, time to go to bed, and they were both emotionally drained. Esther could barely keep her eyes open. "I don't think we can resolve anything right now. This matter can wait until the morning, my dear. It is night all over Russia. Most decent people are asleep at this hour," she added in a comical voice. She hurried to kiss Rebecca on both cheeks and left.

When Ishmael received Mr. Resnik's letter announcing the death of his sister, Miriam, he had only one thing in mind—to contact Rebecca. Free from the promise he made to his sister and aware he owed his daughter an explanation, he planned his trip to Odessa. He must take a place in Rebecca's life and be close to her, as he was long ago. The thought consumed him, and with the passage of the hours, he became obsessed with the idea of seeing Rebecca and his niece, Esther. He was afraid they might reject him. They were ignorant of the truth, but he could tell them now. He was sure they needed his support, and he was ready to give it to them. He was the only family they had in Russia. Ishmael had often talked to his new wife and their two young boys about Rebecca and Esther. Since Resnik's letter, he had secretly hoped to take the girls back to Moscow with him and integrate them into his new family.

The first rays of light of a hazy morning found Rebecca awake. She was afraid to confront her past, she was overwhelmed. After hours of sleeplessness, she got up from her bed, wrapped herself in a wool blanket, and sat in the rocking chair in front of the window. A pale light came through the window, outside, a white fog made the garden phantasmagoric and imprecise. The smell of wet vegetation was deep and almost rancid. When Esther went into her room to get her for breakfast, Rebecca was still in the same position.

"How long have you been up?" she asked, but didn't wait for an answer. "Why didn't you go downstairs for at least a cup of tea if you were not able to sleep? You know Olga has been in the kitchen for more than an hour; she could have made some hot cocoa for you."

"I know, Esther, but I didn't feel like eating."

"I'm sure you can eat now. Why don't you go with me as you are? You can get dressed later." Esther felt sad for her cousin.

"Of course, I will, Esther, I just didn't feel hungry," Rebecca repeated. "I was daydreaming and didn't realize how long I'd been sitting here."

"Becca, cheer up, the news is good. You are not an orphan any longer." Esther was happy for Rebecca. "At least you have your father. It can't be that bad." She waited for a response from her cousin, but Rebecca remained quiet, so she continued, "I'll prepare some tea and toasts while you get ready. Hurry up, I'm hungry."

With the same rapidity in which she had entered, Esther left the room and was on her way downstairs when the front door bell rang. "Who could that be at this time of the morning?" Esther asked herself. Certainly it could not be her uncle, she thought. She rushed to open the door and found a messenger with a brown leather bag strapped to his shoulder and a big envelope in his hand. Madam Perlman's visit crossed her mind and she couldn't repress a very loud, "Oy vey. Not again."

The young man looked at her and smiled with tolerance. His chauvinistic attitude irritated Esther. He gave her a large envelope and a sheet of green paper. The messenger asked her to sign her name in an outlined rectangle. When he retrieved the receipt, he waited for a tip, and placed the coins in his pocket as he walked toward his bicycle, which he had left at the front gate.

The envelope seemed more an invitation card than a letter and was addressed to both of them. What a relief, she thought, just a letter, and with a burst of energy, Esther ran upstairs to her cousin's room. She liked to guess who the letters were from before she read the return address or opened them. She asked her cousin, as she showed her the envelope in her hand, "Who do you think sent us this letter, Becca? Can you guess?"

"My dear, Esther, please don't play games. I'm tired. I did

not sleep well, and I don't need any more excitement," Rebecca said, with a hint of irritation in her voice. "Why don't you open it? That way we'll know immediately." She looked at Esther from the mirror of her vanity. "Let's go for breakfast and then we'll open it."

They sat at the table, and Esther set the envelope aside. Hurriedly, she put a slice of toast on her plate, spread some marmalade on it, and took a big bite. Pensive, she put several lumps of sugar in her cup, stirred it, and with her free hand, reached for the envelope. She used the handle of the teaspoon to open it. She swallowed, read the note, and said, "It is an invitation for dinner and you won't believe who is sending it!"

"Please, no more suspense, my nerves can't take it, dear."

"All right, here it is. Uncle Ishmael is here in Odessa. The invitation is for both of us, for dinner tonight. He will pick us up at seven o'clock."

The news affected Rebecca as if Esther had dropped a kettle full of hot tea on her. She stood so fast her chair toppled to the floor. Her face was tense and her eyes were brilliant with tears.

"With that face, you can participate in a Japanese opera without the aid of face paint. You look terribly pale, darling."

"That is dreadful news. I don't want to hear any more about it. I don't want to go. In fact, I think I won't go."

"Becca, be reasonable. You have to go, my dear."

"How can I look him in the eye without telling him what I think? He abandoned me. I was his child and I needed him."

"My dear Becca, I don't know. I don't have an answer to give you. I understand your feelings, but I believe you have to go." She took a sip of tea and in an almost imperceptible voice, added, "Let's wait. Don't prejudge and don't be a pessimist about it. We'll see what the evening brings us."

For the rest of the day, Esther imagined different strategies and defenses for the evening. One could only stretch a conversation about the weather and other trite subjects for so long. She could, if needed, come up with some other subjects and clever phrases to keep the conversation from dying.

"If worse comes to worse," she said to herself, "I could always faint. As a good artist, I can fake it, but that would be my last recourse." The look on Olga's face made Esther shut up, keeping the rest of her thoughts to herself. She was determined to fight if necessary. She would protect her cousin with her life from that wicked and deceiving father. She was certain her cunning uncle was not motivated by good intentions when he contacted his daughter. "Maybe he is old and dying and now he needs help."

Esther looked for a dark motive below the simple dinner invitation. Why had he waited until now to write, or to even let her know he was alive? She hoped that by the end of the evening, they would get some answers to their long-held questions.

The evening found Esther fully prepared. She had all the tricks she needed to keep not only her uncle, but also a large audience entertained. With Olga's help, she combed her hair up into an elegant chignon. She wore a slick, dark green, long gown, and a shiny silver cape. Her attire was set off by the only piece of jewelry she wore, a diamond broach that had belonged to her mother. It had been passed on to Esther the previous October, just before her eighteenth birthday.

It was early. Rebecca was not yet ready, and Esther hated to wait alone. She walked to the kitchen and expected to find Olga, but she wasn't there. Rita, happy to have a visitor, received her with the usual flap of her wings and a whistle. Intrigued by Olga's absence, Esther hurried to the maid's quarters and was about to knock at her door when it opened. Olga was also dressed in one of her good suits, flat shoes and a flowery hat. She was ready to go out.

"Where are you going, Olga? You are not coming with us for dinner, are you?"

Olga smiled secretively. Since she knew the two girls would not be in the house, she had decided to go out too. George, the carriage driver from the Perlman family, had written to her regularly since the Sunday they went for a ride in the country. He had invited her out many times, but she had never had the opportunity to accept. That morning, she received a letter from him with yet another invitation. He asked her to accompany him on a short walk. She knew Ishmael would arrive at seven and asked George to come to get her not before seven-thirty. George told Olga he had the night free. He was sure Madame Perlman wouldn't need his services that evening.

Esther repressed a smile and an exclamation. She kept it as a tolerant thought, she is too old for this. It would be good if, after all those years, Olga finally found a companion. She would be forty-two that spring, time for her to retire and have her own family and home.

The two women walked together to the kitchen. Olga poured tea from the samovar into two small glasses and gave one to Esther, sighed noisily and sat at the kitchen table. "You look very beautiful tonight, Esther." She was not interested in small talk, so she went directly to the point. "Are you sure you'll be all right without me, little Esther?"

"Olga, you haven't called me that in the longest time."

"Do you want me to go with you? You only have to ask me, I don't mind. I'll defend you both from any harmful plan Mr. Ishmael could have in mind."

"We'll be fine, Olga, believe me."

"Are you sure?" Olga asked again.

"I know that meeting him after fifteen years of thinking him dead creates a difficult situation. Right or wrong, my uncle is our closest living relative. We need to reestablish communication. With time, we'll learn how to love him once more." Esther got up, went to check the time on the big clock, and went back to the kitchen. "It's getting late. Do you think I should go upstairs to see if Rebecca needs my help?" she asked Olga.

After Rebecca placed the last pin in her hair in front of the mirror, she stood and straightened the skirt of her long lilac dress. She didn't turn to take a last look at herself in the oval mirror of the armoire, as she always did before she went out of her bedroom. She put on a long violet cape. From the foot of the bed, she picked up her gloves and a little violet bag and closed the door behind her. She was on the last stair when the clock in the dining room struck the last of the seven bells. The sound of voices directed her to the kitchen, where she found her cousin and Olga in animated conversation. Olga stood at the window in a vigilant position, held the curtain aside and looked out. She saw an enclosed carriage parked in the front of the house. The front door bell rang, seeming louder than ever. The sound froze the three women.

It took a few seconds before Olga hurried to open the door, and she said while she walked, “Stay, don’t move. It is my job, after all, to receive the visitors.”

With her hand gripping the back of a chair so tightly her bones showed through her skin, Rebecca resembled a marble statue. “I don’t want to see him. I’ve nothing to talk to him about.” With repressed tears, she added, “This meeting is a complete mistake, something we’ll regret for the rest of our lives.”

“My dear, I think you are being too melodramatic.” Esther reassured her, “It’ll be all right.”

Momentarily, Olga returned to the kitchen. The interrogative eyes of both girls made her answer their unasked question. “There is a man at the front door. He waits for both of you, and will escort you to meet your father.”

Instantly, the tension in the room decreased, and Rebecca sighed with relief. Olga put her arms on their shoulders and gently pushed them out of the kitchen and toward the front door. She hugged and kissed the two girls. She thought she should go with them and be there to protect them, but knew it was not her place. Instead, she let them go. Olga loved them very much and felt responsible for them. She was the only adult in the household, and in her mind, they were still girls. She couldn’t see them as they were—mature young women, capable of making complex decisions.

The man was dressed in brown clothing and wore black boots and a tall, ridiculous looking black hat. He opened the carriage door and waited for them to enter and sit across from each other. Rapidly, he covered their legs with a wool lap robe. The late winter night was cold and foggy. He jumped on the front seat, and with a click of his tongue and a menacing crack made by the leather whip in the air, the carriage moved away. Olga kept the door ajar and watched them until the carriage, pulled by two black Percherons, disappeared in the distance. Shaking her head in disapproval, she closed the door, going back to her vigil at the kitchen window to wait for George.

The trip was shorter than they expected, and contrary to their prediction, they didn’t end up at a fashionable restaurant or hotel. Instead, they were in a very expensive residential area of

Odessa. The man with the ridiculous hat secured the reins and jumped down onto the wide, oval driveway.

With a long step, he reached the carriage door, opened it and offered his gloved hand first to Esther and then to Rebecca. They were in front of a magnificent neoclassic mansion with white, Italian Travertine marble walls and columns. The front of the house was brightly lit. The two girls waited for him to escort them to the door. The double door opened before they had reached the last of the five marble steps, and a familiar figure came out to meet them.

"Mr. Resnik!" Esther exclaimed. "What are you doing here?"

"My dear lady, for your information I live in this house." He took them by the arm and told them, "Please come in."

Mr. Resnik walked into the entrance hall with them and ushered them to a small parlor in the front part of the house. He invited them to sit, and left the room for a minute.

The parlor had elegant sofas and armchairs and many exquisite French Impressionist paintings on the walls. Esther recognized them and would have loved to point them out to Rebecca, but she did not. She walked around the armchair to look more closely at the art, so she could study the technique.

Rebecca faced Esther and nearly screamed, "I think we should go home right now. I don't wish to see my father."

"Becca, please be reasonable. We cannot go now. They have seen us. It would be too embarrassing, too infantile, and too impossible to explain."

"We never should have accepted his invitation. This is a mistake."

She began to walk back to the door, but it was too late. A tall, thin gentleman walked into the room blocking her escape. Joseph and the tale of the dead girl, Ivana Ivanovna, crossed her mind. Her doubts vanished, and she ran into the opened arms of her father. She smiled with the same delight as she had when she was very young, because she heard his familiar voice saying, "My dearest Rebecca, my zeesa meidel, we are reunited at last."

CHAPTER XIII
THE CONFESSION

Odessa, 1906, days after Ishmael's arrival

"Is Uncle Ishmael coming this morning?" Esther asked.

"He'll come at lunchtime," Rebecca said. "We talked for hours last night; I'm sure he'll sleep late. He looked exhausted when he left; it was past midnight."

Just a few days earlier, Rebecca didn't think it was possible to have a friendly relationship with her father. Then the idea was about as remote as a man walking on the moon. But without effort, Rebecca loved him. She forgot all those painful years she'd cried and wondered where he was. The resentment of growing up without his love faded into her yesterday. Her days were eased by his presence. He was back in her life to stay, but they had a long way to go before they would know each other the way they once did. Rebecca needed to know every detail of what had happened to him before she could leave the past where it belonged. This new man was much older than the one in the photograph inside her locket. He had silver threads in his blond hair, and his moustache became part of his beard. He had lost that arrogant posture. He seemed scarred, but whole, and he smiled more often. They had met every day and talked until dawn. Fatigue did not stop them. Unfortunately, he had to return to Moscow in just one more day. He had to attend to his other life, and the time for saying farewell was near.

That day, Ishmael invited them for lunch, but Esther didn't accept her uncle's invitation. She found a completely credible excuse to decline. "Becca, you go with Uncle Ishmael, I have to study English. As you well know, with so much commotion in our lives in the last few days, I've not opened the book."

Rebecca started to protest, but Esther stopped her. "Gustav is coming this afternoon, remember?"

"No, I didn't; but I'm not sure I'll be back from lunch by then."

"Don't hurry. We can start without you, Becca."

"I won't, Esther, you know that today is our last day together. I won't see Father until November."

"Are you telling me Gustav will have only one student today? He'll pick on me!" Esther exclaimed and laughed.

"Don't be silly. He adores you. He'll be happy to be alone with you."

"That is beside the point," Esther protested. "I have to speak the language before I arrive in America." She wanted to communicate with her Uncle Frank Bernstein in his own language. She was sure her Aunt Sarah would remember Russian and be glad to practice it with both of them.

At ten o'clock, Ishmael came for his daughter. Olga, as she did every time one of the girls left the house, stayed at the door, and watched as Rebecca and her father disappeared.

Father and daughter took a long walk at the edge of the Black Sea. He held her hand, as he had when she was four years old. They had so much to say to one another, they never ceased to talk. When they arrived at the foot of a stone and concrete stairs, they climbed until they found themselves in front of a rotunda. The view was magnificent. From the horizon to the port near by, many ships pierced the waters. On the other side of the concrete circle, opposite the sea, were small shops and restaurants frequented mainly by sailors and prostitutes at night. During the day, the entire area was deserted.

Rebecca and Ishmael continued their walk to a small seafood restaurant near the port. Long ago, he used to eat lunch there with his parents and sister. The place hadn't changed much in over twenty years. They sat in front of a window. The tables had no tablecloths. The bare wood had marks and spots from the wear and tear of years of use. There were even some knife-carved names on them, but the tables were clean.

Their waiter looked like a retired old sailor, one who needed to find a job close to the sea. He took their order, and in less than ten minutes, brought back two steamy cups of fish soup.

Rebecca reached for her father's hand. "I wish you could stay a few more days, Father. I would have liked to get the chance to know you better."

"Oh, Yingele, this is the beginning. I will come back to visit once you have returned from America."

"You'll be teaching then. What will you do with your students?"

"I will make arrangements at the University with another professor. He will substitute for me indefinitely. We will have plenty of time. I'll be able to stay for more than a week then." Ishmael reached into his wallet and pulled out a photograph.

"Are they my brothers?"

"Yes darling, they are."

"They are beautiful!" she shouted. "They look a lot like you, Father. They have your eyes, but my curly hair. How old are they now?"

"This one, Boris, will be seven in May. Alexander will be five in August." He paused a minute to look at the photograph. "I don't think they look like me. Alexander especially, his eyes and hair are the same color as yours, and he talks the way you did when you were his age. He reminds me very much of you."

"You must bring your new wife and my young brothers with you when you come in November. I'd love to meet them. It is not a very long journey, for them, is it?"

"It is true, Rebecca, that traveling these days is easier and so much faster. I remember a time when it was an odyssey to leave town during the winter."

Ishmael looked outside through the restaurant's window, which was whitened with sea salt. His mind revived memory of a summer, when he and his sister Miriam were young. They played on the beach while his parents watched from the terrace's balustrade of that very same restaurant. Ah, the innocent days of careless childhood.

"With the turn of the century," he said, returning to the present of the restaurant with his daughter, "roads have extended to bring cities closer. Tsar Nicholas has kept the progress of the country level with the rest of the European nations. He wants Russia to maintain its status of greatness. Thanks to Nicholas, with the help and ability of Sergey Witte, we now have a very efficient railroad system. Traveling to Odessa or going back to Moscow is no longer as hazardous as it once was, even in the middle of the winter."

The afternoon was dying, and it was dark and rainy when they arrived at the house on Balkovskaya Street. Olga opened the front door for them. Rebecca invited Ishmael in, but he declined and returned to his hotel. Ishmael was physically tired, emotionally exhausted and needed to prepare for the early morning trip back to Moscow.

Olga was glad he was leaving. She didn't like him, and furthermore, didn't trust him. She was still suspicious of his motive for visiting Odessa. She wasn't sure it was inspired by fatherly love. She knew if she was patient, she would discover the real reason that brought him there.

Olga had the crazy idea that Ishmael would abduct his twenty-year-old daughter, but she was sure the girls would laugh if she told them her worries. She resolved to be present to stop any treachery at the time of his departure. Early the next morning before Esther and Rebecca were awake, Olga was ready to go. The three women arrived at the train station and saw the driver from the hotel taking the suitcases to the station platform. Ishmael smiled when he saw the three women and walked over to meet them. The train was not there yet, and they spent a few extra minutes together. Olga was the only one happy to see Ishmael off.

There were just a few days from the first time Rebecca met her father until his departure, but those days dramatically had changed Rebecca's life and her future. Her horizons, once obscured among blinding fogs, had dissipated into clear tomorrows.

Her newfound happiness was dampened by uncertainties. She was no longer sure the trip to America planned for April was a good idea. Leaving Odessa didn't have the same appeal as it once had. When the idea was born, the dear Joseph was only Dr. Feldman, and her father was a phantom. Rebecca was about to cancel the trip, when she realized she had no way to escape the plan. How could she say no to Esther? "I will go to America with Esther," Rebecca decided. "I have so much more than she. I will not deny her that pleasure. I just have to find the moment to tell Joseph about our intentions."

The day was almost over. In the kitchen, Rebecca fed Rita some sunflower seeds. Esther was at the breakfast table with her English book and her homework papers. "I think we are making progress with the language, don't you, Becca?"

"Oh yes indeed, Esther. At this rate, we'll have a huge vocabulary before April."

The classes were a lovely pretext for Gustav to be with Esther. When he left that afternoon, he mentioned his intention to return Sunday with his brother, if he could separate him from Andrew. The relationship that Albert maintained with the young clerk was deeply troublesome for the Perlman family.

"They spend too much time talking to each other, and when they are together the rest of the world vanishes," Gustav mentioned to Esther, afraid to give a name to the relationship between the two men, but close to describing it as somewhat inappropriate.

The truth was that Andrew had made an immense change in the limited life of Gustav's ill brother. Soon after they met, Albert became a bit reconciled with life. Until then, he had been ashamed of the way he looked. He could see pity in his mother's eyes. Her overprotection undercut him psychologically. In front of others, she made him out to be completely crippled. Since the moment he was diagnosed with rheumatism, Madam Perlman had felt more sorry for herself than for her son. She disliked infirmities. She pitied him, and Albert hated her for that. He was always dependent on others to help him, to take him places, to drive him to his medical appointments. His wheelchair was always within arms reach, a symbol of his incapacity. He found refuge and often hid in the large library Mr. Perlman had built for him. Suddenly, life changed for Albert. He felt healthier and happier when at last he found somebody who saw him as just a human being. He was ready to fight against whoever opposed the little independence he had gained. Since Albert had met Andrew, he frequently participated in life outside his books. He was no longer as concerned with his invalid appearance, it didn't much matter in that other outside world.

When Esther finished her English homework, she joined Rebecca and Olga in their animated chat. Although they tried different tactics to make the spinster talk about George, they learned nothing. They were curious and worried for her. She was old, and a man could hurt her and make her suffer. To all the questions the two young women asked, all they got in return were evasive answers from Olga. Defeated, they begged her to at least tell them about her walk with George the night they had gone to dinner.

"Was George on time the other night?" Esther asked.

"Yes, Esther, he was."

"I hope you enjoyed the walk. The night was dreary," Rebecca said.

"It was all right." Olga was about to tell them more when the front door bell rang.

"What time is it? Joseph was coming for a visit after work. I was so tired I completely forgot about it. That must be him at the door," Rebecca said, and looked at the fur clogs on her feet.

"Go to your room, take your time," Esther said. "Change your clothes, wear some shoes instead of those furry stumpers and repair your hair. Your curls are falling, and your bow needs attention. I will entertain him until you come down."

"I'll open the door and ask him if he'd like to drink or eat something," Olga said, grateful the interruption had spared her from telling her story. Many times, when the girls were younger, she had told them love stories that she had invented, but those were not personal affairs. They were tales. What they asked about was another matter. She wasn't ready to tell the girls her most intimate moments with a man. She waited for Rebecca to go upstairs before she opened the door. She let Joseph in, took his hat and overcoat from him and accompanied him to the parlor. She offered him some tea, and asked him to wait while she fetched Rebecca. Esther entered the parlor with her English book and talked about her classes. When she heard her cousin run down the stairs a few minutes later, she disappeared with the excuse she had to study.

Rebecca entered the parlor with her mind firmly set on telling Joseph about the trip to America, but before that, she wanted to tell him about her father. She had to share with him the happiness her father had brought back into her life. But that evening, Rebecca didn't get a chance to talk. That evening, she listened.

Joseph rose from the sofa and walked to meet Rebecca as she entered the room. He kissed her lips without reservation, and holding hands, they sat on the sofa. Olga arrived with the tea service and two delicious pieces of cake. She placed the tray on the coffee table. To minimize her interruption, she was out of the room before they could thank her. Rebecca served the tea and passed a cup to Joseph. She was about to pour her own cup when Joseph, without much preamble, announced, "I've been meaning to talk to you for the longest time, but I did not know how. I could not find the time or the courage."

Rebecca felt alarmed. Her heart began to pound so hard in her chest that it made breathing difficult. She believed she had heard the prelude to an ominous tale. Without her warm smile, her face became darkened by dread. She overcame her fear and asked Joseph, "Are you all right?"

"Yes, darling, completely."

"Are you sure you have to tell me? Should I be worried?"

"No, my dearest, there is no reason to worry," he said. "There is a part of my life you know nothing about, and I need to share it with you. It is from my past life in Moscow, before I came to Odessa. It was long before I met you."

He came from a line of physicians, which began with his great-grandfather. All the males in his family had been or were physicians. His grandfather and father before him studied medicine in Moscow. Joseph finished his studies at the university in 1898. With the help of his father's connections and his own merits, soon after his graduation he began to work in an avant-garde and elegant medical clinic. He had worked for just a month when he met Tatiana Milovich, a nurse that worked with one of his colleagues in the surgical ward at the clinic.

"She was as young as I was," he said. "She was beautiful and extremely intelligent. She was a very efficient nurse. She could have made a good doctor."

"Where is Tatiana now?" Rebecca asked as a burst of jealousy invaded her.

"She died six years ago, in Moscow."

The silence was so absolute that Rebecca thought Joseph could hear her heart beating. She could have killed herself for asking that question. Unconsciously, her hand flew to her chest. Anxiety and jealousy engulfed her, and she wondered if she had a ghost for a rival. "That would be a macabre irony; wouldn't it?" she said to herself, but told him in a whisper, "I'm so very sorry."

Joseph and Tatiana were passionately in love, and before the year ended, they were married. High on their youth, they felt madly happy and believed they were immortal.

"Unlike Odessa, Moscow has a very long winter, there is much snow and it is cold for months. In early spring, when the warmth melts the ice of winter into new life, we run outdoors into the sun." Joseph took Rebecca's hand between his.

Rebecca stopped Joseph from kissing her, but reassured him with a smile. "Please continue. Don't leave me in suspense. You'll kiss me later, I promise."

"Before she accepted my proposal, I had to swear not to ask her to leave her job. She told me that helping the ill was her calling in life. We were married for almost a year and a half when she got irreversibly sick."

In the summertime, and on most weekends, they went to an old country villa that belonged to Tatiana's grandfather. The place was not far from Moscow. One Sunday evening, on the way back home, she became ill. She had contracted typhus. Medications were not enough to save her, and she died consumed by the fever.

The clinic was part of their everyday life. They worked and saw each other many times during those long hours at work. They had lunch together and they rode the same carriage home together every evening. Since her death, the clinic had become a permanent reminder of Tatiana's life. He was haunted by her memory. In the corridors, he thought he saw her turning corners or disappearing behind doors. More than once, he followed the apparition to prove it was just a mirage, a sinister joke of his tormented mind. To keep his sanity, he had to forget the clinic and run away.

"I tried to find another place to work, even though I knew beforehand that Moscow was too small to let me escape from my own pain. I found no place in the region to hide from our history as a couple."

They had grown up in the city and later walked the streets together. He couldn't bear the torment of walking those streets alone. A year had passed when his father's colleague, a friend of Doctor Levin's, informed him about the position that would be open at the hospital upon Dr. Levin's retirement.

"There will be an opening for a general practitioner in a hospital in Odessa," Joseph told his father, and applied for the position. When he got the letter of acceptance, he took only one big suitcase and a small black leather bag with some medical instruments. He asked his father to send the rest of his belongings once he had an address in Odessa, and left Moscow. He hadn't returned home until his father became ill.

The old doctor helped Joseph with his relocation and with his new job at the hospital. Dr. Levin, enchanted by Joseph's personality, intelligence and dedication to his patients, later turned his medical practice over to Joseph.

"When I came to Odessa to work at the hospital, I never imagined that I would also inherit Dr. Levin's office, all the furniture in it, and the files with hundreds of names. I was not here to cure people. I wanted a place to hide from my past," Joseph explained and looked Rebecca in the eyes. He smiled at her, and continued. "I was amazed by the power of working with poor, sick patients. Their own pain healed mine."

Joseph was familiar with tragedies. For as long as he could remember, his life had been marked by the loss of loved ones. He blamed himself for his mother's death. For years he bore the guilt, before he finally understood he was not responsible. He was very young when it happened. He could remember his mother lying at the foot of the stairs. He cried next to her unconscious body, without knowing what to do to help her. He was a doctor when he watched helplessly as Tatiana died. Joseph ignored the fact there was nothing else he could have done.

"At that time, I believed I was guilty for not perishing instead of her. For months, I wondered why I stayed alive to bear so much sorrow."

"It was not your fault, my darling." Rebecca said. "There was no treatment for typhus then; only a miracle could have saved her."

The wise words spoken by Rebecca were filled with love and truth, Joseph thought.

"After Tatiana died, I felt as if I were the victim of an iniquitous destiny. I promised myself to never fall in love again."

"The way you behaved these past months made me think you were not interested in me at all," Rebecca said.

"Do you understand now why I was afraid to be close to you? As ridiculous as it may sound, I did not want any harm to come to you because of me. I love you as I have never loved anyone in my life."

"My silly man, you can love me freely. I will never die. I assure you I'll live forever." She sighed and continued to laugh and talk. "I thought you did not love me. I thought you loved someone else. That was the only way I could explain your distance."

Rebecca was drunk with happiness. Her face was wet with tears when she embraced Joseph and kissed him with unrestricted passion. "Didn't you notice how much I loved you and how miserable I was?" she asked with loving reproach in her voice. "You made me suffer with your indifference."

That night after his confession, they made love on the thick fur carpet of the parlor in front of the fireplace.

Without doubts or reservations and inflamed with all her love, Rebecca gave herself to Joseph. From that moment until Joseph's last breath more than half a century later, no phantoms or memories would ever separate them.

Many pages of history were written as Joseph and Rebecca grew old. The death of the Tsar and the assassination of his family, the triumph of the proletarian October Revolution of 1917, St. Petersburg becoming Leningrad. In their old age, the two of them laughed every time they remembered the first time they made love. That night they drank each other's tears and kept their words to a whisper. That night, they stifled their moans of pleasure for fear that Olga, the guardian, would hear them from the kitchen.

CHAPTER XIV
PREPARATIONS FOR THE TRIP

Odessa, 1906

Esther had not seen her cousin since the night before when she went to bed with a book. The next morning, she knocked lightly on Rebecca's door, but got no answer. She went to the kitchen to find Olga had left for the fish market with Ana. She decided to have breakfast alone. She talked with the only being that was happy to see her, the multicolored, feathered Rita.

It was not until later that morning, when she was absorbed in one of her creations in the studio that Rebecca burst into the room. She raised her head from the canvas to see a radiant Rebecca smiling at her. Her cheeks were aglow, and an indelible smile danced on her lips. She was obviously happy.

"You startled me, Becca." Her concentration lost, Esther rested the palette and the brush on the small table next to her easel, and turned to observe Rebecca thoroughly. "What is it? Tell me, Becca, please." Esther waited for an explanation.

"Last night," Rebecca said, "Joseph asked me to marry him."

"He asked you what?"

"To marry him, and I accepted."

"Dearest, it is marvelous news, but what brought that up so suddenly? Are you engaged? Did he give you a ring? Will you marry him soon?"

Rebecca was so absorbed by her own happiness she neither protested nor answered the questions her cousin asked. At some other time, she may have been irritated by the interrogation, but not that morning, she was too happy. She looked at her finger with the ring on it, and then, without words, she extended her hand to show Esther her diamond.

"Rebecca, that ring is absolutely gorgeous!" Esther overcame her astonishment and hurried to embrace Rebecca, kissing her on both cheeks. But her enthusiasm was forced.

If Rebecca marries Joseph, they will leave forever, she thought.

"This is his mother's ring."

The elder Dr. Feldman was delighted with the news that Joseph, his only son, had walked out of the past and was ready to rebuild his life.

"She must be a wonderful woman," the old man told Joseph and gave him the small velvet case with the priceless jewel inside.

She could not stop looking at the ring on her finger.

"Imagine," she sighed and told Esther, "the old Dr. Feldman had kept the ring for close to thirty years."

"Becca, that's so romantic, and the ring is so beautiful. I'm happy for you." The engagement could change their plans; the trip could even be canceled. She couldn't resist asking her cousin, "You are not suspending the trip to America, are you?"

"Oy vey, no!" Rebecca protested. "Such an idea did not cross my mind."

"Well, things are different now, aren't they?" Esther stated.

"We planned this vacation before we knew Joseph would propose to me. I may consider making a shorter trip, if you're willing to do so, but I won't cancel it." She passed her arm around Esther's shoulders.

Esther agreed with a gesture. She felt a bit betrayed by the unexpected twist in their plan. She had looked forward to the voyage too much to alter her plans, but she knew that within a few days, she would come to accept the change. Soon, she overcame the impact of the unexpected news about the engagement and regained her composure. She should really be happy for Rebecca. She breathed deeply, and after a brief silence, ashamed of her own attitude, asked, "When and where are you getting married? Have you decided on a time? Are you getting married here or in Moscow?"

"You are doing it again, too many questions at once."

"Well, answer me, Becca."

They planned the wedding for the beginning of the winter. They would have a visit with Rabin Zimmerman soon. "Joseph may go to the temple to ask for an appointment this week," Rebecca said. "I prefer to talk to him before we depart for America." Rebecca calmly answered every question. They did not know where. She thought Odessa was the perfect place for the wedding. She planned to buy the fabric for her gown and give it to Madam Petrovky, the seamstress, before starting the trip. She wanted the dress ready by the time she returned to Odessa in October, or September, if she could arrange it. They were not natives to the city, as Esther was, but they loved the town. They hadn't yet had time to discuss the matter, but Rebecca was confident they would stay close to Esther. They would not move away and desert her.

There was no more time to waste on indecisions. It became clear to her from that moment on she had to be in charge of executing the plans. Far away, Rebecca continued to float on a cottony cloud all of her own. Her mind was in a world of white organza and tulle, with wedding blossoms and bows, oblivious of earthly obligations. Esther couldn't trust the decisions her cousin might make. She would go to Mr. Resnik's office and ask him to buy their fares for the trip to America. She knew they needed to depart in mid-April, and to return to Odessa at the end of September. The means of transportation was still a question.

Once again, she daydreamed of traveling across Europe by train, but time was a factor. She couldn't make that decision alone without regretting it later. It would be wise to wait for a few hours to see if Rebecca's euphoria subsided. Convinced that each one of the unresolved matters would have a favorable end, Esther returned to her refuge of canvas and colors. She was still painting when Olga knocked at the door and entered, followed by Gustav.

"Gustav, what are you doing in here?" Esther asked, surprised by his unexpected presence. "I don't receive visitors in my atelier, and you were not supposed to come to the house until it was time for the English lesson this afternoon."

"I do apologize for the intrusion and for the disruption." He smiled with embarrassment. "Believe me, I know, I'm not confused. I'll come back this afternoon for the language class." He stopped and gazed at Olga, who understood. She reluctantly excused herself, but deliberately left the door open. It was not proper for a girl to be alone with a man in a room isolated from the rest of the house, and particularly with a man like Gustav, his fame as a Casanova well known. The cold air from outside crept into the room. Annoyed with so many interruptions, Esther put her painting tools on the table, walked to the door and closed it with a strong push.

"I must control my temper. I'm dangerously close to becoming rude." she said in an imperceptible whisper. Out loud, she asked, "Now what is happening to you? Are you in some kind of trouble?"

"Unfortunately, yes, but it's not I. The problem is with my brother, Albert. He did not come home last night. My mother is devastated."

He told her the problem started the night before, when Albert was on his way out the door with Andrew. They were invited to a poetry reading. A poet friend would read some of his own works in a small gathering. Andrew, who had just arrived to pick up Albert, waited in the entrance hall. Madam Perlman intercepted Albert, who had a ferocious argument with her. Their voices were so loud the servants in the kitchen could hear and clearly understand every single word.

"My mother was ashamed about the scandal. She doesn't approve of Andrew keeping company with my brother. She doesn't understand, nor does she accept their bond. She asked Albert why the two young men spent so many hours by themselves. Andrew could not stand to hear their fight and left the house to wait for Albert outside the door. Deaf to his mother's pleas, Albert left with Andrew. Until late that morning, the Perlman family had not heard from their younger son.

"Have you tried to contact Andrew?" Esther asked. "At this time of the morning he must be working, don't you think?"

She now had a touch of alarm in her voice. “Maybe Albert spent the night at the attic of the bordello where Andrew lives.” After a moment of reflection, she concluded, “I’m sure Andrew is working. He can’t afford to lose his job. If you need to talk to him, you’ll find him there.”

Gustav was of the same opinion. To find Albert, he had to ask Andrew. He used his brother as pretext to go to the house on Balkovskaya Street. What he had in mind was more personal. He went there to implore Esther to accompany him to talk to Andrew. He did not know how to face the clerk alone.

She agreed to accompany him, but there were several things she wanted to do first. Esther asked Gustav to wait. While she cleaned her hands and brushes, she used the time of silence to find an explanation for Albert’s behavior. Albert was old enough to spend a night out if he wanted. At his age, other men had fought in a war and died for their country. He could have had an adult attitude and told his mother not to expect him back until the next day. Obviously the past night’s episode, filled with hostility, made his mother distressed and sick with worry. On the other hand, Madam Perlman also could have used objectivity instead of hysteria. She should be glad that her son, who had suffered a life of illness and pain, had encountered some happiness. A more immediate matter troubled Esther, though. How could they interrogate Andrew without hurting his feelings? How could they ask questions without compromising his integrity or prowling into his personal life?

Once she finished cleaning the last brush, Esther placed them in the holder. As she took off her blouson and apron, hanging them on the wall wooden hanger, she mumbled, “Too many dilemmas, unresolved problems and unanswered questions in one morning for one person to solve.” She turned to Gustav, straightened her clothes, and stuffed loosened strands of hair back into her chignon. In a theatrical voice, she raised an arm, placed the back of her hand over her forehead and informed him, “I’m ready to face the world. Let’s go.”

She sat next to Gustav in his very cold car. The canvas roof was not enough shelter. They had to wait for a four-wheel cart filled with brown sacks pulled by three horses to pass them. Over the noise made by the animals’ hooves and the wheels running over the cobblestone, Esther could hear what the driver shouted loudly to the man seated on top of the cargo. The impatient Gustav, annoyed with the delay, and protesting the inefficiency of the other driver turned the car around. He took a detour and passed close to the old Turkish fort on their way downtown.

"I'm sure Albert is at home," Andrew said when they reached the office. "Before nine o'clock this morning, I accompanied him to the corner of his house before I came to work. I watched him enter the house." He played nervously with some papers and envelopes.

"May I use your telephone to call my mother?" Gustav asked. He needed to find out if Albert was at home, or whether he needed to continue the search. The clerk, with a gesture of his hand, indicated the tall, thin, black telephone on top of his desk.

"One of the commodities that money has bought for Madam Perlman," Esther murmured with a touch of irritation in her voice. Andrew, who heard the remark, smiled with complicity. Her comments were not said loudly enough for Gustav to hear. Esther loved progress. She did not need a telephone, nor did she want one. She couldn't help feeling a bit resentful toward Gustav's mother.

One of the chambermaids answered the phone and informed him Madam Perlman was saddened by her son's display of independence. After she cried for hours in complete loneliness, she'd taken a large dose of laudanum drops and went right to sleep. She had given the order not to be disturbed by anyone, for any reason.

From the moment Esther heard the news about Rebecca's engagement, she thought of visiting Mr. Resnik to see if he could help them purchase the fares for the trip. She saw the opportunity arise that morning. Unfortunately, he was in a very important meeting with a very important client. Esther did not despair; she expected to have the chance to see him later that day. In her purse, she carried a list of questions about the trip, and she would talk to Gustav on the way home. She felt that his many years of travel within Russia and abroad would enable him to give her good advice about her and Rebecca's upcoming trip. She had no other sources of information. He would have to do. Since Rebecca had lost interest in the trip, Esther had taken the initiative in making the decisions. She had to decide on an itinerary map, and for that, she desperately needed Gustav.

On the drive back home, she attempted to bring up the subject of the trip, but Gustav deftly avoided discussing the journey. Instead, he asked to stay for a visit after the English class. Esther told him she had a previous engagement. She couldn't hurt him with a cruel answer, but considering the foul mood she was in, she'd already seen as much of her friend as she could tolerate for one day. They had to leave the visit and the talk about the trip for a less hectic day.

As soon as the car stopped, and before Gustav had the time to run around to open the door for Esther, she opened it, got of the car, and started toward the door. Gustav followed her.

"Good morning, Yuri, it's a beautiful day, isn't it?" Esther shouted to Yuri. He was on a ladder trimming some tree branches damaged by the winter cold. "Yuri is a marvelous gardener," she commented to Gustav. With her hand on the doorknob, she asked him, "Are you coming in?" The straight question took Gustav by surprise. He said good-bye and left.

Esther closed the door and kept her back against it for a few seconds. Suddenly, she felt exhausted. The time spent searching for Albert had taken her away from planning the trip. Her mind worked non-stop. She had to find a safe passage to America. She needed to talk to someone who knew about transatlantic cruises, but she had not yet found the right person.

Olga had lunch ready when Esther went into the kitchen. The conversation at the table turned around Joseph, the wedding and most importantly, the white nuptial gown. The dreamy Rebecca had no space in her brain for anything else. Esther began to realize she wasn't jealous of Rebecca's destiny. Neither was her ugly mood the result of rudeness or sassiness. Since that morning, she had lived with the fear of being left alone.

"Gustav is late," Esther protested. "He should have been here minutes ago; the tea will get cold." She was back in the kitchen, and looked with displeasure at the tray with the tea service and the platter with shortcake and scones she had prepared to take to the parlor.

"It doesn't surprise me," Olga said. "From what you told me, he had a turbulent morning."

Gustav arrived after 3:30 with the English book under his arm. When Esther opened the door, he kissed her on both cheeks with much familiarity. She didn't like it at all. "I'm sorry I'm late." He began to explain, "This morning, you were so insistent on knowing about your trip that I researched several possibilities for you. Once we finish the English lesson, I'll tell you about it."

The caustic mood Esther was in made her impolite. "He found a way to stay after class," she said in a whisper. "I hate his confidence." Her voice was so low not even Rebecca could hear it.

The monotony of the lesson made Esther sleepy. She looked at the wall clock for the fifth time before the English class was over.

"Please, Gustav, tell me how Albert is. Is he well, is he at home?" Esther asked. "Your mother, is she calmer now?"

When Gustav got home, he found his mother lying on her favorite chaise lounge in the privacy of her parlor. She was in a deep sleep, induced by her adored magical laudanum drops. He looked for Albert and found him in the library. He was radiant, and acted calm and secure. He was reading the newspaper, and for the first time, he was smoking a cigar. He had broken the asphyxia of the emotional chains his mother had kept around him and his wheelchair, thus, he looked healthier. Since the moment he accepted his reality, he'd become liberated from the stigma of being a cripple. Enlightened by the previous evening's experience, he became a young man with an egotistic appetite for his independence and his new life.

"I went to Mr. Kopelof's office," Gustav began. "He is the broker who arranges all my travel affairs. I made some inquiries about your voyage."

"Gustav, it was so good of you to take the time," Esther said politely.

"He gave me the information and documents you will need for a trip to America. Do you have a passport?" he asked.

Esther shook her head, and mentally added passport to her long list.

They had to ask Joseph for the small-pox vaccine. When they arrived in America, the authorities required a current certificate, and they did not have one. That evening, Rebecca would talk to Joseph about the vaccine.

Neither Esther nor Rebecca had ever left the country. They did not own a passport. The lawyer could direct their steps on the passports and possible visa matters. Only one piece was missing to complete the puzzle - how to get to America. There were some English and French steamship lines, and they were very safe. However, everyone knew the fastest steamships were German built.

Spending fifteen days on a transatlantic liner did not appeal to Esther. She had never spent even a night on a ship. Being isolated in the middle of the ocean for so many days made her feel a touch insecure. Suddenly, she remembered the many fantastic tales of pirates and sea monsters her father had told her when she was young. She constantly reminded herself that those were just scary stories her father had invented. The information that Gustav brought from Mr. Kopelof, the broker, gave her the choice of two routes. She definitely preferred the short and fast maritime route that started in Germany. The long one was only attractive for its convenience. They could board ship at the port of Odessa and arrive at the port of New York thirty-five days later, after the ship called at Greece and Portugal for a few days. The trip would be perfect if they had extra time to spend sightseeing, but with Rebecca's engagement and imminent marriage, they had to hurry to their final destination.

"They are fashionable transatlantic floating cities," Gustav said. "While aboard, you easily forget you are on a ship,"

"I'll need that. The thought of spending so many days on that ship scares me," Esther said.

"Unfortunately, these two wonders of perfect progress don't include Odessa in their routes. You must go to their point of departure to board them." He suggested going by train to Hamburg, and from there, taking one of the fast German transatlantic steamships, the Kaiser Wilhelm Der Grosse. "She was built in 1897, and holds the record for crossing the Atlantic the quickest."

"Have you crossed the Atlantic in one of them?"

"Yes, I did, Rebecca. In 1903, my family and I visited America on that same steamer." Gustav smiled at both women with reassurance. "For over a week, you'll be pampered in a luxurious floating hotel that has a magnificent architectural design. The menu is worthy of a queen, and you'll love the walking areas on the Promenade Deck."

The ship that eventually took Esther from Germany to America, the Kaiser Wilhelm Der Grosse, was in service across the Atlantic for many years before and after she sailed in it. It was converted into an armed merchant ship when the Great War began. Esther would read in the newspaper and later hear on the radio that the beautiful ship, which she boarded in April of 1906 at the port of Hamburg, was sunk by a British cruiser in a battle off the coast of Africa.

Now she had the information she needed to go to the lawyer's office and ask for his assistance. She could rest, since all uncertainties had disappeared. With Gustav's help, the brilliant future began to unfold before her eyes. The trip to America was a reality and nothing could stop it. One more time, Mr. Pissani and his definitive predictions entered her mind.

"You make your own destiny," she said, and decided to talk to Olga about it. "It cannot happen. I won't let it happen. I'll return to Odessa with Rebecca at the end of September. I'll be with her on her wedding day."

CHAPTER XV
FAREWELL TO ODESSA

Odessa, last week of February, 1906

"Rebecca, come to the beach with me one of these days," Esther implored in an alluring voice. Until then, Esther often had ignored the conventions of her time and walked on the beach alone. It was an intriguing invitation from someone who obviously did not fear for her own safety, or worry about the criticisms of others.

"What brought that urge on at this time of the year? It's still winter, you know."

The weather was far from pleasant. Just a few days earlier, when Rebecca had lunch with her father at the seafood restaurant, the day was cold and gloomy. The sea was enraged, the waves were turbid of sand, and the wind was violent. Rebecca watched as a small sailboat was mercilessly battered against the sandbank. It was not the perfect time to be sightseeing at the seashore. Furthermore, there was still the risk of influenza, but Rebecca assumed that Esther had a very good reason for asking her, and she agreed to accompany her. Some time would pass before Esther could fulfill her desire. In the weeks that followed, their time was completely consumed by making preparations for the trip to America. They had to gather all the documents required for their voyage. It was Esther's stubborn determination that helped them to resolve many unexpected problems. Her strong will made the trip a reality. The fares were bought. They both went to a photographer's studio to have their pictures taken. A clerk placed the photographs in their passports, and soon after, they were completely prepared to set sail. April was less than two months away. Their departure date became imminently closer.

More than ever, the absence of Esther's parents tugged at her heart. She had no one with whom to share her happiness and the excitement about the trip. She had always been close to her mother, and her death had left a painful wound in Esther's soul. The way she felt about her father puzzled her; she didn't feel as if he were dead. He had been such a remote figure in her life, playing the role of an ambiguous father, but often seemed more like a stranger, so dear but forever distant.

Jacob had known he would not be an ideal father before he ever sired Esther. He knew a child would not fit in with his plans or his lifestyle. He dreamed of one day becoming the captain of a naval vessel. For many long years his only desire had been to make it to the top in his career as a naval officer. To become an ensign, he had to conquer many obstacles. When he was twelve, Jacob first had to convince his father of his naval vocation. He spent a full week barricaded inside his bedroom. He didn't even come out for meals, and allowed only the chambermaid to enter his room. He couldn't have succeeded without the help of his sister Sarah, who was two years his junior. Every night, when the household was asleep, Sarah would rush to his bedroom with food she had hidden in her pockets during meals, knock at his door and leave the food on the floor for him to pick up. For fear her father would catch her, Sarah never went into the bedroom with Jacob.

Mr. Vainer, a prominent merchant in St. Petersburg, wanted Jacob to follow in his footsteps and learn the essentials of the trade. At his death, the old man hoped to pass the family business to his son. Mr. Vainer was convinced his two daughters had no head for business. To prove him wrong, after his death, Esther, who never married, took over the family business and made it flourish.

Jacob's second obstacle was almost impossible to overcome. Being accepted at the Tsar's Naval Academy was a much larger hurdle. However, his brilliant mind offset his deficiencies—the lack of nobility in his family tree and the fact that he wasn't a Christian Orthodox Russian.

In June of 1875, in a magnificent ceremony, Jacob joined the ranks of high dignitaries, such as Alexander Alexandrovich Romanov, Tsar Alexander III, when he finished his studies of Naval Sciences and received his commission at the age of eighteen. That same summer, he continued his training as a junior officer aboard a frigate. He left the Port of St. Petersburg to sail the oceans. The ship left en route to Amsterdam, and with that voyage Jacob began his endless passion for the sea that years later, would claim his life.

Given his devotion to the Goddess of the Seas, he was not in search of long lasting romances. A few hours with a woman was the extent of Jacob's relationships. He had no desire to share his life with anyone. Until the moment he met Miriam, he hadn't thought of marriage. For years to come, he would swear that an act of serendipity and the love for the music of Tchaikovsky made it possible for their paths to cross. His ship, anchored in the port of St. Petersburg, was being repaired after a ferocious storm ripped some of her sails apart and cracked one of her three masts. As one of the junior officers, he spent many hours on duty aboard the crippled ship. That weekend, he had liberty to go ashore, an enormous change in his routine after months at sea. Jacob shared the night in the company of land-bound friends. His legs had just become adjusted to walking on firm ground. He missed the eternity of the sky above and the majestic loneliness of the seas. He felt uncomfortable around crowds.

Contrary to those feelings, the magical night he met Miriam, he felt he could spend the rest of his life close to that angelic creature. When they married, Jacob believed he could stay away from his other lover, but his passion for the sea was stronger than his love for his wife, and he didn't have the will to resist it. The baby girl that was born the following October, while he was at sea, came as an unexpected surprise. Esther was not part of her father's plan.

Jacob loved his daughter from the very moment he saw her in Miriam's arms. Mother and child waited for his ship to anchor at the port on that windy day in December of 1888. Esther was already more than two months old then. Before he went back to sea, he took many photographs of his baby daughter with a Leica camera he had bought in Germany during his last trip. He placed each photograph in a large album he kept in his quarters aboard his ship. On each of his visits, Jacob continued to take photographs to mark the milestones along his daughter's way to becoming a young woman. Throughout his long journeys, he would look over and over each one of those photographs. He kept the album a secret until the end. For years to come, Jacob talked of that first time he met Esther at the end of the gangplank. He repeated the same phrases again and again, until young Esther memorized each word. "She was the most beautiful baby I've ever seen in my entire life," he said, and every time he spoke those words, he pulled his daughter toward him, sat her on his lap and kissed her loudly on both cheeks. His short beard scratched her face and made Esther protest. After each one of those effusive raptures, he pulled her away from him and gave her a long gaze filled with fatherly pride.

Jacob had not seen his family for more than six months when his ship was called to join The Great Black Fleet, as it was called in the Navy of the Tsar. In October of 1904, they began their tragic 16,000 mile voyage from the port of Kronshtadt to their annihilation at Tsushima. The entire fleet was ordered to defend Port Arthur in Manchuria, which was besieged by the Japanese. Driven by an ominous foreboding, he wrote unusually long letters to Miriam during every free moment he had.

The naval vessels stopped at Tangier. In that Mediterranean port, the smaller ships transferred their heavy gunnery and ammunition to the larger and heavier ships. From Tangier, the Russian Fleet separated to follow two routes. The lighter vessels, without delays or major difficulties, traversed the Suez Canal to arrive at the Indian Ocean. The heavier ships had to round the continent of Africa to arrive at Capetown in South Africa. To follow, they crossed the treacherous waters where the Atlantic tumultuously mingled with the Indian Ocean, off the Cape of Good Hope. It was a long time before they reached the rest of the fleet, which waited in Madagascar. Destiny was against their success. To ensure they had enough fuel, they had stored coal in every possible place, even in the officers' cabins. Adding to their problems, the trip was slowed to a halt on many occasions by breakdowns of the engines. The confinement, impossibility of privacy and excessive work hours, made the men extremely irritable, and the inevitable began to happen. The entire crew suffered from malnutrition. Diseases began to propagate among the lower ranks, as well as among the officers. Insurrection, mutiny and executions were frequent occurrences. Life became cheap, and death by aggression and suicides darkened the seven-month ordeal with tragedy.

Jacob was discouraged, exhausted by the excess of responsibility and powerless to change the situation. In one of his last letters to Miriam, he told her he intended to resign from the Navy once they arrived in Vladivostok. He confessed that he wished to remain at home for the rest of his life. He was tired of the voyages. The time to settle down was near. Miriam never received that letter; Jacob never mailed it.

News that Port Arthur had fallen to the Japanese reached The Black Fleet. Aware of their disadvantageous position against the superiority of the Japanese Navy, the Tsar's Navy was ordered to wait for reinforcements in Indochina. There were changes of plans and a new route to follow. The flotilla was to continue to the port of Vladivostok in Siberia and force their passage through the Straits of Tsushima on the Yellow Sea. At that crucial moment, the Russian Navy fatally misjudged the strength of the Japanese fleet and its commandant, Admiral Togo's, tenacity. The admiral, Japan's national naval hero, blockaded the Tsushima Straits off Korean waters. On May 27, 1905, the devastation inflicted on the Russian fleet was absolute. Of the thirty-seven initial components of the Tsar's naval group that engaged in battle, only nine were saved. The rest of the vessels were badly crippled or sunk. The loss of human lives was excessive.

Jacob died with the name of his wife and daughter on his lips. His ship, The Borodino, under the command of Commandant Captain Serebriacoff, was one of the twenty-eight ships sunk in the battle. The crew and the modern vessel were engulfed by the heavier firepower of the Japanese twelve-inch guns and swallowed by the turbulent water.

The news of Jacob's death traveled very slowly. It took weeks to reach the house on Balkovskaya Street.

Boris Prusky, Miriam's father, was the perfect grandfather and frequently filled the void left by Jacob's absence. He was already old when Esther came into this world and into his arms. He was weakened by rheumatism and a chronic cough, which his wife said was caused by, "too many years of smoking those smelly cigars." He died of pneumonia at the age of seventy-one. Esther was five years old.

Esther remembered her grandfather very well, but had very vague memories of her own father before the age of six. Often, she felt envious of the seas. She used to long for her father during times of crisis, but she always knew he was on some distant sea of a mysterious country, too far away to help her. Finding solutions for the unexpected problems on her own made her a much stronger and more independent person. Unquestionably, she had always loved her father very much, even though she never really got to know him well. Their time together was too small a bridge to connect the long spaces of absence. When he was at home, Esther protected herself with an ethereal shield of indifference to avoid suffering when he left again to go to sea.

Esther's mother lived for the moments when Jacob was home. Her entire existence was shaken by violent emotions that spun around her husband's visits. She felt anxiety mixed with joy when he arrived, and she welcomed him back into the warmth of her heart. She fell into an abyss of solitude and sorrow with each of his departures. In the course of those long years of political instability, wars and violent changes, her mother was in constant agony, afraid for the life of her husband during his absences at sea.

All Esther knew of her father was what her mother told her and what she could learn while he was at home between farewells. She remembered him as a tall man who was too thin, or at least, that was the way he appeared to her then. He had the kindest smile, and beautiful blue eyes. Everyone said her eyes were just like his.

When she was very young, Esther disliked the announcement of his imminent arrivals. The attention was shifted, the house was shaken, and her mother had no time for motherly games. Miriam had to become the woman she'd once been, and had fewer hours to spare. Esther saw her father as a rival and detested having to share her mother with him. She slowly understood his role as a father, husband and provider, but it wasn't until she was older that she allowed him in her heart. She loved him, and eventually accepted his phantom figure as part of her reality.

His death was as mysterious and abstract for her as his life had been. "I never saw him dead," she frequently said to herself. "I was there when my mother took her last deep breath. Perhaps if I'd buried my father's body, I'd not feel this way about him."

She kept a box full of mementos and presents her father brought her from his voyages. She had many albums filled with photographs they'd taken together during his visits. Those were the few brief moments of complete happiness she'd shared with her parents.

With nostalgia, Esther looked at some of the photographs she had helped to place in the album when she was younger. She adored one group of pictures in particular, from when she was six and the whole family had visited a carnival that came to Odessa. Her father spent almost that entire fall at home. Her favorite was a picture with her father on the merry-go-round. In many of the photographs she had of him, he wore the impeccable uniform that gave him a distant air of severity, but not in that picture. Her father, in civilian clothes, stood next to her on the carousel horse, smiling at the camera with his arm around her shoulders. Unlike other times, when both girls sat side by side on the carrousel, Rebecca wanted to be on the silver horse on the opposite side from the white horse Esther had chosen.

"This white horse is for my beautiful princess," her father said. He kissed her on both cheeks and helped her to mount the horse. Esther was so happy and thankful for that magical moment. She would remember that day forever; the music playing on the merry-go-round and the words her father told her.

Days had passed since Esther mentioned the walk on the beach. The rainy weather kept her from walking on the white dunes close to the water. It was Friday morning and they were still at breakfast, when abruptly Esther said, "I've been having dreams of Father, and he was the center figure of very intricate tales."

"Do you remember what they were about?" Rebecca asked.

"No, I don't completely remember them or understand their meaning."

"Is Uncle Jacob talking to you? Are they bad dreams, Esther?" Rebecca wanted to know.

"I know they are not nightmares. Sometimes these dreams happen in the middle of the night when I'm deeply asleep. To further confuse me, parts of them later become woven into other dreams. They transform into shreds of vanishing pink gauze that burns with the first light of the morning sun, and I don't quite remember them when I awaken," she sighed, drank some tea and continued, "Do you think there is a message in these dreams?"

"You haven't mentioned those dreams to me before. Why?" It took seconds before Rebecca reacted to the startling revelation and words came to her mouth, "When did these dreams start?"

"There was nothing to mention, I just know that it is Father who talks to me. I wish I'd remember enough of it to tell."

Esther never had talked of her apparitions to anybody. Until then, she kept her dreams of ghostly figures secret even from Rebecca. What could she have said? That maybe those fragments of her imagination had frightened her. Besides, she was not sure her apparitions would make sense to anyone else. At first, she interpreted the dreams as hallucinations or fabrications of her own stressed mind. She doubted she was completely asleep when they appeared. She considered going to one of the much in fashion psychiatrists. The new science had revolutionized the medical field and made headlines in the newspapers almost daily. She read that the very famous composer, Rachkmaninoff, after he finished his second symphony, was depressed. Doctor Dahl, a psychiatrist, treated the composer and kept him in a psychiatric clinic for six months. She read in another article that those specialists could study and break into pieces any enigma of the mind, and arrive at the core of the problem. In the same article, one of the psychiatrists stated that the root of a disturbance factor is frequently found in the adult individual, but was clawed into the patient's mind during infancy. The idea tempted her, but what could she tell them, that she was seeing ghosts? She did not need a psychiatrist to decide she was not insane. She knew she was not. Dreaming of her dead father was not that unusual.

"You were not prepared for his unexpected death. The way your father perished would bring nightmares to a bearded man," Olga told her once. "You are strong, my dear, but you are no more than a little girl."

He had been at sea for over a year when the Japanese Navy sank his ship.

Esther never received the little treasures her father, with his refined taste, had bought for them on that trip to Indochina. For his dearest Miriam, he bought a black lacquer chest with red engraved landscape. She loved oriental furniture. Also, for Miriam, Rebecca and Esther, he bought the most exquisite silks, exotic perfumes and pearls that came from China. Esther would never know that she was in her father's thoughts until his last breath when his ship was devoured by flames and disappeared in the waters that swallowed his life and his presents.

Esther needed to say her farewell to her father. To talk to his spirit, she had to go where his body was buried. One early morning, a few days after she confessed her recurring dreams to Rebecca, they walked together on the beach. The salty sea wetted their feet while drunk by the thirsty sand. The wind that blew from the east dried her tears. The same east wind took the prayer from her lips to her Father. On that wintry morning, Esther left a white flower on a wave knowing that the Black Sea would take it back to her father's eternal rest.

In a murmur, she said her farewell to him, until the time they would meet again. She could swear it was not the east wind that played with her hair and whistled in her ears, because in that east wind that came from the Yellow Sea, she felt the lips of her father kissing her on the forehead, and she clearly heard his voice when he whispered her name.

CHAPTER XVI
A PROMISE

Odessa, 1906

Yuri saw them from afar and abandoned his warm place inside the carriage. Since he believed they would come in to find shelter from the inclement weather, he jumped down and waited with the door open. The young women walked together with their heads down and their shoes in their hands. They had to push against the wind that wanted to take them back to the edge of the sea. They reached the end of the dunes, and sat on one of the long benches along the sidewalk to clean their feet. In happier times, in the late spring, they used to go to the beach and sit on those same benches. In the company of Miriam, they watched the seagulls play on the golden sand and dive into the sea to catch fish.

Yuri reached into the trunk in the back of the carriage, and took out a towel and a small basket with some porcelain cups and a thermos. He hurried to the bench, and, as if they were still children, he kneeled and attempted to help them to clean their feet.

"Thank you, Yuri, but we can do it." Rebecca said, and instinctively hid her feet under the bench. "Maybe you can give me a cup of that hot chocolate and offer one to Esther. We're freezing."

They both got inside the carriage and covered their legs. "It is very cold, isn't it?" Esther observed. "Before I leave Odessa I must go visit the place where my mother is buried."

She asked even when she knew the answer, “Would it be too much to ask you to accompany me to the cemetery, Becca?”

“I would go with you even if you didn’t ask me.”

“Thank you. I never liked the place, and I don’t want to go alone.”

“I know, I know, dear.” Rebecca smiled, and reached for Esther’s hand. “Oy vey, your hand is so cold.”

They spent the rest of the short way home in silence. Yuri understood their grief and demanded a fast gallop from the old horse. With a “whoa” and a click of his tongue, he made the horse stop in front of the house. In rapid succession, he secured the reins, jumped down and opened the small door for the girls to come down. Then he asked, “Will you need the carriage this afternoon, Miss Esther?”

“Oh no, Yuri, thank you for asking, but Esther and I are too cold to go back out today,” Rebecca hurried to answer.

For a change, the eternal door greeter was not there to receive them. On that late morning, Olga was just outside the back door of the kitchen. From the entrance hall, they could hear her laughing and chatting with Mr. Kurt, the knife sharpener. The dark, bearded man used his left foot to push the side pedal on the cart in a rhythmic and steady motion. On top of the table and attached to the pedal by a belt, a large sharpening wheel spun on its axle. Olga had to shout over the noise it made. A river of stars flowed freely from the blade. The tiny universe was stopped only when Mr. Kurt, with his foot still on the pedal, removed the blade from the stone and submerged it in a bucket filled with cold water. The bucket hung from the other side of the cart, and swung to the same rhythm with which the wheel moved. The man allowed the stone to rest only when he took his foot away from the pedal to stand up. With his eyes closed, he held the blade in one hand and passed a finger from the other hand over the sharp edge to check the effectiveness of his job. Olga was one of his devoted clients and assured whoever wanted to hear that he was the best knife sharpener in Odessa.

Mr. Kurt, with his wheeled cart full of tools and sharpening stones, came through the neighborhood once every three months to take care of scissors and kitchen knives. He was also very good with a hammer and rivets. He could patch tiny holes or replace handles in some of the too-used copper, iron and aluminum pots. As usual, his dogs accompanied him. Two of his dogs were given to him by a client when her husband passed away. The others were strays who had picked him as their master.

While the knife sharpener worked under the vigilant eye of Olga, Katiuska, a beautiful young female dog, oblivious of the world around her, went into labor. Mr. Kurt didn't know she was pregnant. He had found her close to the train station a month earlier, abandoned and very hungry. "Even if I had known, it would have made no difference to me. She is beautiful and needed a home," he explained to Olga. Katiuska was obviously young and scared. She acted as if she was new to having puppies. She was a small dog with wavy, honey-colored hair, a long tail and very large ears. Not completely sure of what was about to happen, the poor female found refuge under the sink Ana used to do the laundry. Olga, who anticipated the situation, ran to help the unprotected mother. She went to the carriage house and looked for one of the cardboard boxes she had seen Yuri put away in the basement. From one of the shelves, she took an old blanket and arranged it inside the box. In violation of her own principle to 'Never become involved with animals,' she returned to the kitchen with the box. Olga placed the improvised maternity bed beside the fireplace.

"Katiuska and the puppies will be warm and protected in that corner," she told the knife sharpener. Then the strong Olga, with infinite care, picked up the panting Katiuska in her arms, brought her in the house and placed the honey-colored animal in the box. Rita joined the excitement by whistling, flapping her wings and chanting "good dog, good dog."

The first puppy was born just as Esther and Rebecca entered the kitchen. The two girls spent over an hour kneeling next to the box, mesmerized by the violent yet sublime act of one being giving life to another. By early afternoon, Katiuska, tired by the effort of giving birth, was the proud mother of five puppies. Only one of the tiny animals, another female, resembled her mother. She was pretty and had the same golden color and long ears.

"If the babies look like the father, I would say Katiuska doesn't have good taste in selecting her mates. The puppies are very ugly," Rebecca said with a laugh.

"Olga, do you know what will happen to them? Can you ask Mr. Kurt if he has a place to leave them, or someone to look after them while he is sharpening knives at his clients' houses? They'll die outdoors, and Katiuska is still weak. Besides, it's winter cold," Esther worried.

"I don't know, Esther. It is hard to imagine the man would have a warm place for the new family, but I'll ask him." Olga left the kitchen and went to investigate the plans Mr. Kurt had for Katiuska.

"This has been an experience. Before today I never saw the birth of a being. It's fascinating, isn't it? We must take care of them," Esther decided.

When Olga was about to enter the kitchen with both hands full of very sharp blades and repaired pots, the two girls stopped her at the door. After they kissed and embraced her, as they always did when they wanted something from her, Esther pleaded on behalf of the babies and mother. Without any resistance, Olga agreed, and Mr. Kurt was delighted to let Katiuska recuperate in such a loving home.

"You may leave them here a month or two," Esther told Mr. Kurt. "That will give the puppies the time they need to grow up. Their legs will be strong enough to follow you and the rest of the dogs on your daily rounds."

Olga would never confess that she was afraid of solitude, and expected to feel lonely as soon the girls left for America. She had come to work for the family before Esther was born. George was there for her, but not as often as she needed him to be. She wanted to have someone with whom to share her love and attention more frequently than one or two evenings a week. A guardian angel had placed those puppies in her kitchen. That day, before she served a late lunch for Esther and Rebecca, Olga prepared a succulent meal for Katiuska. Olga had no idea when she allowed the animals to enter the kitchen that Katiuska and her puppies would become part of the family and would stay with her for the rest of their lives.

The commotion produced by the birth of the puppies made

Esther forget her sorrow. They were still in search of names for the five furry youngsters when Olga entered the kitchen. "Esther, you have a visitor waiting for you in the parlor." The old maid stopped to talk to the puppies, making little noises with her mouth and kissing the air to get their attention.

"Who is in there? I'm not expecting visitors," Esther remarked with hint of irritation.

"I'm sorry, but the person made me swear not to say his name," Olga said.

"Why would anyone who is inconsiderate enough to arrive unannounced expect to be seen?" She mimicked a protagonist in a dramatic play. She rose from the floor near the puppies' cardboard box and almost shouted, "Look at me. Look at my hair, I've sand and salt on my clothes, I need a bath, not a visitor."

"Who is it? Tell us, Olga," urged Rebecca, amused by her cousin's tantrum.

"It's Mr. Gustav."

"What is he doing here?" Esther asked.

"He is bringing you flowers, a very big bouquet. I have never seen so many beautiful flowers." Olga thought for a moment and added, "Well, except for funeral wreaths."

"Maybe what he has to tell me can wait until four o'clock. I hate ask you to do this, Olga, but would you please ask Gustav to come back this afternoon?" Esther implored. "We'll be back from the temple by then." She was not eager to see Gustav, but curiosity led her to invite him for tea. "Tell him that if he would like to leave the flowers, you'll see that I receive them," she said with a touch of humor and a big smile.

At two, she went to the synagogue for an appointment with Rabbi Zimmerman to discuss the fact there was no synagogue aboard the transatlantic ship. The wise man always had an answer ready for each question his parishioners asked him. She was sure he would have a solution to this small problem.

"Rebecca, if our talk with Rabbi Zimmerman doesn't take too long, I would like to stop at the bookstore," Esther said, before she opened the side door of the synagogue. The temple was empty and looked larger. The smell that emanated from the waxed wood floor and benches was familiar and evocative. The history of the temple was entwined with their own history. They had come to that synagogue for almost every Shabbat service through the course of their lives. There, they had celebrated every religious holiday and festival. Just before the death of her father last May, they went to the synagogue to celebrate the bar mitzvahs of the younger son of their neighbor.

Their strong ties with the temple would continue. Once they returned from America, Rebecca and Joseph had planned to be married in that same synagogue.

The complete silence revealed their respiration. The light filtering through the high, stained-glass windows above the women's section was gold and warm. It was enough to keep the vast room illuminated. The solemnity of the building made them walk on tiptoe. It was the only way they could keep their high-heeled shoes from tapping on the floor. The side corridor led them to the office where Rabbi Zimmerman studied the Torah, read books, newspapers, and received people. Esther knocked at the slightly open door. It took some effort for the rabbi to break away from his book to greet the visitors.

Rabbi Zimmerman was not an old man, but his hair and beard were gray. For as long as they could remember, Esther and Rebecca had seen him wear a black yarmulke on his head. He wore a black suit and a white shirt with too-long sleeves. The white cuffs sticking out of the sleeves of his jacket. His shoes were made of soft, black leather, and his wife kept them shiny. The two girls were convinced the rabbi had chosen shoes with thick rubber soles to keep the temple silent when he walked. His gold-rimmed glasses still sat half way down his aquiline nose. When he talked to people, he rested his chin on his chest to lower his head and look over his glasses. He smiled with ease, always listening attentively and gave the right advice. However, his most remarkable feature was his voice; it was like a magnet to his congregation. When he sang or spoke, everyone fell silent and listened to what he had to say

Rabbi Zimmerman, who was expecting Esther and Rebecca, was happy to see them. As they sat around the fireplace, one of his daughters brought a tray covered with a white napkin. The young girl smiled, said hello and quickly exited the room. The rabbi ceremoniously folded the large napkin and offered them a very sweet glass of tea, and almond cookies his wife had just made that afternoon.

"Please have some. They are still warm." He passed a plate filled with the golden medallions under Rebecca's nose so she could inhale their delicious aroma. "Have some, Esther. I know you like them." Then, he left the plate with the cookies on the edge of the table, pushed up his glasses, and continued, "I understand your concern, but it is nothing to worry about. During the crossing of the Atlantic, continue to pray in your quarters twice a day, just as you are doing now in the temple. Once you arrive in New York, go back to praying in the synagogue. Ask your aunt. She will know of one." They continued the chat a bit longer. He was told about Katiuska and her puppies and they learned Madam Zimmerman was pregnant with her fifth child. They congratulated the rabbi and kissed him. They both left the synagogue feeling relieved.

"Do I have to remind you that Gustav is coming to the house for tea?" Rebecca told Esther.

"You know I can't go to sleep if I don't read at bedtime," Esther argued. She insisted and they went by the bookstore, even thought she knew they would arrive home after four. "I was thinking we should stock up on books. I wonder if there will be any books in our language in the ship's library."

They returned home at half past four with two big packets of books, which were all printed in Russian. Gustav, who had arrived at four o'clock, was undeterred by their delay, waiting in the kitchen with Olga, sipping a cup of Turkish coffee she had made for him.

"I'm very sorry we are late," Esther apologized, placing the package with the books on the kitchen table, and walked toward the cardboard box where the puppies were. "We tried to hurry, but our appointment with Rabbi Zimmerman took much longer than expected."

Rebecca, who had entered the kitchen at the same time, couldn't believe what she just heard. Her cousin didn't quite lie, but she had certainly exaggerated the truth. Never before had she heard Esther lie. It took a few minutes for her to get over the shock and speak. "Is there still tea in the samovar?" she asked Olga.

"I'd love to have some tea, Becca. Please serve some for me," Esther said.

"Would you like a cup of tea or would you prefer some more coffee?" Rebecca asked Gustav. She saw the cake that Olga had made for tea time, and offered, "Perhaps a piece of cake?" She attempted to make small talk to compensate for the annoying lack of interest being shown by Esther. Then she had one more suggestion, "Why don't we move to the parlor, and Olga will bring us the tea and cake as soon as she prepares it?"

With the last word, without waiting for an answer, she began to walk toward the door. Gustav rose from his chair and followed. Olga stayed in the kitchen to prepare the tea and had the most enigmatic smile on her lips.

"I'll be there with both of you in just a minute," Esther said. She, who had remained silent until then, picked up the package from the table and used it as an excuse. "I have to take this upstairs."

"I'll take it after I prepare the tea," offered Olga

"Oh no, Olga, thanks, I'll do it now." She had a strange foreboding she wasn't sure she wanted to hear why Gustav had come to the house for a second time that day. Once she deposited the package with the books on her secretary, she looked at her image in the armoire mirror. She wondered why Gustav brought out such ugly conduct in her. She felt perversely compelled to hurt him and to be rude to him. Without finding an answer, she went to the window and watched the progress of a blue bird building a nest. Then, Esther slowly walked downstairs and into the parlor.

Rebecca saw her and an involuntary breath of relief escaped before she could stop it. "Good, now you are here, I'll leave you."

"Sorry it took me so long," Esther apologized.

"I need to write a note to Joseph, and make sure he receives it before he leaves the hospital."

"Would you come back for another cup of tea?" Esther asked.

"Oh no, sweetheart, thank you, but, afterwards I'll go ask Mikhail to take the note to the hospital." She stopped at the door and turned to face them. "Gustav, dear, it is awfully nice that you came to visit. I hope to see you before you go." Rebecca left the room convinced Esther wasn't in love with Gustav. Her Aunt Miriam's affirmation: "marry first, love will come later," was wrong. She knew Esther would never love him.

"Tell me, how is Albert? I haven't seen him in ages. Is he all right?" Esther asked.

"He is much better, thank you for asking," Gustav replied.

"Is he still having problems at home?" Esther did not like to pry into her friend's life. She was truly interested in his welfare. She really missed Albert and wanted to hear that he was happy. Since she had introduced him to Andrew, his visits to the house were more sporadic.

"He is much happier, I would say," Gustav admitted.

"Is your mother better?"

Madam Perlman's health didn't really concern her. Esther hoped that superfluous conversation would make Gustav forget the reason for his visit.

He mentioned that in the few days following the first argument, Madam Perlman used all her motherly tricks. She wept loudly enough to be heard, had headaches and fainting spells. She used prolonged silences and the aid of several small bottles of laudanum, but didn't get the results she expected. She finally realized that all her tricks were a waste of time. They had gotten her nowhere.

Madam Perlman changed her tactics. In a renewed effort to tempt Albert, she had soirées at home, inviting many of the young beauties from their group of friends, hoping her son would become interested in one of the young ladies. Albert detested those parties. He embarrassed his mother by refusing to attend the gatherings, even though they were in his honor and in his own home. He would use a previous engagement or a sudden painful burst of his rheumatoid arthritis to excuse himself from the parties. He fled the house through a back door, or went to bed without telling anyone. Then, the resourceful Madam Perlman, aware of her son's eternal adoration with the theater and the plays of Anton Chekhov, invited Albert to the theater. Every new evasion she plotted to distract Albert failed, and slowly she accepted the inevitable. Andrew the goy, with his dark, curly hair and second hand clothes, was there to stay. He became a frequent visitor in the rich mansion and Albert became almost healthy for the first time in his life.

"He is very much alive," Gustav said. Then he made an attempt to talk with Esther about politics. "What do you think of the replacement of the Prime Minister Witte? Tsar Nicholas himself has chosen Peter Stolypin to replace him. I wonder if Stolypin will bring the much needed changes."

"In my opinion," Esther said, "Witte lost the favor of the Tsar when he forced him into signing the 1905 October Manifest. I also think that Stolypin is not as strong minded as Witte was."

"You're right, Esther. I think the Tsar can easily manipulate him. He lacks kishkes."

"We'll see what the new Duma can do." After a moment of reflection Esther added, "So much propaganda for the election of the new Duma. So much violence, we are certainly ready for a change."

The first Duma, which was elected in March of 1906, didn't meet the expectations of the people. Even when it was integrated by many of the different political factions and parties, it was not able to accomplish positive changes. Unfortunately, it did not succeed in pacifying the unrest. As Gustav mentioned, Peter Stolypin was elected Prime Minister.

Convinced that Gustav would not leave until he said what was on his mind, Esther brought up the subject, and asked, "My dear Gustav, I know you like politics very much. I also know you don't like to talk politics with women. Am I right?" Gustav was about to protest when Esther pressed on, "Furthermore, I don't think you came just to discuss politics with me today. So you must tell me what it is that you have come to tell me."

"Esther, you're right. But I wish I could have talked to one of your elders before telling you what I am about to tell you." He stopped and tried to put his thoughts in order before he could continue.

"Go on. Don't stop now," Esther insisted, showing interest in the hesitant Gustav.

"I thought to write to your Uncle Ishmael and explain the situation, but the truth is, I did not know if you would have approved of such an act." Gustav no longer had his characteristic superior tone of voice when he spoke. He appeared to be very agitated, almost confused.

"Are you nervous, Gustav?" Esther seemed amused by his display of weakness.

"Well, no. Not really," he said with a touch of embarrassment.

"Can I help you, Gustav?"

She followed each one of his movements, watching as he got up from the armchair and went to the window. He combed his hair with both hands, and kept them for an instant on the back of his head. The open curtains let him see the last reds and purples painted in the clouds and the golden light of the dying day.

"What I have to tell you, I have never before said to anyone."

You may need to hurry. Olga serves dinner in an hour, she thought and the comical sarcasm made her smile. The Gustav she knew had vanished. This unknown man completely confused her, and she had no idea what to tell him.

To help him and give him some encouragement, she said, "Don't be afraid of words. Just tell me what is on your mind. You are making me nervous."

He again sat next to Esther and faced her. He picked up the cup from the table, took a sip, then pushed to his feet and walked back to the window. He breathed deeply, filled his lungs with air and began to talk. "As you know I have been a bachelor for a long time now. I never found a woman with whom I wanted to share my life or begin a family."

The smile was erased and the amusement Esther felt quickly subsided. Her back tensed, she clasped her hands together, becoming seriously concerned with the direction the conversation was taking.

He took a sip of cold tea from the cup he held and continued, "I know I have been known by many as a womanizer, and maybe I was one. I know some mothers keep their daughters from me, talking about me behind my back and categorizing me as a libertine."

Why is he telling me this? Is he having an act of contri-

tion? she quietly asked herself. *If he was Catholic, I would believe he was confusing me with a priest.* She coughed and said in a louder voice, "Gustav, I understand, but I don't want to know any more of that. Tell me what you came to tell me, please."

With hurried steps Gustav was next to her. He moved in such a brusque way he astonished Esther. She was witnessing an unknown facet of her friend. He was being completely emotional, and she liked that. He knelt at her feet. Before Esther could react, he placed his hand over hers. "My beloved Esther, it may not come as a surprise to you that I love you with all my heart." He stopped, reached into the inside pocket of his jacket and took out a small, black velvet case. He opened it, and inside was the largest diamond ring Esther had ever seen. The sight of it took her breath away.

"Oh my God, that ring is dazzling!"

Gustav smiled at her. With the ring in his hand, he continued, "I would like to ask you to marry me, Esther. If you accept, you will make me immensely happy." He reached for her other hand, which was now unguarded, and began to place the ring on it.

Esther, moved by his words and staggered by his unexpected declaration of love, lost her composure. Never before had a man proposed to her. Maybe Gustav used that moment of vacillation in his favor, but Esther did not offer resistance. The ring was on her finger before she could retrieve her hand.

"My dear Gustav, it is so sweet of you to ask me to marry you, but I'm not ready to give you an answer at this moment."

"My beloved Esther, I'm willing to wait for your answer as long as it takes you to decide. I do love you."

"I'm afraid I don't love you as much as you love me." She began to take the ring off her finger, but was stopped by Gustav.

"Please keep the ring until you give me an answer."

"It may take some time." Esther grew quiet. When she spoke all the amusement had disappeared from her now almost-sad face. She was certain she didn't love him, but was moved by his sincerity and love. Esther was close to tears when she said with a truly emotional voice, "Gustav, I can promise you this much, my dear, you'll have my answer when I come back from America." She sighed and repeated, "I promise."

CHAPTER XVII
THE VOYAGE

Odessa, April, 1906

"I think this is it. I'm finished!" Esther exclaimed. She danced in front of her bed where a suitcase lay open, too full with clothes. "This is the last piece of luggage to be sent to the station. Please, Olga, help me close it. Rebecca is not strong enough," shouted Esther from the second floor, trying to get the maid's attention.

"I can sit on it if you want me to, but I can't pull. It is so full I can't do it even if I try, my hands are tired," Rebecca protested.

An effervescent excitement ran through the household. In three days, they would be finished with the preparations. They would begin the anticipated trip to America. No doubt, Rebecca was sorry to have to part with Joseph; she would have preferred for him to accompany them, but that was impossible. She became enthusiastic and was ready to go in the last few weeks, when all the procedures and decisions were completed.

"I consider the train trip to Hamburg nothing more than an inconvenience," Esther said, irritated with the idea. They had to begin the transatlantic journey in the train station rather than the port.

"You're right. The trip won't truly begin until we pass the gangway and step on the deck aboard the Kaiser Wilhelm Der Grosse," Rebecca agreed and left the room with a small bag in her hand.

The two girls were tired, but the trip was a reality. There were no more preambles. They had passports, visas and vaccinations. Esther, more practical, would be the one in charge and would keep and carry all documents and fares in her handbag. Most of the clothes were in two big, green wardrobe trunks with brass hinges. They had labeled every piece of luggage with their names, as well as the addresses in America and Russia. "Just in case one gets lost," Esther said.

Yuri, strong as a bear, picked up four bags at a time, and had them downstairs in minutes. He placed them in the big, flat cart, the one he used to fetch firewood, and drove them to the train station that afternoon. The luggage had to be dispatched as cargo in a freight train. All their baggage would arrive a day or two before them and would be taken to their cabin aboard the ship. They had yet to prepare their carry-on suitcases.

Under the advice of the expert, Gustav, they would keep their jewels with them until they could lock them in the safe in their quarters, along with their documents. He had suggested they put most of their money away with the rest of the valuables. "You'll see, there is not much you can do with money aboard," he explained to Esther. "You may use it to pay for a drink or to tip your chamber maid or the boy who will clean your shoes, that's all."

Esther had searched all over her bedroom for the amethyst pendant she inherited from her grandmother and mother. One last time, she looked into her jewelry case on top of the tall chest of drawers.

"It has to be here. There is no other place I would put it," she thought out loud, as she frequently did. She was noticeably agitated. Once again, Mr. Pissani and his prophesy continued to interfere and intruded on her thoughts. She wanted to forget, but contrary to her will, the prediction played with her emotions. She felt irritable and tired. "I knew the pendant was in the box," she screamed when she finally found it. Drained by the effort, with the pendant in hand, she sat on the black, lacquered trunk at the foot of her bed.

"Who are you talking to?" Rebecca asked as she entered the bedroom. She looked around with curiosity. "Nobody's here."

"I was thinking out loud, that's all." She sighed, picked up her skirt and dried her tears with it. "We must go to the cemetery. You have to go with me, Becca," she pleaded. "I get almost hysterical when I think we are about to leave the country, and I haven't visited my mother's grave."

"Esther, you act as if you were about to leave the country forever." Rebecca had a touch of irritation in her voice. She reflected over her last words and repented for her burst of irritation. She continued her talk in a softer and more loving voice. "Of course, I'll go with you. We can go as soon Olga comes to help you to close that suitcase."

"It is very important for me to visit her tomb, do you understand? But I'm afraid to go alone."

"Oh don't even think of going alone! I'll go with you. We have time to spare. Joseph will come for dinner, but not before six-thirty."

Since their engagement, Joseph had visited Rebecca every evening and had frequently joined the two young women for supper. The trip had made Joseph unhappy. He wanted Rebecca in Odessa with him, not in America. He complained they had a big job ahead of them. Without her, it was impossible to begin preparations for their wedding. He suggested that Esther take the trip by herself, while Rebecca remained with him. They would take the same trip later, for their honeymoon. Her answer was a final "No!" He and the wedding would have to wait for her to come back.

Just as Esther was about to go downstairs to look for her, Olga arrived. She closed the last suitcase. "You can go to the graveyard now," she said as she turned to carry the suitcase downstairs. As always, the girls were flabbergasted. They did not understand how Olga knew everything. They had not mentioned the cemetery in her presence.

The place was not too far from the house. Esther and Rebecca could not count on Yuri to drive them. He would be busy. He had to deliver the baggage to the train station and fill out the necessary paperwork. A job that would take most of the day. The two young women resorted to public transportation.

April was in bloom. The streets were perfumed with the fragrance of new greenery. They hired a young man with a shay to take them to the cemetery. They had no need for a carriage with a roof, the air was no longer cool. The trip was shorter than they remembered. Unlike that dismal day in December, this afternoon the streets were clear of snow, and they were bathed in the sun's warmth. Esther asked the shay driver to wait for them at the gate. They preferred to walk the distance to Miriam's grave. Along the way, Esther stopped for an instant, attracted by a shiny object on the road. She leaned forward and picked up a small white stone. Carefully, she examined it and grasped the pebble tightly in her hand. Then, she extended the length of her steps to reach Rebecca and continued on their way together.

They arrived at the grave, which did not yet have a headstone. Esther sat on the ground on one side of the grave. Rebecca sat across from her cousin. They did not cry. Esther caressed the green grass that had grown since the early winter. Just before she got up, she kissed the ground and whispered, "I will never forget you. You'll be in my heart forever." She left the white stone at her mother's grave, got up, and walked away. She never looked back.

Rebecca, who had not expected her quick reaction, was left behind. "Esther, dear, wait for me!"

Esther slowed her pace so Rebecca could catch up with her, but she did not stop. "Thank you, Becca. You made it possible. I was terrified. I could not have come alone." Esther sighed and reached for Rebecca's hand. "Now, I can go to America."

The driver had cut a handful of fresh grass and gave some to the brown mare. When he saw the girls nearing, he stood at the side of the shay and waited to help them in. The ride back was uneventful. The driver sat on the side of the sulky and spurred on the young mare to a fast gallop. "She loves to run," he told them.

The bright sun and the spring breeze reminded Esther she was alive and that death, as spring with its rebirth in the cycle of the seasons, was part of that miraculous circle of life.

When they arrived home, Rebecca continued her way upstairs. Esther heard conversation in the kitchen, and went to find Yuri with a cup of coffee in his right hand while Olga bandaged his left. "What happened?" Esther asked in alarm.

"It is no more than a small scratch," Yuri explained. "Olga is pampering me and you know how she gets when she sees a drop of blood," he said with a smile. "Believe me, it's nothing."

He had just finished unloading the baggage from the cart and giving it to a porter. To be sure the man did the job right, he watched while the railroad worker carried them to a wagon. He saw the last suitcase disappear inside the wagon, when a cold sensation on his hand made him look down. It was a dog. The animal's wet nose touched his palm when it began to lick his hand. It was then he noticed the deep cut on his hand. "You must be careful with the brass hinges on both of the green trunks. They are sharp."

Two days spun by like a cyclone. Esther stood by the window, gazing at the languid vermilion flashes of the sky on her last day in Odessa before the journey. The light began to slide into the soft velvet of the night. She detested her sentimentality. It made her feel weak. Against her will, she felt sorry for Gustav. That day, more than anything else in the world, she wanted to love him. She knew Gustav would be with Albert at the train station early the next morning. However, she understood how important it was for them to have a moment alone, a time to say goodbye privately. She invited him to come over for coffee and dessert. She had just sat in the parlor with a book when the doorbell rang.

He arrived with another bouquet of flowers for her. For the trip, he gave her a box of Swiss chocolates and the most recent book written by Chekhov: Chayka, The Sea-Gull. "I'm sure you'll find it as entertaining as all the other books he wrote." He looked tired and nervous. He sat for an instant and got up before Esther could serve him a cup of coffee. He sat again, and before he accepted his cup, he reached inside his jacket pocket and pulled out a long, black velvet case. He opened the case and took a wide gold bracelet from it and placed it on her wrist. When Esther began to protest, he insisted that she wear it. "Please, Esther, you must wear it for my sake."

"Gustav, the bracelet is beautiful, but I can't accept it."

"You have chosen not to wear the ring I gave you until you come back, and I accept that. Permit me this pleasure." He asked her to wear it until they met again. Then he pulled her tightly against him. He held her and kissed her passionately for the longest time, and, before she could react or say a word, he was at the door.

She was about to say something, but Gustav placed a finger over her lips, and stopped her. He kissed her once more, lightly this time, and left with a promise to be at the train station the next morning. Esther watched him go. With her hand on the doorknob, she wept and wondered why she could not love him the way he loved her. She was convinced he could have been a perfect husband and could have made her completely happy. "I'll wear this bracelet forever." Maybe because she cried and her voice was no more than a whisper, Gustav never heard her last words.

Feeling tired and sad, her face wet with tears, she climbed up the last step to be surprised by the figure of Rebecca, who appeared in the doorway of her bedroom. "Oy, you startled me!" Esther gasped.

"I'm so sorry, dear, I should have kept the light stronger. I needed to see that you were well." They kissed each other. "We must go to bed. Tomorrow will be a very long and exhausting day. The train leaves the station at eight o'clock."

"Yes, we'll have an early morning and an uncomfortable two day ride." Before she kissed Rebecca goodnight, Esther showed her the gold bracelet. "Isn't it beautiful? Gustav gave it to me." As a litany, she added, "I wish I could love him."

"Maybe you prejudged him before he could demonstrate who he could be for you," Rebecca suggested as she embraced her. "He'll have another chance when we come back." Then she ordered, "Go to bed, darling. We have to get up in a few hours. You'll be too sleepy tomorrow to enjoy the panorama from the train."

It was early. The sun had not yet warmed the air that spring morning. The mating songs of the birds came in the open window of the bedroom and made her smile. Esther awakened to what she suspected, but did not know, would be her last day in Odessa. "I'm taking a prediction as a reality. I love my country and my life. I wish to be back." She got out of bed and walked to the window, whispering to herself, "I'll be back if that is my destiny."

She wore her winter robe and started her way downstairs. The smell of bread fresh from the oven made her hurry. The table was set for breakfast, the tea prepared and a very pensive Olga awaited her. Esther walked to the wooden box Yuri had made for Katiuska and her pups. "They are big and fat, aren't they?" she said. "Soon they will need a larger place to sleep."

Olga nodded, but did not reply.

"The smell of your bread has made me feel famished."

Olga ignored every word Esther had said and told her, "I was waiting for you." She walked toward Esther until she was no more than an inch from the young woman. She placed her large hands over Esther's shoulders and spoke to her in a soft and maternal voice. "Don't cry and don't look back."

"What are you talking about?" Esther asked, but realized Olga knew as much as she about the prediction of Mr. Pissani. It was time to stop pretending. "Oh, my dearest Olga, what should I do?"

"The universe," Olga continued, "with its infinite kindness, is opening a door to the future, your future, Esther. Don't ignore it. Don't fear it. Run, if you must, to catch it. Press it in your hand and hold it. It has been born. Take it to your breast and feed it. Sing for it a lullaby. Don't let it go. Fly with it. It is your new life."

CHAPTER XVIII
THE FIRST STEP

Odessa April 21st, 1906

The Chinese Taoist Philosopher Lao Tzu wrote in 604 BC: "A journey of a thousand miles starts with a first step." That day in Odessa, in April of 1906, Esther took the first step of an extraordinary journey.

"Rebecca, don't miss this view, it's breathtaking. Look at those imposing mountains to the west. They are white with snow. The spring has not yet arrived in the Carpathian Mountains," Esther exclaimed to her sleepy cousin. They had left Odessa early that morning.

Yuri and his family had come to the house to say goodbye before breakfast. Mikhail had picked some wildflowers in the field behind their home and made a small sheaf for them.

Olga did not accompany them and said goodbye from the door of the house on Balkovskaya Street. She refused to go to the train station. "I've been there too many times," she protested. She carried both their handbags and helped them get in the car. From the sidewalk, she watched them leave. Olga was petrified; her hands were wrapped in the white apron, her eyes were lost in the far street corner where the car had turned and vanished. She could have stood there forever, but Katiuska's barks and the puppies' cries summoned Olga to back to the house and her kitchen.

There was no sign of movement at the train station. The silence was broken only by discreet coughs and whispering voices. Sleepy people sat on long wooden benches. The room was big, with no windows and had the peculiar smelled of urine. The lack of light and clean air forced Gustav and Albert outside. They saw Joseph's car from afar and hurried to help Esther and Rebecca. That day, Albert seemed taller to Esther. Joseph and Gustav waved their kerchiefs until their figures melted in the background and became one with the distant scene. The two men and Odessa would wait for the young ladies' return.

The train traveled for hours and stopped in Vinnitsa and Ternopol. The monotonous noise produced by the wagons running over the rails, and the constant undulating movement made Rebecca fall into a hypnotic trance. She closed her eyes in abandonment. Esther, not completely convinced of her destiny, needed to stay connected with the land she might never see again. She was too excited to waste her time on dreams. The scenery outside the train had changed many times since early morning. The mountains were close to the railroad now, and the landscape became rustic and more dramatic. High grasses, moved by the wind, touched the train on its passage.

The conductor was a short, thin man, no older than Yuri. He was dressed in a gray uniform with gold buttons and a black hat, which was similar to a military hat. He came by soon after the train left the station at Odessa, knocked on their compartment door, asked for their train tickets and punched a hole in them. He continued with his rounds every time the train was close to the next stop and for a few minutes after. He told the passengers the name of the next town and gave them the time the train would arrive at the station. Over an hour earlier, he had announced they had left their beloved Russia and entered Poland.

The rail cars, as expected, were extremely comfortable and ornate, with spacious corridors and large glass windows that let in much light. Bored, Esther made a small excursion through the cars while Rebecca was asleep. On her walk, she found the dining car and the public bathrooms. Toward the end of the line, she found several other cars with many people in them. Those passengers were seated quite close together, without privacy or comfort. Overhead racks packed with luggage, had taken away part of the large windows and the light.

The two young women were alone in compartment A-243.The conductor pleaded with them to share their compartment with an older couple for a few hours. Mr. and Mrs. Agustiniak had not reserved their seats in advance, and were seated in the public first class car. Unfortunately, Madam Agustiniak suffered from acute headaches and the excess noise disturbed her. Since they had so much space, Esther and Rebecca agreed. Soon after, the conductor brought in the couple, who sat across from them. Without malicious intention, Esther observed their reflection in the window glass. They were old enough to be their grandparents.

Madame Agustiniak wore a large hat adorned with fruits and flowers. *Take that horrible, heavy burden from your head, and your headache will go away*, Esther thought and smiled at the old lady. Madam Agustiniak smiled back. After that first smile, the old lady engaged Esther in a pleasant conversation for the rest of the couples' trip. She told Esther they were Poles from a small town near Krakow. They had spent the last month with Mr. Agustiniak's younger brother. The younger Agustiniak had celebrated his fiftieth birthday the week before. As had Esther and Rebecca, they also started the trip in Odessa.

The train would arrive in Krakow before the evening ended. Mr. and Mrs. Agustiniak would leave the train then. "Our older son will be at the train station waiting for us," the woman told Esther.

"We are actually on the first part of our trip to America," Esther exclaimed with joy. "It took such a long time to make the preparations for it. I thought it would never happen, but here we are."

With much effort, Rebecca began to come out of her drowsy state. She smiled with benevolence at her cousin's outburst. "I think I need a cup of tea," she said and stood up. She invited Mr. and Mrs. Agustiniak to join them. Mr. Agustiniak never opened his mouth, his wife talked for both of them. She thanked them for the invitation, but they chose to stay in the relative silence of the enclosed room.

Their compartment was in the second passenger car behind the locomotive. To reach the tea room, they had to walk toward the rear of the train and walk through two more passenger cars. They went through the lounge car, where some passengers stood around a table and watched a game of chess. In the center of the car sat a green, felt billiards table.

Esther gestured at a few burnished tables and chairs under the windows. “We can come here and play dominoes or cards if we are bored,” she said. “We have a long way to go before we arrive in Germany.”

The next car, the smoking car, was elegant and much adorned. The sun light was impeded by heavy velvet curtains edged with gold fringes placed over thin voile ones. There were several armchairs, a few of the burnished tables and in the corner a mirrored stand with glass shelves lined with liquor bottles. There were many male travelers in the car. Their eyes followed the two young women. Esther and Rebecca had to open one more door to arrive at their destination. A gallant man got up from his armchair, and after leaving his cigar in the ashtray, opened the door for them. For an instant, they found themselves on a platform between the two cars. It was cold, and the noise deafened them. Esther reached the door, opened it and they stepped inside the dining car. The sobriety of the place contrasted sharply with the car they had just left behind. It had dark green, leather booths and tables with white tablecloths. The only adornments were a candelabrum and fresh flowers on each table. The light from the windows was filtered by voile curtains.

A waiter dressed in white came to take their order. The tea made Rebecca come out of her lethargic state. The sandwiches and cake they ate had a different flavor than those they were familiar with. The time without hurries pleased them, and Esther and Rebecca experienced their first relaxed conversation in days.

The sun, its rays stopped by the mountains, had disappeared several hours earlier. The train arrived in Krakow in complete darkness. The porter had passed to announce they would remain at the station for fifteen minutes.

Mr. and Mrs. Agustiniak were ready to leave the train ten minutes before the train stopped. When they saw the light of the station, they took their backs from the upper shelf and said goodbye before the train had even stopped then left compartment A-243 just as fast as they had entered it earlier.

Esther was impatient, she had been sitting for hours. She left the book on the seat and stood. "Do you think we can go for a walk on the platform, just—?" Her question was interrupted by the way Rebecca looked at her.

"Are you out of your mind, Esther? What do we do if the train starts before we get back?"

Once the chance to go outside vanished, Esther paced the short distance between the window and the door of the compartment countless times before the train restarted its march. It was not until seven-thirty that the train left Krakow.

"Genug shoyn," Esther said. She closed the book noisily and got up. "Are you hungry, Becca?" Until sundown she had enjoyed the change in the landscape. The night had brought a dull darkness, and the only thing Esther could see was her reflection on the glass.

"Sweet Esther, we had tea after five. I'm not ready to eat yet," Rebecca said, the book pressed against her chest.

Esther opened the cover of a tiny watch that hung from a chain around her neck and checked the hour. "Can you see the time from there?" She leaned forward to place the watch in front of Rebecca. "It is already past dinnertime in Odessa."

Krakow had been left behind over an hour earlier, but the train would be in Polish territory until dawn. The porter told Esther when she asked, that he expected the train to be in German territory by seven the next morning and the first stop was Berlin soon after.

"All right, let me go to the bathroom to repair my chignon. I've not combed my hair since early this morning in Odessa."

"Do you think we are wearing the proper clothes? Maybe we should change to go to the dining car," Esther asked as she used the window as a mirror to repair her undone hair.

"I'll go as I am, if you don't mind." Rebecca did not know if they were properly attired, but had no inclination to wear anything else. The clothes she had in her case were reserved for the next day.

When they went back to the dining car that evening, many of the tables were occupied. The place was well-illuminated and the crowd was formal. The waiter in white took them to a booth on the right side of the car. There was nothing to see outside. Esther felt nostalgic. The darkness was absolute and came to the edge of the penumbra left by the passing train. There was not even the moon in the sky to provide light, only distant stars.

Dinner was served with efficiency by the waiter in white. He described the dishes he recommended to Esther and Rebecca. They were unfamiliar with Italian cuisine and never had tasted anything like that at home, but they loved the scaloppini and the pasta. After the most delicious French mousse, they were ready to go back to their compartment. Under the indiscreet gaze of many, the girls left the dining car. It was extremely unusual to see young, pretty and obviously unmarried women without the company of a chaperone. When they arrived at compartment A-243, they found the place totally changed. There were two berths ready for them. They took off their clothes and hung them in the very small closet, then took their nightgowns out of their handbags. Before they climbed into bed, Rebecca locked the door.

"These beds are comfortable," Rebecca said. "When I saw them, I believed they were hard and thought I couldn't sleep a wink. I misjudged them. Goodnight, Esther." With those words, Rebecca rolled onto her side with her back to the wall.

"Good night, Becca. I'm very tired. I think I'll sleep forever." That last phrase did not reach Rebecca's ears in time. She was already asleep in the lower berth.

The next morning, loud voices and fast steps in the corridor interrupted their sleep before they received the early call by the porter. He knocked at every door to announce the train would arrive at Berlin in fifteen minutes. Sleepy, they lay in bed until the train braked and its noisy wheels skated over the rails. The light of the new day was still scarce. They expected silence, but they heard the same kind of nervous rumpus they had heard many times at the port of Odessa. The shouts of the conductors and porters dominated the sound of the fast footsteps of the crowd.

Curiosity made Esther jump down from the top bunk. She opened the curtain just enough to see the platform. "This place looks like an anthill that was stepped on," she shrieked. "Everybody is moving in a different direction. There is so much hurry. Come here and see, Becca. What a confusion!"

Many hundreds of people were about to embark on the same journey. The multitude converged at the station in Berlin from different countries. They would take a train to Hamburg to later board a ship to America. She remembered the trunks and luggage Yuri had taken to the train station three days earlier. She felt ashamed when she compared the one bag each one of those poor people carried with the excess of clothing they had in their trunks.

"Where did they leave all their treasures?" she wondered. "How can they start a new life with just a suitcase?" They wore used clothes and appeared to be poor. She felt sorry for those men and women. Esther was surprised to see how grievous they seemed to be on their way to the Promised Land. "It must be very painful to have to leave your country believing in just yourself, and taking chances on the promise of a future." Esther was moved and at the edge of tears. "Becca, we are so very, very fortunate. We have so much."

Rebecca was intrigued by Esther's sentiment, and moved the curtain on the other side of the window to see what Esther had described to her. "There is not enough work in Europe. Too many wars have left many countries impoverished. There is so much famine." A chill shook her body. Maybe her beloved Joseph's ideas about medicine and helping the poor were right.

The stop in Berlin was a long one, and by the time the train restarted the march, the station was empty. Again, they were on the way to their destination before they abandoned the window.

"What kind of future will they have there, Rebecca?" Esther asked as she sat on the bed beside her cousin.

"Oh my dear, I'm sure they will have a better life in America. It is such a big country. The new continent has much to offer. There is so much unclaimed land. They will be happier there." She noticed that despite her words, her cousin remained sad, and she changed the conversation. "We have to get dressed and go for breakfast."

"I hope you are right, Becca, and America receives them with open arms." She reflected for a second and said, "I'm not very hungry, just thirsty. I'd love a cup of tea." She looked at Rebecca through the mirror while she combed her long hair and tried to avoid hitting her elbows on the bathroom door. "The space in this compartment is quite limited, isn't it?" she complained with a frown.

"Tonight we'll sleep in the transatlantic ship's stateroom, Esther. I expect to have a lot more room there."

At breakfast, the dining car was completely full. Every table was in use by other passengers having their meal. Even the small table they used the night before was occupied. They stayed at the entrance and waited. The waiter with the white clothes came to ask if they would share a table with another young lady. With a flourishing gesture, he showed them to a table where a woman in a pale green suit was already seated. Esther and Rebecca exchanged a gaze of approval and nodded to the waiter. "Please follow me," he told them. A woman about Rebecca's age was seated alone in one of the green booths. They had to overcome the language barrier to find a way to communicate.

"Do you speak Russian?" Esther asked the young lady. The movement of her head and the incomprehension reflected in her eyes made Esther try her not-too-perfect German.

"I'm Esther Vainer, and this is my cousin, Rebecca Prusky. It is so awfully nice of you to share your table with us." She sat and moved toward the window to leave space for Rebecca. The waiter came, they ordered breakfast, and Esther was again the one to talk. "We took the train yesterday early morning in Odessa. We go to Hamburg." This time Esther spoke in Yiddish.

"That is a coincidence, me too," Ruth said and smiled, answering in a velvety Yiddish.

"We are on our way to the New World," Rebecca told her. "We'll take the ship in Hamburg, the Wilhelm Der Grosse. We'll depart tomorrow."

The young woman's name was Ruth Grossman. She lived in America, and was on her way back home. She had boarded the train the night before in Krakow. As Rebecca and Esther, she too would leave the train in Hamburg. There she would board the ship that would take her back to New York. She was married to Abraham Grossman. Her husband was the manager of the family's business. She had been married for two and a half years and she had no children yet. She had come to Poland to visit some relatives.

"My grandmother was sick," she said. "She implored my family to let me come. She needed to see me," Ruth continued in a very low voice and a somber shadow darkened her green eyes. "I left Warsaw when I was a child. When I came back last month to visit her, my grandmother did not recognize me, even though she knew I was on my way to see her."

"Don't feel bad. She must be an old woman. She remembers you the way you were before you left for America," Rebecca soothed.

"Is your grandmother well now?" Esther asked.

"Oh she is beyond help, grumpy and very stubborn, but she is well," Ruth said sadly.

"Does she live in Krakow?" Rebecca asked.

"Yes, she lived her entire life in Warsaw, as we did before leaving for America. I went south to visit an aunt, sister of my mother. She still teaches in a girls' school on the outskirts of Krakow."

The three women were so entertained with their chat that it was close to noon when they walked out of the dining car. The waiter in white was relieved to see them go. He had to clean and prepare the table for lunchtime. Esther invited Ruth to their compartment and they continued to learn about each other, cultivate the new friendship, a link that would grow and flourish for the next half-century, until the day Rebecca would learn of Ruth's death. She was in Moscow when she received a letter from one of Ruth's children with the sad news of Ruth's passing. She was seventy-eight then. The two world wars, the millions of deaths and the abyss created by political animosity that their countries showed toward each other could not break the tenacious friendship created between Ruth, Esther and Rebecca. They wrote to each other until the end.

Ruth was delighted to know that Esther and Rebecca would cross the Atlantic on the same German ship that she would be on. "I felt very much alone when I took the trip to Europe. My husband couldn't find the time to come with me. He had to remain in New York," Ruth told them. Abraham was the older son in the family. With her father-in-law, they owned a large factory. They manufactured fabrics for many clothing factories in the country. They had not yet finished with the spring and summer stock when Ruth left.

Abraham had a younger brother, Natan, the rebel of the family. Natan worked for a Jewish newspaper in Manhattan. In the opinion of his father, Natan, a Socialist, was always too involved in politics and not enough with his own family. He offered to help in the factory while Abraham was away, an offer that was immediately refused by his father. Mr. Grossman did not want to give Natan the chance to place revolutionary ideas in the minds of the workers at his factory. Ruth had also a young sister-in-law, Bertha, who would finish school that June.

"How long will you be in America? It is such a beautiful country to visit."

"We'll be there until the beginning of September," Rebecca answered.

"As you, we will also be in New York," Esther told Rebecca.

They could hear the voice of the porter down the corridor as he announced their arrival in Wittenberg. Rebecca had finished a letter to Joseph, and hurried to close the envelope. She opened the door in time to talk to the porter in the gray uniform.

"Do you think it is possible to mail this letter from the train station here in Wittenberg? Do I have time to leave the train and mail it?"

"I'm not sure you would, madam," said the porter.

"Maybe you would be kind enough to do it for me?" The man agreed, and left after he received the letter, money for the postage and a generous tip.

Before she joined Esther and Ruth in their game of backgammon, Rebecca folded the clothes they had worn and placed them back in the two brown leather handbags. Then she walked through the cars that separated her from the entertainment car.

Night had fallen when they heard the porter call the next stop. Hamburg was near. Esther and Rebecca moved closer together. They felt the apprehension of the unknown. The largest vessel they had ever been in was the small sailboat her father had on the harbor. They had sailed on the Black Sea and always very close to the coast. They had never stepped in a seven hundred seven foot-long ship that had two propellers and four enormous smokestacks. They had read all that information in the papers they received from Mr. Pulaski.

Ruth, who had made the trip once before, had the anxiety of one who was ready to go home. She felt happy. She was closer to that final stop, but experienced the fatigue of one who knows there is still a long way to go.

The train station at Hamburg was not well lit, and it was very crowded. Newspaper and magazine stands were at the end of the platforms. A flower shop and a restaurant were on the right, close to a central hall. Many trains arrived, while many others were about to leave. Passengers were in a chaotic rush, and moved quickly in every possible direction. Esther and Rebecca felt overwhelmed by the unknown place and the language barrier, and held each other's arms to find security. The crowd moved in waves, and pushed and dragged them toward the near exit.

Ruth also felt suffocated by the multitude. On the brink of a panic attack, she clung to Esther's arm. The porter, a tall, blond Aryan, pushed a wheeled cart with the luggage that belonged to Ruth plus the two brown leather handbags. The young man slowly followed the three women. When he realized their consternation, he pushed his way around them and opened a path for the three foreigners to follow.

When they arrived outside, they were shocked by the cold wind and snow that fell on their new hats and shoes. Esther hurried to put on her gloves. "Oy shney! I can't believe it!"

The porter signaled them to wait. He went to where the drivers were and talked to an older man who drove a large carriage. He explained the language barrier and their destination. He asked the driver to take the three women to the pier where the Kaiser Wilhelm Der Grosse was anchored. Then he placed the suitcases in the back trunk and on the roof. Ruth paid the porter and sat across from Esther and Rebecca, who were already inside the coach. She closed the door, and almost immediately they were on their way. The carriage, pulled by two shiny white Percherons still in their winter coats, took them to the edge of the Baltic Sea where the majestic German cruiser awaited them.

CHAPTER IXX
ELLIS ISLAND

Last day of April, 1906

Rebecca and Esther were on one of the upper decks reclined on canvas long chaises basking in the morning sun when Ruth arrived, her face lit with joy. She had to secure her hard straw hat with her hand. The wind wanted to take it away from her. "Good morning, girls," Ruth greeted. "I'd been looking for you all over the ship, and I ended asking the steward."

"Good morning, Ruth. Rebecca and I waited for you for a while, but we were hungry," Esther said as she placed the book on her lap. "When we saw that you were not coming we went for breakfast." Rebecca shaded her eyes with her hand to look at Ruth. "I hope your headache is gone."

"I'm just fine, Rebecca. Thank you for asking. I took a long bath and my headache went away."

"Did you have breakfast yet?"

"Yes, Esther. Thank you. I asked the steward to bring breakfast to my stateroom."

"You look radiant. Is it our proximity to New York that makes you so cheerful?" Esther asked.

The end of the transatlantic trip was near, and with it, the apprehension Rebecca had felt since the start began to ease. Unlike her cousin, Esther even enjoyed the tempest they experienced the second day after the ship left Hamburg. The vessel had just entered the vastnesses of the Atlantic Ocean when strong winds kept the passengers indoors. The high waves and the rain converged as one to sweep the lower decks. Rebecca struggled to remain calm, but dizziness overtook her, and throughout the ordeal, she stayed in bed with a cold cloth over her forehead. The only time she got up was to look at the life-boats through the porthole. Comforted by their presence on the ship, she went back to bed. In twenty-four hours the seas re-gained their relative calm, and Esther and Rebecca were able to walk on the promenade, sit on the deck with a book, and sigh with the beautiful sunsets.

"Have you noticed any changes in the surroundings? Have you examined the sky today?" Esther asked Ruth, but got no answer. She pushed up her dark green sunglasses and asked again, "Well, have you?" Esther just didn't see the transparent blue air and the beautiful clouds, as she had the previous day. That morning she saw the first marine birds. "We are close to land, Ruth. We are arriving in America!"

"I know, I know, but let me tell you what happened. Last night, as you know, I went to my stateroom after dinner with a headache. After putting on my nightgown, I sat down and placed an ice cold bag over my eyes and forehead. I don't know how long I sat, but I became very sleepy. I was not able to keep my eyes open, and I slept until an hour ago." The night before, when Ruth entered her room, sickened with pain, she over-looked a cable the steward left for her on the night table.

"I read it this morning. It was from my husband, Abraham. I'm so happy!"

"I wonder why the steward took the cable to your cabin in-stead of delivering it to you," Rebecca commented. "Did you ask him?"

"It's not important. I received my husband's message, and that's all I care about. It makes me feel like telling it to the whole word." She missed Abraham terribly. This was the first time they had been separated since their wedding night. She put her hand in the pocket of her crepe-de-Chine brown dress and took out a sheet of carefully folded white paper. Ruth unfolded it and said, "Let me read it to you." 'I am counting the hours. Stop. The family will be at the pier. Stop. I love you, my dear-est. Stop. Abraham.'" She folded the cable and placed it back in her pocket.

"My aunt and her husband will be waiting for Rebecca and me." To make herself easily recognizable, Sarah told Esther what she would be wearing: a cobalt-blue dress and coat, with a black hat, purse, gloves and shoes. Esther was sure she would recognize her aunt. The contrast and definition was perfect in the small black and white photograph Sarah had sent to Odessa. The picture showed a woman in her thirties. She knew her Aunt Sarah was the younger of the two aunts, but she was about her mother's age. Her aunt would be forty that same year. Esther was sure to discover her among the rest of the people on the pier.

Her aunt had mentioned in several of the letters, the apprehensions she felt with the trip. Esther had to convince Sarah that nothing would happen to either of them.

"We are two responsible grown-up women. We're not the babies you remember," she wrote in response to her aunt's worries.

Sarah believed it wasn't safe for two young ladies to do such a long trip without a chaperone. She'd even gone as far to speak to her husband, Frank, about her concerns and he came up with a marvelous idea. "How do you feel if I sent Mrs. Coleman to meet you in Hamburg?"

Mrs. Coleman, a respectable widow, had much experience and would be a perfect chaperone for Esther. Aside from the chaperone business, Sarah had expressed one more fear. "What would happen if I don't see you. If we can't find each other when you arrive?" Sarah was afraid of what could happen in the crowded port. Any unpredictable event could make the encounter impossible. She thought of every possible scenario and crisis. In each one of the last three letters she sent their telephone number at home and at work and the addresses of their house and the factory. She also sent them a very generous amount of dollars to have. "Just in case."

"Would you ladies like to go to the promenade deck for a walk?" Rebecca's voice startled Esther and brought her back into the moment.

"Yes," she agreed enthusiastically, "and maybe we can play a game of ping-pong." She patted her stomach. "The food is so delicious, and I have been eating so much that, unless I do more exercises I'll be fat by the end of the cruise." The remark made Rebecca and Ruth laugh. Still laughing, they climbed the metal stairs to the promenade deck.

The architectural design in the upper decks was quite elegant. Esther had to agree with Gustav, the ship's ambiance was disguised as a comfortable hotel. The public spaces were remarkably beautiful. Unlike the staterooms in the lower decks, which were either too small and dark or general dormitories, their cabins were spacious and airy. Esther knew the immigrants had not the same kind of comfort or foods.

The décor of the dining room was simple but harmonious. The foods and desserts were completely delicious. From the Russian caviar, Italian antipasti and sauces, Spanish paellas, French bouillabaisse and desserts, to the delightful Portuguese wines and seafood, the international cuisine exuded refinement and distinction. Herr Albert Ballin, one of the designers of the Hamburg-America Line, used the foods served in the restaurant at the Ritz Hotel in Paris as inspiration for their menus.

"I can become addicted to this kind of life, I feel so pampered," Esther told Rebecca the first night at sea. Some days, when the waves were not too furious and the transatlantic ship had just an imperceptible roll, they could forget the soft confinement and pretend they were dining in France. The dining room had a large stage between the galley doors. As a perfect gift for the diners, a symphonic orchestra played in the evenings after seven-thirty. To entertain the passengers, busty sopranos and round tenors in elaborate costumes sang lover's duets from Italian operas.

The first class travelers had many entertainments for the evenings, but the most popular attraction was a typical German cabaret. To the gentlemen's delight, a lightly dressed line of young women danced and sung for the noisy audience. The bartender worked to exhaustion to keep his customers happy. The cabaret stayed open well into the first lights of dawn.

Esther's curiosity made her wonder about the other part of the ship. They were not supposed to visit the lower decks. More than once, but without success, she lured Rebecca downstairs to listen closer to the violin music that rose to their ears.

Most evenings, after dinner, Esther and Rebecca, accom-

"Look to the left. I think I can see the famous Statue of Liberty, Rebecca, can you?"

"Where do you see it? It is too far away to see anything. You are imagining it."

Ruth, next to them, had to rest her back against one of the white metal stanchion on the deck. Her knees felt weak and failed to support her weight. She was at the end of her trip. She had gone all the way to the eastern part of Europe and now she was almost home. Some place in that city her husband awaited her.

"I would like to go for breakfast," Rebecca said. "I'm hungry. Are you ladies ready to join me?" To totally break the enchantment, she asked, "Esther, do you have your suitcases ready?" Rebecca was amazed to find out her cousin had most of her clothes packed. Esther had not decided what to wear for the afternoon, but had put away most things; even her books. She didn't want to be folding clothes when the ship entered into the New York harbor. It was imperative for her to be on the deck when the vessel passed the Statue of Liberty. She had seen photographs and heard too much wonderful talk about it. She had to see the masterpiece.

It was close to one o'clock when the Kaiser Wilhelm Der Grosse was met by two tugboats. From the taller ship some crewmen on the bow and stern threw lines to the seamen who had positioned their tugboats immediately below. With that maneuver the unwieldy giant began the tedious and slow end of the trip guided by the nimble dwarfs. Not much time had passed when the trip was interrupted one more time. A ferryboat came alongside the ship, and immediately a flurry of activity began. The crews communicated to each other by flag signals. Repeated attempts in the approach were needed until the ferryboat was parallel and very close to the liner. Many lines were thrown to secure both ships tight together. Once the operation was completed a gangplank reached from a lower deck of the big ship to the ferryboat. Despite all the efforts, the plank was in a dangerously inclined plane. An officer in a blue uniform with folder under his arm crossed from the German ship into smaller vessel. Several minutes passed before the same of came back aboard the Wilhelm Der Grosse. The ocean r panied by Ruth, went for a walk. They chose the dark opennes of the decks to the noisy confinement. The immense dome of the sky, the progress of the new moon and the sharpness of the stars in such an obscurity, appealed to the romantic sensibility of the three women.

Leaning over the railing of the forecastle, they could see the crescent moon shattered into a thousand pieces on the mirrored water and on the path of foamy waves, reflected lights from the lower decks. The pounding of the waves on the metal of the prow was not a strong enough noise to silence the music and laughter that arrived to their ears.

"They are having much fun, aren't they?" Ruth said.

"They are their own entertainment," Esther said with a smile. "They have three more days to be themselves."

"What are you talking about?" Ruth asked.

"When they arrive on Ellis Island, they'll die," Esther affirmed with anguish.

"My dearest cousin, are you crazy? Has so much water affected your good sense? Please explain to me with clarity the meaning of your words."

"Until the moment we anchor off Ellis Island the day after tomorrow, those people have a name, a language and a tradition. As soon as they go through the arrival table, where they will be checked into the country, their names will be changed by an ignorant scriber, who could not spell them correctly. Their precious language will be useless in the new country. To communicate, they will have to embrace the new language." Her voice trembled when she spoke the last sentence. "The bag of rich heritage they bring with them must be left aside to permit them to melt, to disappear in their effort to become Americans. To belong, they will have to embrace the new culture." Esther was saddened by her own words. It would not be until two days later when the ship anchored to transfer the immigrants to a smaller ship to be taken to Ellis Island that Rebecca and Ruth would understand.

Although the arrival at the port was not expected until early afternoon, they began to see the silhouette of the city of New York in front of them, lit by the yellowed rays of a mid morning sun. Esther and Rebecca were mesmerized by the view.

the ships in an unsynchronized pattern. The waves, way below, pounded on both ships, and produced a white bubbly rug under the plank. Suddenly a somber procession of drunken moving figures began to pass aboard the ferryboat. The people had to walk across an insecure gangplank. Some of them held children in their arms. All of them carried bags. Many were pushed with force from one to the other handrail. Stoic women, with their heads wrapped in dark shawls, carried their own bags. At that instant they showed the spirit of the strong pioneer and as the men, they kept the queue uninterrupted. Suddenly a man fell overboard, a nondescript man, just one that looked much like the others. From both ships, sailors threw life rings on the choppy waters. The poor soul had no chance. The ships were too close together to attempt a rescue. His body never would be found. His life cut short by a stupid accident.

Esther did not notice the tragedy. She had left her watch placed on the balustrade to respond to a desperate call from Ruth. Esther went to help her to search her cabin for a lost piece of jewelry. Ruth had lost an emerald and diamond ring. Abraham gave it to her when he proposed.

"Please, Ruth, think. When was the last time you wore it? Do you remember?" Esther asked impatiently, an arm curled around her waist and a bit irritated by the waste of time.

"I think I had it on last night," Ruth called from under the vanity. She sat on the floor. "Do you think the chamber steward has taken it?" she asked in an alarmed voice.

"I don't think so. What would he do with your ring? Sell it? He would lose his job." Esther went down on all fours, to look under the chairs and table in the room. "I'm sure we'll find it."

Esther was right. She found the ring on the bathroom lavatory, hidden by the bar of soap. Ruth had taken it off to wash her hands and never placed it back on her finger. With relief, Ruth closed the last suitcase at the same time that, with a lurch that made them lose their balance, the ship restarted the slow approach into the harbor of the city of New York.

The activity and noise had increased considerably in the passageways. The excitement among the passengers rose and made them sparkly. Even for those who went to bed after sunrise, the proximity of the city made them awaken in a euphoric mood. They ran around half awake and crowded the staircases. All the travelers who had someone at the pier were on deck. Everyone looked for a perfect space along the railing. People wanted to see as much as to be seen.

A happy group of men and women with champagne glasses in their hands, laughed loudly as they pushed away the people at the rail to open a place big enough to hold them all. They ignored the protests. The group celebrated with anticipation of their arrival. Some first time photographers, in their eagerness to capture the last hour aboard the vessel with their cameras, trampled and disturbed other voyagers.

The pier was still far away, when Esther suggested they go above to the promenade deck. "Maybe we'll find more space there. My panorama is composed mostly of all sized heads. I can't see much of the city of New York from here." Before the other women agreed, she began to climb the wide metal stairs. Many others travelers had the same idea. Esther arrived on the last step to see just a few spaces left on the balustrade. She pressed the other two women to climb the steps faster and rushed to the rail. The view was magnificent and the deck quieter without the happy drinkers from below. The transparent light of the early afternoon shone on the colossal symbol of the Statue of Liberty. Esther became silent. The Statue of Liberty, the vigilant guardian of the bay and protector of the harbor, was before her eyes.

The end of their voyage was near. Slowly they began to divide, to shift, and to break their dependency. Destiny had brought them together, but was now separating them. Two different paths waited for them ashore.

Ruth gave her address and telephone number to Esther and Rebecca. "Please call me soon. I'd like to invite you for dinner and introduce you to my family. I'd love for them to know you."

"We'll get together, don't worry," Rebecca said, placing the calling card in her purse.

Ruth held Esther and Rebecca by the arm and smiled. "I can be your Cicerone, and show you the city."

"You can call us here." Esther wrote their telephone number on a card and gave it to Ruth. As her aunt told her when she sent it to her, just in case, and she had learned the number well. "You must know the city. We'll visit New York together, it will be fun."

The late April afternoon was pleasant. To catch the food thrown to them, thousands of marine birds flew around the ship performing elaborated air dances. Some of the most audacious dared to land on top of the lifeboats, the squeaking seagulls waited to be fed by the spectators from aboard. Esther and Rebecca were happy to see nature's creatures after so many days of high seas loneliness. Irremediably, the ship continued to advance to its final destination. The faces on the pier slowly came out of the nebulae. A magical brush gave them shape and color. Esther took out the old picture of her Aunt Sarah. Suddenly she decided the photograph was too old. People change in five years. She wasn't as sure as she had been before to isolate the face of her aunt in the multitude. She didn't know the port would have such a tremendous crowd. Her concern marked a deep frown on her forehead.

"What's the matter, dear?"

"Oh nothing, Becca, I'm fine." Esther did not mention her recent worry.

Ruth wasn't troubled by the crowded pier. If there was a face she could recognize in that mob, it was the one of her beloved husband, Abraham.

Before the crowd and very close to the water next to the iron bollards, pairs of mariners were waiting for the ship to moor. Esther could hear names shouted from the impatient. She could see people who waved their arms in semicircles to attract attention. Many others waved white handkerchiefs in the air. Men with children in their arms showing those still on the ship the continuation of their lineage. The expressions of happiness and the excitement produced disorder and a commotion among the waiting gatherers. The barriers installed by the Port Authority to keep the people safe and contained became a broken dam, and a human torrent soon was next to the sailors at the edge of the pier.

"I can see Abraham," Ruth said as she screamed his name. With a smile she asked Esther, "Do you see the tall man with a beige tweed jacket? That's Natan and Bertha with him."

Esther followed the direction Ruth pointed, but it was impossible to separate one unknown face from the crowd in a multitude of strangers.

"I'm sorry, Ruth, I can't see him." She continued the search for the tweed jacket when she said, "Aunt Sarah?" then shouted "Aunt Sarah, Aunt Sarah here we are!" She couldn't help herself and imitated other passengers. She waved her arms and screamed from the top of her lungs, "Aunt Sarah! Here! Up here! I'm Esther!"

From the pier, an older woman in a thick blue overcoat too heavy for the warm April afternoon took off her black hat and, holding it with her black gloved hand, waved it in the air and shouted almost as loud as Esther, "My dear child, I see you!"

CHAPTER XX
NEW YORK CAROUSEL

May, 1906

"Are you sure you don't need more rest?" Sarah asked. "It is only your first day in New York. We have months ahead of us."

"We are perfectly well, Aunty, anxious to visit places," Esther answered.

"I know, but you may need some time to adjust. We can just go for a stroll in Central Park."

"Oh no, Aunty Sarah, please! We are certainly ready to go out. We spent too much time resting on the ship with nothing to do," protested Esther emphatically.

"Something light then," continued Sarah. "We could visit the Bethesda Fountain. It's not far from here, just over ten blocks to Park and 73rd Street."

"I would like to go out too, and at some point, if it's possible, I have to go to the post office. Is it very far from here?" Rebecca asked as she showed Sarah all the letters she had written to Joseph, and a sepia postcard. Before America, she had never seen photographs of public places made into a postcard to be mailed. She wanted Joseph to receive one.

"Maybe we can go by the post office on the way to the synagogue?" Esther asked her aunt.

"That's a good idea, Esther. We'll go in the afternoon. Is that all right with you, Rebecca?"

Esther embraced and kissed her aunt on both cheeks. "I'm

so delighted we came to visit you Aunty Sarah," she exclaimed loudly, short of shouting.

The encounter at the port was terribly emotional. For Sarah, Esther was the link to her past and her beloved brother. Since she never had children, Esther was also her continuation into the future. Sarah was the female replica of Jacob. Esther was delighted to find so much resemblance to her father in her aunt's features. She loved Sarah instantly.

Rebecca began to enjoy the American cuisine. Her stomach never felt completely well on the trip across the ocean. Unlike Esther, she didn't eat much aboard the ship. She was happy to be on firm soil and to walk again without the ship moving under her feet. "This arrival would have been perfect if Joseph was with me," she whispered to Esther when they were on the gangway. "I miss him so."

Frank Bernstein, upset his wife by hiring a driver with a cart to transport the trunks and the rest of the luggage. His new automobile was not big enough. Besides, as he told Sarah, "The porter can scratch the paint," and when Sarah gave him a severe gaze, he explained, "Also the weight of those heavy bags will ruin the leather of the interior."

"You could have brought one of the trucks from the factory," Sarah argued.

The trip from the port to the house was not long. In the short ride, Esther and Rebecca had a taste of the uniqueness of the city. The cobblestone streets were broad and full of cars, trams, carriages and heavy wooden carts pulled by pairs of horses. The sidewalks were spacious, tiled, and trees were planted close to the curb. The many unconcerned pedestrians were not afraid of anarchists' bombs. Elegant houses with green lawns and pretty gardens framed the background. The architecture was quite modern, such a difference from the one found in historical Odessa. Even the smell in the streets was different. There was an aroma of fresh baked bread in the air. The change was radical.

"What kind of sport is baseball, Uncle Frank?" Esther asked.

Some short brick walls were covered with posters. The picture of a pitcher and large black letters readable from the street, advertised the next Sunday game. The posters were glued over, but not covered completely by some others which advertised a boxing match in Madison Square Garden.

"Baseball is a hard sport to explain, Esther. I'm not sure I can. Your aunt is still learning about it."

"I never heard of it."

"I know. It was born last century in America and is loved by everyone including myself. It is our national sport," her uncle said while driving, his eyes fixed on the road. Just a few days earlier, he had read a statistic that alarmed him. More people had died in car accidents in those last five months than in the entire Spanish-American war. He was constantly reminded by Sarah to drive carefully. "Slow down. Otherwise you will kill us all." He never drove too fast anywhere when he was with his family. It was not his purpose to increase the number of fatalities and become part of the statistics. He bought the automobile for comfort.

Sarah shared with Miriam the birth year, 1886. She became Sarah Bernstein when she married her husband Frank. She left St. Petersburg with the certainty that it was forever. She did not go back when her parents died. When she received the first telegram, Frank offered to go with her, but she became agitated and categorically refused his idea. "I'll keep the past where it belongs. I don't wish to revive it." When her mother died, Frank accompanied her to place a telegram of condolences, without asking or saying a word.

They lived in Manhattan for over ten years in the same home at East 60th Street, half a block from Park Avenue. For long time they waited to be blessed with a baby but to their regret, they had no children. With the same motherly care, Sarah had placed all her loving attention and time to make her home beautiful. She regularly attended services at the temple and belonged to several charity groups. She spent many afternoons, when Frank was in his factory, at the new nickelodeon. At the end of the past year, a new movie theater had opened on Broadway Street, not far from their home. She was a fervent fan of the motion pictures and never missed a premiere.

Frank was four years his wife's senior. He was born in a family of German immigrants from Bremen. They rose before dawn every morning and worked very hard in their profitable Coney Island bakery. He and his three brothers and sister were first-generation Americans. Frank was still at school when he had the dream to own his own factory. He would provide buttons for all the garments made in New York. His siblings used to laugh about, "such a little dream," as his sister, Emma, jokingly called it. Frank worked very hard for the first two years before The Little Dream as he called the line of buttons produced in his factory became known. Soon after, his dream was a very profitable reality, and he sold as many buttons as he was able to produce. He invited two of his older brothers to work for him. Before the century ended, his little dream had made him wealthy. A jolly man, he adored his wife and enjoyed the good life. Frank had only one regret, the lack of children of his own. Often he had the presentiment that the same kind of loneliness was in Sarah's heart, a void beyond his love. Since the thought often made him worry for her well-being, he welcomed the introduction of Esther and Rebecca into their lives. He delegated the responsibilities in The Little Dream to his older brother and took some time off from the factory. He wanted to be there to help Sarah entertain their nieces.

The enclosed winter garden with exuberant vegetation and exotic flowers was extravagant and lovely. From a shell, a marble Venus was pouring water in the cupped hands of a chubby cupid. The silvery stream cascaded into the eternally disturbed surface of the fountain. The curious Esther sat on the edge of the tiny lake and had her hand in the water, and tried to lure the elusive red fish.

"Yingele, come for breakfast," Sarah called, still in her purple silk negligee, seated at the table next to Rebecca.

"I'll be there in a minute."

"As you know, Frank loves Coney Island. He thought you both may like to go there for a visit. He was born there, and he thinks it is the best sea resort in the world." She served a cup of tea for Esther. "It's two weeks from your arrival. We don't have all that much time. Before you know, every day will be used, and the moment to go back to Odessa will be here."

"I'll go to every place you'll take me, Aunty. I love this country!"

"Well, then, maybe we go for the day and see if you like it. We can go for lunch to Feltman's." She stopped abruptly and smiled. "Have you ever had hotdogs?" When she saw their blank expressions, she explained, "Feltman's is a good restaurant and has the novelty of a Bavarian garden at Surf Avenue in Coney Island. They serve sausages with mustard and sauerkraut on soft bread, and they are delicious."

"We never had anything like you are describing, but I'm sure I'll love to try it," Rebecca said.

"Good, you will. Coney Island has several elegant hotels. If you girls like the idea, we'll spend the night there."

"I like that." Esther hurried to sit at the breakfast table. She kissed her aunt, and reached to touch the hand of her quiet cousin. "Would you like to go, Becca?" Esther sat on a rattan chair next to her. She felt sad for Rebecca. "Do you know if the mail has arrived yet?" Without waiting for the answer, she asked, "Have you written to Joseph today? He should come and join us."

After breakfast and for the rest of the day, the three women continued their preparations for the trip to Coney Island. To avoid the crowded weekends, that same Wednesday they arrived at the train station at the fashionable sea resort. The porter took their bags to a carriage. "To the Brighton Hotel," Frank told the driver. "Did you know that a few years ago, the hotel had to be moved inland?"

"That is pretty unbelievable, Uncle Frank. Are you telling us the truth?"

"Yes I am," Frank said. He laughed, amused by the disbelief of his niece. "They made the mistake of building the Brighton Hotel too close to the ocean. A few years ago we had some terrible storms in this part of Brooklyn." He relit his half-smoked cigar and continued, "Those storms produced much damage and erosion on the beaches and the ocean was pounding on the hotel threatening to bring its walls down. The owners and the engineers debated for weeks before they decided that, unless moved, the structure would be swallowed by the sea. The whole hotel at once was placed on railcars and transported six hundred feet inland. The operation took less than two months. I saw some of the preparations. Since then, the hotel has been working nonstop. I thought you would be interested in knowing, because this is where we will spend the night."

"Aunty, is that true?" Esther asked, laughing with incredulity.

"I'm afraid it is, darling. Your uncle is telling you the truth."

Coney Island was perceived as a place out of a dream for the girls. Rebecca and Esther had never seen such a display of wealth and elegance, not even from Madam Perlman. It was not a playground to entertain that upper crust.

Now Frank's family was ready to relocate. The old way was almost gone since the arrival of the railroads. They disliked the changes that began to happen in the resort with the turn of the century. His father told Frank there were too many gamblers, too much illegal betting at the horse track. He was aggravated by the latest development—bordellos in the outskirts of the island. Frank took the complaints as the reaction of an old man's inflexibility to embrace progress.

"Don't you think we should visit your family?" Sarah asked him when they arrived at the hotel.

"Sarah dear, they don't need to know we are in town. They are not expecting me," and immediately he corrected, "Or you. We'll see them soon."

It was afternoon when they arrived for lunch at Feltman's restaurant. It was not late for lunch at the sea resort. Everyone there played hard and went to bed way past midnight and got up close to noon. They sat in the famous Bavarian garden their aunt had mentioned. Almost immediately, a waiter appeared. He was blond and red-faced, dressed in a white shirt, and a white apron that covered him from his big stomach to just a few inches above the hem of his black pants. He took their order and vanished with the same rapidity, but not before he recommended their clam chowder. Frank and Sarah refused the suggestion, since they had other foods in mind.

"What is clam chowder, Aunty?" The unknown dish awakened curiosity in Esther.

"Oh, it is nothing much, just a soup made with heavy cream. Would you like to try some?" The soup was one of the specialties of the town and was offered in most of the restaurants. In the less expensive places, a big plate of clam chowder was only ten cents and it was so big, a diner could make a meal of it.

When the waiter returned, he carried a round metal tray on one hand, balancing it between his shoulder and head. He lowered it and placed a platter with hotdogs on the table, followed by four gray and blue ceramic steins and a large glass pitcher overflowing with beer.

"I never had beer before," Esther announced. "What an experience!"

"Neither have I," Rebecca confessed. She extended her arm to take a hotdog from the platter Frank held for her. Under the supervision of Sarah, she got a spoonful of mustard from a glass container, put some on the frankfurter. Then she took the first bite before she thanked them for their assistance.

"Well?" Frank asked and waited for their reaction. He enjoyed food very much and wanted everyone to experience the same pleasure.

"Ummm, I think it's delicious!" Rebecca wiped a smear of mustard from her lips. "I do like the beer too."

"L'chaim!" Esther held the stein with both hands. "It is good." she concluded.

The town, built with the idea of entertainment, had many attractions the two Russian women had never seen before. They were amazed and happy to follow Frank's planned tour. "Have you ever seen a horse race?" he asked and was pleased with the answer … they never had. The two young women had given Frank the unexpected opportunity to play father for a few months, and he used it fully.

It was past four when they came out of the race track. Since Sarah had gone through the same itinerary before and was tired from the trip, she insinuated it was time to go back to the hotel and rest, but the inexhaustible uncle took them for an ice cream. "Best ice cream parlor in the world," as he phrased it. He reserved the visit to Steeplechase for last. The amusement park was so crowded they chose a meeting point in case they got separated from each other and lost among the multitude. They saw the heated swimming pool and Sarah told them it was one of the largest in the world. They ate cotton candy. Esther won a stuffed brown bear as a prize after she caught several fish with a magnetized hook that hung from a fishing line. Uncle Frank explained to Esther that since the year before, the toy was mass produced and called Teddy bears in honor of President Roosevelt.

"Come here, Becca, and play this game. It's fun!"

Rebecca, disinterested in the offered attractions, bought several postcards to send abroad. From the very beginning, Frank meant to invite them for a ride on the roller coaster. The roller coaster at Steeplechase claimed to be the fastest and the one with the deepest drop.

Sarah complained, "Such a brusque ride! They are little girls. It could hurt them."

Frank was deaf to his wife's overprotective attitude and bought four tickets, including one for her. Esther and Rebecca sat in one of the cars on the front seat and Frank, with a very disappointed Sarah, in the one behind them. Each of them would have a different tale about that ride. From beginning to end, the two girls screamed in Russian, Yiddish and even the few English words they knew. Sarah was so scared that her mouth was unable to modulate sounds, much less a complaint. With one hand, she held on to the bar in front and used the other to press her hat against her head. When the roller coaster arrived at the end and came to a complete stop, Frank noticed he had lost his beloved cigar. It took several minutes for the group to overcome the panic and the hysterical laughs produced by the ride. Soon after, Frank was ready to go to the next game. They had to drag him out of the entertainment park and to the hotel. He protested. He wanted to continue the tour.

"Aunt Sarah looked a little dazed when she came off the roller coaster, didn't she?" Esther commented later to Rebecca.

"We were too, dear," Rebecca laughed. "We were too."

They were in the elegant hotel lobby ready to go for dinner, but the older couple had not come down yet. The walls were painted in a gold color, the windows had night blue velvet curtains, and the armchairs and sofas in the lobby were upholstered in blue, gold, and cream striped silk. The wooden floors were covered with gigantic Turkish rugs. The décor was fashionable and quite expensive, but almost unsuitable for a place just a few yards from the sand and the water in a sea resort. Despite the permanent effort of the maids who constantly swept the floors, careless guests tracked sand from the beach to the hotel. Esther and Rebecca felt provincial in front of so much opulence.

Frank and the refreshed Sarah came out of the elevator and were next to them, waving their hand to call the girls' attention. They walked together to the front desk, left the room keys with the concierge and walked out. The evening was cooled by a strong breeze that carried with it the smell of the salty sea and the noise of the waves breaking on the shore.

"What a beautiful evening!" Esther whispered. A gust of wind made her shiver, and she closed her short cape. "It's a bit too windy, isn't it?"

"Yes, it is" Sarah agreed.

"All right, girls, where would you like to go now?" Frank asked. "If you don't have any other suggestion, maybe we can go to the Bowery for a walk and for an aperitif. Later we'll have dinner at Stauch's."

"I thought we'd have dinner here in the restaurant at the hotel," Rebecca said. She was tired and had taken an aspirin for her headache. She would prefer not to go back out, but to remain alone in the hotel did not appeal to her. Besides, she wanted to be part of the excursion planned for the evening.

The trip from New York early that morning and the sightseeing on Coney Island for so many hours had worn Esther and Rebecca out. They got out of the taxi and knew it was impossible for them to walk one more step, but they were wrong. The flamboyant airs at the Bowery were contagious. With the view of beautiful people in front of them and the happy atmosphere, Esther regained her strength, while Rebecca lost her headache.

The Bowery was a place to see and make others see you. No car or carriages were there, just people who walked in very elegant attires. Small tables were occupied by noisy customers on the sidewalk next to the establishments.

"So much *joie de vivre*," Esther shouted to be heard. "Everybody is happy in this street." She felt warm and unbuttoned her short cape, took it off and folded it over her arm. She would remember years later with infinite nostalgia and longing, the visit to the bustling street. She didn't know that part of her future then and imbued by the happiness of that moment, she breathed deeply and an aroma of expensive perfumes and tobacco filled her lungs. Content and free of preoccupations, she began to walk next to her dearest family.

"This is it. Ocean's Shells," said Sarah. The place Frank had chosen to take the ladies for the aperitif was on one side of a narrow and long bar that was illuminated with gaslights. On a small dance floor, people moved to the music played by an orchestra. On the other half, and divided by shelves adorned with shells and corals, was a well-lit mix of an ice-cream parlor and candy store. The place was mobbed. Every table inside was occupied. They stopped and looked for an outside table and sat. Esther and Rebecca rested their tired feet and had a completely new experience. Since Frank enjoyed astonishing them, he ordered a drink the girls' had never heard of, or tasted before. Vermouth on ice with a slice of lemon.

"The hors d'oeuvres were delicious, *a sheynem dank*," Rebecca said, thanking them.

"And this vermouth has made me tipsy," Esther added.

"I think we should go for dinner before the kitchen closes," Sarah advised.

"We don't have to hurry. It's close by." Frank took the cigar out of his mouth and held it between the index and the thumb of his left hand. When he finished talking, he placed the chewed end of the cigar, darkened by the saliva, back in his mouth. He never mentioned his bad habit and laughed every time his wife protested.

"If he is not drinking, eating or talking, he is smoking," she complained.

"Sweetheart," he told his wife, ignoring her comment, "as you know, the owner is a friend of mine, and he lives in the restaurant. He will feed us even if the kitchen is closed for others."

Once they finished the drinks, Frank paid, and they abandoned their refuge to walk in the unwanted company of strangers moving in the same direction. There were so many people and so close together they could hear their conversations.

"Stauch," Esther read, "Is that the place, Uncle?" A lighted long sign on the façade of the restaurant stretched from the top of the door to the roof and three feet out. A circumspect host dressed in a black suit came to receive them. It surprised Esther and Rebecca to see the respect and familiarity the man showed their uncle. They followed the pompous dressed man to a well-illuminated room. He took them to a table and asked, "Is this table to your likeness, Mr. Bernstein?"

"Yes it is. Very good, Anton." He held the chair for Sarah and Rebecca, while Frank helped Esther. After Anton told Frank the waiter would take their order momentarily, he bowed to them and said, "Madam Bernstein, ladies, Mr. Bernstein," and went back to his position as host.

Frank ordered French white wine and a succulent dinner of crab bisque, sauté filet of sole with capers, and the buttery tender asparagus in a magnificent creamy wine sauce.

"We should write the name of all these delicious foods and tell Olga later. She'll love to know about them," Rebecca said while she tasted some of the bisque.

"Where is the music coming from, Aunty? Is there an orchestra and a dance floor in the restaurant?"

The restaurant claimed to have the largest dance floor in the world, but Esther's question died without an answer. A waiter with a dessert cart with a breath-taking chocolate cake and some French named delights came to the table and, even when he did not mean to, interrupted the conversation. The young man recommended a very American pecan pie ala mode, a dessert new to Esther and Rebecca. The same waiter brought them coffee and liqueurs. Sarah sat across from her husband and coughed repeatedly under a cloud of smoke from Frank's cigar.

The room was too warm and noisy, considerably aggravated by the music that escaped from the upper floor. Esther thought she had heard a familiar voice calling her.

"Is it my imagination or do I hear my name?"

The second time the voice called, Rebecca heard it too. "Esther, look at the table across and to the right of the door. Is that Ruth?"

They looked toward the direction the voice came from and saw Ruth waving at them.

Ruth, their journey's companion, was accompanied by a

young, but formal gentleman. The couple was in the next row of tables not far from where they were seated. Rebecca excused herself, rose and walked to the other table, quickly followed by Esther. Ruth came to meet them. She ignored the rest of the people around and their judgmental gazes. They shouted, laughed, held hands and kissed each other on the cheeks. They were nudged by Ruth toward her table. "Come with me. I'd like to introduce you to my husband, Abraham."

"Ladies, Ruth has talked so much about you, I feel I know you," Abraham told them as he stood to greet them. He kissed their hands and invited them to have coffee with them.

"Maybe some other time," Esther answered. "My relatives wait for us now. We had a very long and exhausting day."

"Would you like to come for dinner to our home on Sunday?" Ruth asked. "The whole family will be at the house. It's my birthday."

"Oh, how awfully nice, Ruth. Thank you for the invitation. We'd love to be there."

"I'll be waiting for both of you."

CHAPTER XXI
A LARGE FAMILY

New York, last days of spring, 1906

"Macy's is not far from the house. If you like, we can go this afternoon." Sarah offered.

"I love it! I wanted to buy some intimate clothes in preparation for my wedding trousseau," Rebecca confessed with a touch of a blush on her cheeks.

"Oh honey, you'll find smashing lingerie there." Sarah was in her bedroom in front of the mirror of her vanity, putting on the last touches of her makeup as she talked to Rebecca. When she finished, she placed the lipstick on the shell-shaped glass table next to other cosmetics. "You'll find the most beautiful undergarments there as well. Do you know that department store has a whole section dedicated to lingerie made here in America and also imported from Paris?"

Esther erupted into the bedroom with a letter in her hand. "Guess where this letter comes from?" She jumped to avoid Rebecca reaching it. Esther and Rebecca had left Odessa over a month earlier, and this was the first letter to arrive from the Old to the New World since they left Russia.

"Esther, give me the letter at once," Rebecca frowned, ordering her cousin with irritation. She took the envelope that now was offered and looked for a chair to sit in.

With curiosity, Sarah and Esther followed each one of her movements. She opened the envelope with impatience and unfolded the sheets of white paper. A smile lit her face when she read out loud for them to hear it too.

In the letter Joseph wrote that Gustav and he had remained immobile on the station platform for a long time after the train was no longer visible. When he reacted, he had to drag the hopeless Gustav out of the station and into his car where the gracious Albert patiently waited all that time. Gustav was still in shock when Albert drove him home.

"Two good things happened at that moment," Joseph wrote. "The first was that Gustav did not care about his car. He was too sad to pay attention to material things. The other, and just as important, was that Albert showed to the entire world, and to his mother, that he could drive. Driving home, he gained the last shred of his independence."

No more than a week had passed since Esther and Rebecca began their trip to America when Albert got his first car. He asked his grandmother to accompany him. Together they bought the car from the same car salesman where the other cars in the family were bought. He drove his grandmother back home. Albert never asked for permission or money. He had his own and almost unused checkbook.

"Imagine?" Esther exclaimed, excited, "Albert driving! I told him many times, I knew he could do anything he wanted!"

Rebecca ignored the interruption and continued to read the letter. From the train station Joseph went to the house on Balkovskaya Street to find comfort in the kitchen where Olga awaited with a cup of strong Turkish coffee and the understanding of a Russian matrushka. He felt less lonely in the company of Olga. He gladly accepted each invitation delivered to him by Yuri and was always ready to go back to the house for a visit, for a cup of coffee and a piece of cake from the magnificent cook.

The wise Olga helped him to know Rebecca better and to miss her less. With motherly love, she told Joseph some of the family anecdotes and little secrets and showed him some of the family photographs from the time when Rebecca was still a young child.

Esther and Sarah kept silent and waited for Rebecca to continue to read out loud. A short pause made Esther ask, "Is that all?"

"Well, no," responded a much happier Rebecca, "that is not all. The rest of the letter is private. Joseph wrote it just for me."

After that first letter, the mail for Rebecca continued to arrive quite frequently and the news from Odessa formed part of the daily conversation.

Sarah was in the parlor, a cup of coffee on the table next to her, the New York Times opened on the sofa. She had some peculiarities. She read the paper, but did not touch it, disliking the leftover ink on her hands. She also commented aloud on the news. It was the end of May, but the paper continued to write about the April earthquake that devastated San Francisco. An article talked about the effect the quake had on Enrico Caruso, and mentioned that for days after the first tremor, he slept outdoors. Still, over a month later, he could not sleep through the night. "I'm sure he is not the only person affected by such a disaster of catastrophic proportions. At least he did not lose his home, did he?"

She was outraged with the news about automobiles and the new national speed limit of twenty miles per hour. She had just predicted millions of accidents everyday, and was blaming the authorities for such a bad decision when the telephone rang insistently. The maid with a light blue uniform, a white ruffled apron and coif on her tightly combed hair arrived in the room. She had a telephone in her hand, and walked to the wall. She kneeled and plugged the end of the cable into an outlet.

"Pardon me for the interruption, madam, but you have a call. Madam Grossman is on the phone. She asked me to speak to Miss Esther. When I told Madam Grossman that Miss Esther had gone out with Miss Rebecca, the lady asked to talk to you." The dark skin of the maid contrasted with the very white and well manicured hand of Sarah when she received the receiver.

"Thank you, Rose."

The young woman stood next to her, and held the other part of the very modern telephone.

"Thank you, Rose," she repeated. "You may go now. I'll call you if I need you." She had the mouthpiece covered with her hand to avoid being heard at the other end of the line. Rose placed the device on the side table and excused herself. She began to leave the parlor when Sarah called, “And Rose, when my nieces return, please tell them that I need to see them.”

“Yes, madam, I will,” Rose answered and left the parlor in the same complete silence she had entered before, not even her shoes made a sound.

Sarah was still in the parlor when Esther and Rebecca returned from the walk in Central Park. Rose told them as soon as she opened the door with words and signals to be sure they understood their aunt waited for them in the parlor. They gave the maid their parasols, purses and gloves and headed for the parlor.

“Is something wrong, Aunty?”

“I have some messages for you, but nothing that can’t wait. Tell me, how was your walk? You were in the park a long time. I was a bit worried.”

“I’m sorry, Aunty.” Esther reached for her aunt’s hand. “We had a wonderful time, everything is blooming, and there are so many birds I’d never seen before. You are privileged to live here.”

“I believe so, Esther. And you know? The winters are as beautiful as the springs.” Sarah changed the subject and informed the girls there had been a call from Mr. Harmon, their English language teacher. “He won’t come until five this afternoon. He told me he suffered a minor accident with his bicycle this morning.”

“We can cancel today’s class, if he needs to,” Rebecca offered.

“Oh no. No need for it. I know he counts on that money. He said the incident was unimportant, but made his bicycle useless. As consequence, he has to use public transportation, and that has slowed him some.”

“He’s not hurt, is he?” Esther asked. “You said there was more news for us, perhaps letters from Russia?” she concluded in a comic tone of voice.

“I’m afraid not.” Sarah smiled at Rebecca. “Mrs. Grossman called. She is a nice young woman, isn’t she? We talked for several minutes. She invited me and Frank to go to her home with you the twenty-seventh of May.”

“The twenty-seventh is this coming Sunday, Aunty.”

"Yes, it's that soon, I know. She'd like for you to call her back. She said she'll be home all day, and you can call any time you want."

Esther went to the entrance hall where Rose had left her purse. She retrieved a small address book with a red leather cover from inside it. She left the purse on the chair and went back to the parlor. Taking a seat next to her aunt, she opened the red booklet at the letter G and found Ruth's address and telephone number. She picked up the phone from the table, and, for first time, she realized that she had to talk to an operator who would not understand Russian or Yiddish. She had to ask for the number in English. "I can do it," she thought with determination.

She picked up the receiver, lifted it to her ear and soon a woman's voice asked her for the number. With an unusually timid voice and in broken English, Esther slowly spoke the number. She was connected without delay. "She understood me!" she screamed so loud that it startled Sarah and made Rebecca laugh.

Ruth told Esther she would be in Manhattan the next day. "I'll have lunch with Abraham, and, since he has to work I have the afternoon free."

They made plans to visit the Metropolitan Museum together and have tea afterwards. They continued to chat a few more minutes. Before she hung up Ruth reminded Esther about her party on Sunday. "It means a lot to me to celebrate my birthday with both of you."

Next morning, and under Mr. Harmon's recommendation, they went to the bookstore in search of several books. He told them, "Reading English literature will enrich your vocabulary." They opened the door of the shop and the bell that was moved by the motion announced their arrival. The familiar smell of paper and ink of the books rushed them back to the old bookshop in Odessa, but this place was twice as big and packed with books, magazines, and special shelves with black and white postcards.

A clerk, owner of a big smile, came to meet Sarah. "Madam Bernstein, welcome, how may I be of service?"

He was pale, thin and wore worn clothes. Esther whispered sadly to Rebecca, "If his eyes were not so blue and his hair dark instead of red, I would think he is Andrew's American brother. How horrible, they're separated by so much water, and united by the same path in life, the same fate." Esther wondered if the red haired clerk also lived in an attic of some cheap bordello. With an awakened interest in the young man, she asked her aunt about the young salesman's wages and education.

Sarah told her it was out of reach for a person of his condition to have a degree from a university. "It is way too expensive."

The regular salary for services such as his was fifty-two dollars a month. To earn that much money, people had to work close to sixty hours a week. Very few had the stamina and the ambition to find time to study in the evenings after work. Besides, it was almost impossible to find a night school.

Sarah decided to leave the bags full of books at the button factory. "Frank will bring them home tonight. The museum is too big to visit carrying those heavy bags." She was quiet for an instant and said, "I know a small restaurant on Canal Street that serves delicious Italian food. How would you like to go there for lunch?"

With the unanimous approval of her nieces, Sarah hired a carriage that took them straight to the factory, where a clerk received the books from them. In animated conversation, Sarah and her two nieces continued their trip in the roofless carriage to Canal Street. The driver stopped in front of a restaurant decorated with Italian flags by the name of Italia Mia.

The early afternoon was warm, the spring air transparent, and they enjoyed the ride, the meal and the company of one another. Esther was happy. She began to let go of the tragedy she had lived for the past year. When they abandoned the restaurant after a perfect meal of antipasto, veal, a delicious Italian wine, and zabaglione ice cream, she was not aware that a time of uncertainty was about to unfold. Fate had prepared events for her that would change the rest of her life.

"This is the Metropolitan Museum," Sarah said, before she stepped down from the carriage. "Isn't it magnificent? Inside you'll find the history of ancient extinct civilizations shown with drama. We'll see the past, present and future depicted in the expressions of artists of the world. Such exuberance of beauty is exhilarating. I hope you both like the museum as much as I do." Sarah delivered the short speech with enthusiasm. She stood between Esther and Rebecca, both her hands holding the parasol in front of her as a cane.

Her nieces, applauded, and laughed a bit at her dramatic unconventional flair. They climbed the gray steps passed the columns that supported the portico and entered the immense lobby. Ruth, who had arrived before them, was in animated conversation with a man. She saw them from a distance and waved her hand, smiled at the group and walked toward them.

"This is Natan, my brother-in-law." Ruth held the young man's arm. "He was gathering information about some new acquisition of European paintings when he saw me. He has to go back to work, but refused to leave me alone."

"I'll go now that your friends are here," Natan said quietly. "I only wish I could stay." He looked deep into Esther's blue eyes as he spoke, his gaze making her feel oddly weak. Her eyes hid under the shield of an involuntary blinking and a warm blush tinted her cheeks.

"Ladies, I'm forced to wait until Sunday to have the pleasure of your company. I must return to work. I'll count the hours until then," he said in a comical tone to conceal the effect that Esther had on him. That next Sunday he would confess his secret to Esther. "Back from the trip to Coney Island, Abraham had described you in such a way that I fell in love with you even before we met."

The museum encounter was not an accident. The night before at the dinner table, Ruth mentioned Esther, and their meeting for the next afternoon at two o'clock. The rest was simple for Natan. Since he had been asked at work to check on some new French paintings and to write an article, he needed to find the information at the museum. He used the excuse of the painting just to be in the lobby at the time of their meeting.

Natan was the younger brother of Abraham. He was twenty-three years old and had finished college with a degree in journalism. He was gifted with languages. He spoke French, Spanish and perfect German. "I want to talk to my grandparents in their native German language, and Spanish with the Argentineans when I visit my relatives in Buenos Aires," he often said.

He was an accomplished violinist and had an orchestra with some friends. They played Jewish folk music at weddings and bar mitzvahs. He worked as a reporter and covered most subjects for a small Yiddish newspaper. Many times he had to also be their photographer and, when needed, he was one of their typesetters. His passions were classical music and the theater, and he was a participant of a Yiddish theater group. He became vehement each time he talked politics or defended a labor position. Natan frequently argued with his father over his election of a job.

"Ideas are wonderful, but they won't feed you or your family if you ever have one," Mr. Grossman told Natan more than once, his fists clenched in anger. Since the moment Natan graduated, his father reminded him often that it was time for him to become a productive adult as his brother Abraham was. He had to find a good woman, get married, and settle down. Mr. Grossman did not approve of his son's political ideas, nor his low paying job or his artistic inclination. "I don't like your Bohemian life style or your friendship with those people of the theater." Only his grandmother and mother could ease the tension between father and son.

Natan wished to move out of the family home. He attempted to do so many times. Every time he had an argument with his father, he went back to his room and began throwing clothes into his bags only to be stopped by his mother's silent tears. He was his mother's favorite and she could not bear the pain to see him leave the family home.

On that early afternoon of May at the museum, since Natan had no excuse to stay, and no one to stop him, he was forced to say goodbye. The irreversible wheel of destiny started to turn. Sarah, unaware of the recent event, moved toward the information desk. She asked for the directions to the gallery that held the exhibition of the new acquired pieces of art from the French Impressionists. Ruth followed her with an unsettled sensation in her stomach. Only Rebecca knew what had just happened and whispered to Esther, "I think Gustav is farfalen and definitely out of the question, isn't he?"

The afternoon flew by as the museum entertained them with its magnificent world of wonders. "As much as I could enjoy a cup of tea, I may need to start my way home," Ruth said apologetically. She checked the time on the big clock on the wall of the lobby. "Brooklyn is over an hour away from here. I don't want to be late for dinner. Mr. Grossman would be upset and Abraham very nervous, thinking something terrible happened to me. He is very protective."

"Would you like for us to accompany you?" Sarah offered.

"Oh no, thank you, Mrs. Bernstein," Ruth said emphatically. "Before I go, let me tell you how to get to the house on Sunday. The address is 2315 Tillary Street, just before the corner at the intersection with Adams. It's not too far after you cross the Brooklyn Bridge." Before she kissed them goodbye, Ruth added, "Please come Sunday for dinner at six. It's just my family, you are the only friends I've invited."

Since the afternoon at the museum, Esther had changed. She lay for hours on her bed with her eyes fixated on the ceiling. She was not able to concentrate or read a book for more than ten minutes at a time and found herself reading the same paragraph over and over. She sat alone in silence in the winter garden at the edge of the water fountain. She gazed into the distance, unaware that her hand in the water had finally attracted the red fish. She sighed frequently. Rebecca was amused by the sudden shift in her cousin's moods.

From early morning on Sunday the twenty-seventh, Esther went through her entire wardrobe, tried many dresses and could not decide on the appropriate clothes for the dinner. Before the evening arrived, Esther had changed her attire and her hair style many times. She cried over her rebellious curls, and lost gloves, which Rebecca found inside the drawer mixed with other gloves next to her embroidery handkerchiefs, just where she kept them.

Frank was downstairs in the large living room dressed and ready to go. He had a glass with scotch on ice in one hand. In the other he held the last edition of the newspaper. The rising thin blue-gray line of smoke announced his forgotten cigar; it lay in an ashtray on the table next to his velvet armchair. Across from him, Sarah was reading a book. She sat on the edge of the seat completely straight. "I must be careful. This chiffon becomes wrinkled in an instant," she told Frank. Sarah was still a beautiful woman. She wore a blue taffeta and chiffon dress as elaborate as her dark blue hat. Blue was her favorite color.

Frank put the newspaper down when he heard high-heeled steps. He lowered his head to see over his reading glasses and observed Rebecca entering the room. "You look lovely in that silver dress, Rebecca." He drank the rest of the scotch, left the glass on the table, and picked up his cigar. Still looking at Rebecca, he said, "Your Dr. Joseph is a very lucky man. You are a fine young lady."

Rebecca thanked her uncle. She sat on the sofa, and selected a magazine from the side table to wait, hoping Esther would be downstairs soon. Frank went back to his newspaper. He pulled his watch out of his pocket twice and checked the time, moved on his seat uncomfortably, folded the paper and placed it beside the glass on the side table and got up noisily. He walked to the dark fireplace and rested his elbow on the mantel. Impatiently, once more, he opened the lid of his watch and checked the time. "We'll be late. We must go soon," he affirmed.

"If you like, I can go and see if Esther is ready," Rebecca offered.

Five more minutes passed before Esther appeared at the foot of the stairs,

"I'm sorry I'm late. I apologize for making you wait." She turned around for her uncle to see her and said, "I'm ready now, we can go."

"My dearest child, you look completely beautiful." He walked toward Sarah, helped her up and they went out. Lewis, one of the servants and many times the driver, helped the ladies to get in and closed the door of the black automobile. He was ready to sit at the wheel, but Frank told him to stay in the house.

"I'll drive, Lewis. In today's cars, we don't have enough space for five people."

The drive through Manhattan was exciting. Fifth Avenue was lighted, and the late spring evening was warm and inviting. Most New Yorkers didn't work on Sunday, and there were people everywhere.

The traffic on the Brooklyn Bridge was extremely congested. "I wonder what the problem is. We'll be really late." Frank moved his head to the side and looked out to stare into the distance. Uncomfortably, his hands tensed around the wheel. He was about to swallow his chewed cigar when he repeated, "Really late."

It took minutes to realize the problem ahead wasn't just the heavy flow of traffic but a bad accident. An automobile had collided with a large carriage. The carriage had a broken axle, its horse dead and the upside-down automobile partially blocked the road. On the ground were several police plus a police car. An ambulance with some nurses had to push through the crowd to arrive at the scene. The curious spectators around the accident weren't enough to hide the gruesome sight, and Frank advised the women not to look.

"Keep your heads to your right. The view on your left is too horrid and quite shocking, I would say," he advised and passed the scene without stopping at all, as did the other cars.

They parked the car in front of the home of the Grossman family ten minutes after six. Frank checked the time in his pocket watch and didn't utter a word, only shook his head in displeasure. Frank had opened the gate and they were about to enter the front garden when Ruth came out to meet them.

"I'm so happy to see you, *vos machtsu*." Ruth embraced Esther and Rebecca at once. A little girl, who accompanied her, was scared by the unfamiliar faces of the strangers and found refuge behind Ruth's skirt.

They wished Ruth a happy birthday and entered the hall. The house was bursting with the hum of murmurs. To the right of the wide open front door in a small parlor were no less than six people, all men. A child was crying. Two others passed by chasing after a white and black dog. The animal, that was not too eager to be caught, ran and hid among the bushes outside. Music and laughter from a back garden came through two open glass doors. The just arrived guests were still engaged in conversation with Ruth when Abraham saw them from afar and came to greet them.

Until that moment, neither Esther nor Rebecca could imagine a family with so many relatives. They all looked so happy together and seemed to enjoy one another's company. One thing was clear to Esther, they all were noisy. "Oy vey, Ruth! You do have a large family," she shouted to be heard, overwhelmed by the multitude.

CHAPTER XXII
A LEAP INTO TOMORROW

The summer of 1906

"Come with me to the back garden," Ruth said to Esther and Rebecca.

"Oh yes, it is crowded here," Rebecca said.

"And also too noisy to hear what I want to tell you, Esther," Ruth added.

Sarah was in animated conversation with Bertha, Ruth's mother in-law, as if they had known each other forever. They wouldn't notice their absence. Frank had joined the men in the parlor. He was obviously discussing his most favorite subject after baseball: business. Abraham, the Patriarch of the Grossman family listened to him, and nodded his head in agreement.

Ruth took Esther and Rebecca by the arm and continued to walk with them. She was stopped several times on their way into the back garden. "Since Friday, Natan has never ceased to talk about you." She glanced at Esther, looking directly into her eyes, and smiled. "What did you do to him? He is bewitched," she said in a low tone to avoid being heard by others.

"What do you mean, Ruth?" Esther protested, a bit embarrassed.

"We didn't see Natan when we arrived. Where is he?" Rebecca asked.

"I don't know, but I'm surprised he is not here," Ruth answered. "He told me he planned to be home before you arrived.

He wanted to leave the newspaper by five and since it's Sunday, there's not much traffic. I don't understand. I hope nothing happened to him."

Natan had written an article about President Roosevelt and the positive influence his image as world leader exercised in the international arena. In the same article he mentioned that other world political and church leaders had nominated the American President as a candidate for a Nobel Peace Prize that year. The complex piece had to be finished that afternoon and kept Natan in the office later than expected. He was on his way home and midway over the Brooklyn Bridge when the accident developed in front of his eyes. There was not much time for second thoughts. The collision happened so unexpectedly that it demanded a quick reaction from the driver of the carriage he was in. The man made an enormous effort; he halted his horse just in time and avoided a crush into the misfortunate carriage ahead. Natan noted when the driver of the car, who was going much faster than the twenty miles per hour limit, lost control of his vehicle. The car driver veered into the adjacent lane and hit the unoccupied carriage going in the same direction. On impact, the carriage lost a wheel and catapulted the driver forward. The automobile continued its tragic ride, drove over the unconscious man and was stopped by the body of the horse. The injured animal later died. The force of the impact sent the car into a spin and flips. Finally the vehicle, completely wrecked, stopped fifteen feet away upside-down, but not before it crashed into two more vehicles. The unfortunate carriage driver was gravely injured and lay in a pool of blood on the pavement.

Natan forgot his hurry to see Esther. He kneeled at the driver's side and stayed with him until the police and the ambulance arrived. Nobody knew how serious the injured automobile driver was. He was taken unconscious by the ambulance to Memorial Hospital. Many of the spectators assured him that he was no longer breathing.

As any good journalist, he loved news coming to him, such as this tragic life and death event. However, on that 27th of May, he had a date with destiny. He was no longer the writer; he was the protagonist. He wanted to be home. He wanted to be with Esther from the very first moment she arrived. The accident altered his plans. The injured carriage driver asked him to go to his house and tell his wife. The man lived in Brooklyn, not too far from his own family. Natan agreed to do so, and finally reached the front gate of his house after seven. His father, his brother and two of his uncles were in the parlor with a man he didn't know. "He must be Esther's uncle," he muttered to himself. He entered the room and inevitably interrupted the conversation. He went to the window and opened it. "There's too much smoke in here. You'll choke with it." He kissed his relatives and introduced himself to Frank. To explain his tardiness, Natan commented about the accident in the bridge.

"What a remarkable coincidence," said Frank, "we passed the same accident just after it happened. It was very macabre, blood everywhere, and that enormous horse was blocking the pass. The traffic was slow and people wanted to see the horrid sight while driving. We drove looking in the other direction. Blood bothers me. The presence of the police made every driver cautious and delayed us on our way here."

"That's not a good excuse. You are always late, son," Mr. Grossman reproached Natan in an acid tone while he filled his pipe with fresh tobacco. He wasn't convinced the accident was the cause for his son's late arrival."

"It's not an excuse, Father, it is the truth."

"Are you sure you were not writing one of your articles or distracted somewhere by some labor meeting?"

Natan didn't answer. He left the room before the rebuke of his father could upset him. He had to see Esther. His search was interrupted when his mother called his name.

Bertha saw her son and felt relieved. Her husband had asked her several times in the last hour where he was and each time she answered with many vague words, as mothers do when they don't want to tell. She knew Abraham would be angry at her son, and she could not allow a disagreement to mar the evening. Natan was too independent to be ruled by his intransigent elder. He was not intimidated by his patriarchal figure, and he expressed his own opinions or dislikes. On the other hand, Bertha understood her husband. He expected to have from Natan the same kind of silent respect and docility that his son, Abraham, showed him.

Natan walked into the glassed porch where his mother was with Sarah and other women relatives. He searched among the faces, but Esther was not there. The smell of the lilac was deep and entered the room with the cool breeze. He would forever associate the aroma of the flowers with the anxiety of that first evening. "I'm sorry I'm late, Mother."

"I was worried, darling, but everything is all right now that you're home." She said, turning to Sarah, "This is my son, Natan, but I think you met him at the museum the other day, didn't you?"

Natan sat next to his mother, kissed her and whispered in her ear, "Have you seen Esther?"

Before his mother had the time to form an answer, he went around the group of ladies. He kissed each one of the cheek and had a word with each one of the women there. Some of those women, second and third cousins of his mother, saw Natan as the perfect candidate for some of their own unmarried daughters.

When he approached Sarah, he reached for her hand and told her, "Madam Bernstein, your niece is the most adorable creature I have ever seen. I love her with all my soul, and I will marry her one day." Then he kissed her hand.

Sarah, overcame her stupefaction, and managed to ask, "Which one of my nieces has captivated your heart?"

Bertha knew her son too well, he was too honest to the detriment of his own good. Her intervention managed to save the moment. "Both of your nieces are enchanting girls. Ruth has told us how talented they are." With ability, Bertha shifted the conversation and ignored the tension brought by her son's candor. "What a blessing it was they met in Poland. Esther and Rebecca made the trip back to America for my daughter, easier and no doubt, pleasant."

Natan's remarks about his love, expressed so uninhibitedly to Sarah, created great curiosity in the group of women. With condescending smiles, the ladies followed each of his movements and gossiped to each other. Conscious of being observed, Natan awkwardly pulled his watch from the end of the silvery chain, checked the time, closed the lid and placed the watch back in the pocket of his black vest.

Bertha loved her free spirited son. To spare him from more scrutiny and embarrassment, she said, "Earlier, I saw Ruth and her friends walking toward the back garden. I haven't seen them coming this way. They may still be there." She smiled at him and raised her arm in the direction of the back garden. "Go and find them, darling."

Natan excused himself with the women, thanked and kissed his mother and began his way to the back garden. He was detained at every step by an older member of the family that hadn't seen him in a long time. Each one assured him he looked thinner, fatter, younger and older. He had an immense affection and respect for all and each one of them, but he had no time to linger for a chat. He was on his way to find Esther. To aggravate the situation and complete his misery, he was almost outside when the lights went off. He could have shouted out her name in the dark, but the touch of a warm hand slipping into his stopped him.

In frenzy, the women ran through the house lighting candles and searched for kerosene lamps almost forgotten on shelves since the instant the city changed the light system from gas to electricity. The unexpected darkness made the young children cry, and prompted the older children to join the adults in playing pranks on others. The dogs barked at every menacing shadow. Everyone spoke curiously louder and the three musicians attacked a military march composed by Sousa with gusto. Over that chaos, Natan heard a soft voice calling his name, and felt the warmth of the body close to his.

"Where were you?" Esther asked in a whisper. "I've been waiting for you since Friday."

To stop the confusion that surrounded the darkened house and restore order, Bertha went into action. She asked some of the women for help and placed most of the lamps and candelabra in the dining room and called the complete family for dinner.

The rest of the night would elapse unoticed for Esther. She could only remember when Natan pulled her against him and kissed her. Taking advantage of the moment and with the complicity of the darkness that enveloped them, he kissed her with passion and new love. With that kiss, Esther surrendered her will. She would adore him the rest of her life, but she didn't know it then. His first kiss left her drunk with happiness and unable to think of anything else. Ruth and her family vanished, and the rest of the world became a nebulous … for Esther, only Natan and his love were real.

The electricity fault was repaired and the light restored by the time Frank began his goodbyes. Esther and Natan had a date for the next afternoon. He would come to the house and have tea with Esther and her family.

Logically, their romantic love wasn't meant to be. Their lives were divided by most of the continent of Europe and the Atlantic Ocean. In a few months, Esther would return to Russia, and, as his father often said, who knew where his job would take Natan? Oblivious of time, distances and continents, Natan and Esther fell in love. Without concern for the future, they dated under the vigilant eye of her aunt. Rebecca often found a family story to distract Sarah. They had so much to tell to each other. They had to unveil each other's mysteries and histories of those many years before they met. They had to learn each other's traditions and rituals. Esther and Natan were intoxicated with their love and only interested in seizing an instant of intimacy for the avid pleasure of a stolen kiss. To satiate their senses was more important than to foresee into the events of tomorrow.

As the spring melded into summer in exuberant splendor, Esther was in love and saw the parks and the trees greener, the flowers more beautiful and their aroma deeper than ever, and she swore it was not her imagination. There was even more music in the song of the birds since that first kiss.

Esther didn't know that such a state of harmony and happiness could exist in one life. It was perfect. They had long walks in Central Park, accompanied by Rebecca, but she always tired soon. After a few steps she needed a shady bench to rest. She read her books, wrote letters to Joseph, and patiently waited for their return.

The late summer morning was warmer than usual, and a maid, with the help of Lewis, had opened all the windows of the enclosed garden.

"I believe it won't be enough. Maybe we should have

breakfast in the back garden," Sarah told Lewis.

"There are many pretty butterflies out here," Esther said. She got close to the flowers, and attempted to catch one. "They're attracted by the honeysuckle. Look, Rebecca, they are lovely, aren't they?"

As every day since their arrival, they were in the garden for breakfast with their aunt when Rose brought in the morning mail to Sarah. From afar Rebecca saw that one of the many letters was for her. She recognized the envelopes Joseph used for his letters. At the risk of being rude, she reached across the table, retrieved the envelope, and opened it with noticeable impatience. The mail from Europe was slow. Sometimes it took almost a month for a letter to reach its destination. This was the first news from Joseph she had received in over a week. A dark thought crossed her mind and she read the pages with a bit of apprehension. Once she finished reading, she folded the sheets of paper and placed them back into the envelope. She was very quiet, her face pale and her hands trembled when she lay the envelope on the table.

"Is it there something wrong, Becca?"

"No, not really, Esther. Just some changes."

In the letter Joseph told Rebecca he had an offer for a job as director in a private clinic. The salary was double of what he had made in Odessa, but the clinic was in Moscow. They had to move there once they married, if he accepted the job. "Both of our fathers are in Moscow and both of them are becoming elderly. It is logical to think they will need our help soon. It will be a beneficial change for us to move close to them," he wrote. He tried not to preoccupy Rebecca with the possibility of such a drastic turn in their lives, and assured her he wouldn't make any decisions alone. Nothing would be done unless they talked and agreed over the future step and she was happy with the changes.

"Your home is in Odessa," Esther protested, suddenly afraid.

"I know."

Esther remained quiet. She imagined her life tomorrow. It would not be the same alone in her ancestral house. She felt selfish and ashamed of her thoughts. She had no right to ask her cousin to stay in Odessa. Rebecca had to follow her own path in life. After all, Moscow wasn't that far away, certainly closer than America. In the worst case scenario, she could visit them in Moscow as often as she desired. She looked at life again with optimism, and embraced Rebecca.

"I think you'll be happy close to Uncle Ishmael and his new family." She kissed her cousin on both cheeks and to encourage her, she said, "You must go to him, Becca."

With those words, Esther helped Rebecca immensely. She found in her younger cousin the needed strength to break away. From the very first day she arrived at the house on Balkovskaya Street, Esther had become her baby sister, her playmate, and her friend. She would not do anything to hurt her or make her unhappy. Esther had had enough unpleasantness in her young life. She would write to Joseph in the evening once they were back from the synagogue. Her plans would be reversed by destiny.

Three weeks earlier, in Odessa, afraid the letter was not clear enough for Rebecca to make a decision, Joseph went to the house on Balkovskaya Street to say goodbye. He would leave for America. Olga had not enough reasons to convince him to wait for Rebecca in Odessa. He could not wait. He refused to live without Rebecca any longer, and though Olga tried to stop him, Joseph left. That same late summer afternoon, he arrived at the home of Sarah and Frank Bernstein in Manhattan.

Rose entered the winter garden where Sarah slept on a recliner away from the heat. The maid announced there was a man at the front door. "When he speaks, he has the same kind of accent your nieces have. He is asking in very weird English to talk to Miss Rebecca. I think," and the confused Rose concluded, "What do I do, Madam Sarah? Do I let him in the house?"

"Don't stand there. See him in," Sarah said as she got up at once and straightened her skirt.

On the early morning of that same day in Brooklyn, Natan had a ferocious quarrel with his father. This would be the last time they argued, he promised himself. He could not stand another confrontation or live in the house much longer. He wanted to run away, but his love for Esther stopped that impulse. She was the only reason for him to remain in New York, but she would soon leave to go back to Odessa. He resolved not to move out. He would not upset his mother, but would go abroad for a year or so. Bertha would be happier with that idea. It was easier to believe that her son would take a vacation instead of moving out. He would go to Argentina to visit his aunt Mary. In every one of her visits to the family in New York, Aunt Mary had raved about Buenos Aires and all the opportunities that constantly opened there for educated young people.

On that same complex day, Natan picked up Esther and Rebecca after lunch. He had promised to take them to the synagogue and later for ice creams in Greenwich Village. He sat in silence in the shadows of the temple, while Esther and Rebecca were at prayer. Impatient and unable to contain his secret much longer, he went to the women's section. Rebecca watched with amused astonishment how Natan took Esther by the hand and led her out the door. Their steps were amplified by the void in the temple and the echo lingered after they were already bedazzled by the brilliancy of the outside.

"What is the matter with you?" Esther demanded. "Are you losing your mind?

"I'm sorry," Natan said. "I have to talk to you, Esther."

"How could you take me out of the temple, running? Shame on you!"

"I apologize for my rudeness, but I have to talk to you now. It can't wait." They both sat on one of the many steps that linked the temple with the sidewalk. Natan told her in detail about the dreadful argument he had had with his father. He needed some time and space between them to heal the damage caused by their words. He mentioned he had decided to go to Argentina for maybe a year, but he had yet to buy the fare. "There is a line of Hollandaise ships that makes the trip to the port of Buenos Aires from New York. Some of the vessels only stop in Bahia de San Salvador in Brazil for a little more than a few hours."

Esther's tears ran down her face and wet her dress and her hands.

Natan avoided looking at her. "I know there are more companies that do the trip. I have to find the one that leaves no later than tomorrow." He was silent for an instant, held her hand, took a deep breath and said, "Come with me, Esther."

Natan saw panic in her teary eyes and placed his hand over the lips opening in protest. "Please marry me. I promise you I'll love you forever. I'll make you happy."

"Nothing would please me more than to marry you." She looked inside her purse for a handkerchief to dry her tears. "Rebecca came to America because I wanted to come. I would not abandon her now." She dried her eyes and, in a sad whisper, said, "I know you can't go to Russia. You don't speak the language, and you won't find a job there. Maybe next year we'll meet again here in New York."

Rebecca came out of the temple early enough to hear part of the conversation. When she saw the sadness on their faces, she invented a headache and suggested they leave the ice cream for some other time and return to the house. The silence of the farewell loomed over their souls. Natan called a taxi, and helped them into the carriage. No one said anything on the way back. There was nothing else to be said. They arrived too soon; the trip seemed shorter than before.

Without waiting for help, Rebecca jumped down and hurried into the house. Natan helped Esther down, kissed her for the last time and without a word, got back into the carriage and departed. Esther was shattered; sobs shook her shoulders, and her legs refused to move. She felt paralyzed by grief and could only rest her back against the thick trunk of the oak tree at the edge of the street. Her knees, unable to sustain her, yielded to the weight of her body. She was still in the same position, seated at the foot of the oak tree when Rebecca and Joseph went to look for her outside.

"My dearest Esther, what on earth happened?" Rebecca asked. She held her cousin's hand to help her up. "Where is Natan?"

Joseph reached for the purse that had slid from Esther's hand and was lost among the thick roots. "Sweet Esther, what is the matter?" he asked as he embraced her.

"Joseph?" Esther asked in a whisper. "Joseph?" she repeated without understanding. "Am I dreaming? Is this our Joseph?" she shrieked, overcome with new emotions. "What are you doing in New York?" she asked. "This is not a dream, is it?"

Alarmed by her rapid change, Rebecca and Joseph believed Esther was hysterical and in immediate need of a large dosage of laudanum. Rebecca dried the tears from the now laughing Esther, and they began to walk toward the house.

Rose, who had kept the door open for them, thought the three foreigners were completely mad. They had not yet reached first of the five white marble steps of the front door when Esther stopped abruptly and faced the couple. Her decision was made. Enigmatically, she pulled her purse from Joseph's hand and removed two folded pieces of white paper from inside. "This is the letter and the prophecy Mr. Pissani wrote for me." She handed it to the amazed Rebecca. "This is what he told me when he looked at the lines of my hands. Later at home, I wrote his words on this other paper."

She breathed deeply. "My dearest Becca, I know you wanted to know before." Esther gave her cousin the second sheet of paper. Here, you can read it now." She embraced them and kissed them with some of her noisy kisses. They entered the house, and Rosa, who couldn't understand a word spoken by those insane foreigners, closed the door behind them.

Esther had much to do if she wanted to be aboard that ship at the New York harbor. Rushed by the lack of time, she arrived at the foot of the marble stairs, and before she started her usual race upstairs, she stopped, turned to face the young couple and said, "Rebecca, you know how much I hate to pack. I'll need your help. I'm leaving for Argentina tomorrow.

LaVergne, TN USA
19 November 2009
164664LV00001B/2/P

9 780984 187027